ABOUT THE AUTHOR

Steven P. Moysey, PhD, is an organizational psychologist who specializes in the areas of conflict resolution and negotiation. He holds a PhD from Tufts University in Management and Psychology, and spent several years as an adjunct member of the graduate school faculty focusing on the psychological and behavioral aspects of leadership and team management. His research and writing centers on conflict and negotiation with a particular emphasis on law enforcement hostage stand-off situation. Dr. Moysey has previously published on the Balcombe Street siege in the *Journal of Police Crisis Negotiations.* Born and raised in the UK, Dr. Moysey now manages his consulting practice from Grafton, Massachusetts, where he lives with his wife, musician Monica Hatch, and their two Welsh Springer spaniels, while shuttling back and forth to London on research and consulting trips.

The Road to Balcombe Street: The IRA Reign of Terror in London

The Road to Balcombe Street: The IRA Reign of Terror in London has been co-published simultaneously as *Journal of Police Crisis Negotiations,* Volume 8, Numbers 1 and 2 2008.

Monographic Separates from the *Journal of Police Crisis Negotiations*™

For additional information on these and other Haworth Press titles, including descriptions, tables of contents, reviews, and prices, use the QuickSearch catalog at http://www.HaworthPress.com.

The Road to Balcombe Street: The IRA Reign of Terror in London, by Steven P. Moysey, PhD (Vol. 8, No. 1 and 2, 2008). *A comprehensive account of the build-up to and events of the Balcombe Street siege–the six-day standoff between London's Metropolitan Police and the IRA in 1975.*

The Road to Balcombe Street: The IRA Reign of Terror in London

Steven P. Moysey, PhD

The Road to Balcombe Street: The IRA Reign of Terror in London has been co-published simultaneously as *Journal of Police Crisis Negotiations,* Volume 8, Numbers 1 and 2 2008.

Routledge
Taylor & Francis Group
NEW YORK AND LONDON

First Published by

The Haworth Press, 10 Alice Street, Binghamton, NY 13904-1580 USA

Transferred to Digital Printing 2009 by Routledge
270 Madison Ave, New York NY 10016
2 Park Square, Milton Park, Abingdon, Oxon, OX14 4RN

The Road to Balcombe Street: The IRA Reign of Terror in London has been co-published simultaneously as *Journal of Police Crisis Negotiations,*™ Volume 8, Numbers 1 and 2 2008.

Library of Congress Cataloging-in-Publication Data

Moysey, Steven P.
    The road to Balcombe Street : the IRA reign of terror in London / by Steven P. Moysey.
      p. cm.
    "A comprehensive account of the build-up to and events of the Balcombe Street siege : the six-day standoff between London's Metropolitan Police and the IRA in 1975. Co-published simultaneously as Journal of Police Crisis NegotiationsTM Volume 8, Numbers 1 and 2 2008."
    Includes bibliographical references and index.
    ISBN 978-0-7890-2912-6 (hard cover : alk. paper) – ISBN 978-0-7890-2913-3 (soft cover :)
    1. Provisional IRA. 2. Political violence–England. 3. Terrorism–England. 4. Hostages–England–London. I. Title.
HV6433.G712P766 2008
942.1'0857–dc22

                                        2007036559

Publisher's Note
The publisher has gone to great lengths to ensure the quality of this reprint
but points out that some imperfections in the original may be apparent.

The HAWORTH PRESS *Inc*
Abstracting, Indexing & Outward Linking
PRINT *and* ELECTRONIC BOOKS & JOURNALS

This section provides you with a list of major indexing & abstracting services and other tools for bibliographic access. That is to say, each service began covering this periodical during the year noted in the right column. Most Websites which are listed below have indicated that they will either post, disseminate, compile, archive, cite or alert their own Website users with research-based content from this work. (This list is as current as the copyright date of this publication.)

Abstracting, Website/Indexing Coverage . . . . Year When Coverage Began

- **Academic Search Premier (EBSCO)**
  <http://www.epnet.com/academic/acasearchprem.asp> 2006

- **MasterFILE Premier (EBSCO)**
  <http://www.epnet.com/government/mfpremier.asp> 2006

- *(IBR) International Bibliography of Book Reviews*
  on the Humanities and Social Sciences (Thomson)
  <http://www.saur.de> 2006

- *(IBZ) International Bibliography of Periodical Literature*
  on the Humanities and Social Sciences (Thomson)
  <http://www.saur.de> 2001

- *Academic Source Premier (EBSCO)* 2007

- *British Library Inside (The British Library)*
  <http://www.bl.uk/services/current/inside.html> 2006

- *Cambridge Scientific Abstracts <http://www.csa.com>* 2001

- *Criminal Justice Abstracts (Sage & CSA)* 2001

- *Current Abstracts (EBSCO)*
  <http://www.epnet.com/academic/currentabs.asp> 2007

- *EBSCOhost Electronic Journals Service (EJS)*
  <http://ejournals.ebsco.com>. 2001

- *Electronic Collections Online (OCLC)*
  <http://www.oclc.org/electroniccollections/> 2006

- *Elsevier Eflow-D <http://www.elsevier.com>* .2006

(continued)

(continued)

Bibliographic Access

- *MediaFinder <http://www.mediafinder.com/>*

- *Ulrich's Periodicals Directory: International Periodicals Information Since 1932 <http://www.Bowkerlink.com>*

Special Bibliographic Notes related to special journal issues (separates) and indexing/abstracting:

- indexing/abstracting services in this list will also cover material in any "separate" that is co-published simultaneously with Haworth's special thematic journal issue or DocuSerial. Indexing/abstracting usually covers material at the article/chapter level.
- monographic co-editions are intended for either non-subscribers or libraries which intend to purchase a second copy for their circulating collections.
- monographic co-editions are reported to all jobbers/wholesalers/approval plans. The source journal is listed as the "series" to assist the prevention of duplicate purchasing in the same manner utilized for books-in-series.
- to facilitate user/access services all indexing/abstracting services are encouraged to utilize the co-indexing entry note indicated at the bottom of the first page of each article/chapter/contribution.
- this is intended to assist a library user of any reference tool (whether print, electronic, online, or CD-ROM) to locate the monographic version if the library has purchased this version but not a subscription to the source journal.
- individual articles/chapters in any Haworth publication are also available through the Haworth Document Delivery Service (HDDS).

As part of Haworth's continuing commitment to better serve our library patrons, we are proud to be working with the following electronic services:

AGGREGATOR SERVICES

EBSCOhost

Ingenta

J-Gate

Minerva

OCLC FirstSearch

Oxmill

SwetsWise

FirstSearch

Oxmill Publishing

SwetsWise

LINK RESOLVER SERVICES

1Cate (Openly Informatics)

ChemPort
(American Chemical Society)

CrossRef

Gold Rush (Coalliance)

LinkOut (PubMed)

LINKplus (Atypon)

LinkSolver (Ovid)

LinkSource with A-to-Z (EBSCO)

Resource Linker (Ulrich)

SerialsSolutions (ProQuest)

SFX (Ex Libris)

Sirsi Resolver (SirsiDynix)

Tour (TDnet)

Vlink (Extensity, formerly Geac)

WebBridge (Innovative Interfaces)

ChemPort·

Gold Rush

LinkOut.
LINKING TO A WORLD OF RESOURCES

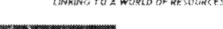
atypon

LinkSolver

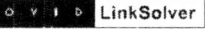
ULRICH'S
RESOURCE LINKER

SerialsSolutions

S·F·X

SirsiDynix

TOUR

(extensity)

WebBridge

The Road to Balcombe Street: The IRA Reign of Terror in London

CONTENTS

Foreword

Acts of terrorism, by their very nature, are intended to appear random and unpredictable designed to cause maximum psychological impact. In this well-researched and well-written book, psychologist Dr. Steven Moysey traces the destructive and apparently random path taken by one of the most ruthless and murderous gangs of IRA terrorists ever to operate with such vicious consistency on the mainland of Great Britain. He covers the bombing, shooting and kidnapping offences carried out by this small group of determined killers and outlines in authentic (and dare I say exciting detail, as he triggers my own memory) the events leading up to their eventual capture when they were caught in a trap carefully placed and sprung by the London Metropolitan Police on 6th December 1975. Moysey clearly outlines the randomness and unpredictability which was the hallmark of this particular Active Service Unit and which was epitomised by: bombs left in shop doorways on one day; a doorstep shooting and killing the next; the murder of a child cancer physician, by placing a booby trapped bomb under the wheels of his neighbour's car; and opening fire from an automatic weapon on crowded restaurants and hotels while speeding past in a stolen car. In one evening alone in early 1975 no less than seven timed bombs were placed in shop doorways and under fuel storage dumps in and around London.

But although this almost daily switch of methods and likely targets helped them evade early identification and capture, their continued success, (which included the death of one of our top explosives experts), the very randomness itself contained a pattern which allowed the Metropolitan Police Anti-terrorist Squad to set a sophisticated trap into which, on the cold and damp evening of 6th December 1975, the most murderous IRA gang which had ever operated on the British mainland inadvertently entered as they attempted to carry out yet another deadly

[Haworth co-indexing entry note]: "Foreword." Imbert, Lord Peter. Co-published simultaneously in *Journal of Police Crisis Negotiations* (The Haworth Press, Inc.) Vol. 8, No. 1, 2008, pp. xxi-xxii; and: *The Road to Balcombe Street: The IRA Reign of Terror in London* (Steven P. Moysey) The Haworth Press, Inc., 2008, pp. xiii-xiv. Single or multiple copies of this article are available for a fee from The Haworth Document Delivery Service [1-800-HAWORTH, 9:00 a.m. - 5:00 p.m. (EST). E-mail address: docdelivery@haworthpress.com].

shooting by opening fire on a high class West End restaurant crowded with pre-Christmas diners. The terrorists, facing armed officers for the first time in their campaign of violence and finding themselves cut off in a part of the City, ran into a small block of Council flats, entered No. 22b, placed a gun to the head of the woman occupant and called to the pursuing officers that they would shoot her if the officers made a move to enter. The officers, knowing of the murders already committed by the terrorists knew this was no idle threat; they would carry it out. So began the siege of 22b Balcombe Street which with armed terrorists inside, who were more than capable of killing their hostages, and armed police covering the premises from the outside, presenting the police, and indeed the government, with a grave dilemma as to how this situation could be resolved.

Steven Moysey tells the story of the build up to the siege, which was to last six days, with great skill and thoroughness. He examines the state of mind of the hostage takers and the hostages during the stand off, and particularly the terrorists' psychological motivations for their actions and what drove them to stay the course of a hopeless siege and resist the relentless negotiation tactics employed by the police for a whole week.

Moysey's research included perusal of all press reports and pictures by journalists at the scene and lengthy and probing interviews with the main players on the police side. I admit to enjoying the exercise of casting my mind back 30 years and, with him, re-reading the transcripts of the many hours of interviews which my then boss, Detective Chief Superintendent Jim Nevill and I had with the four terrorists following their capture.

This is the first comprehensive and all embracing account of the events leading up to the hostage taking incident at Balcombe Street and the successful and peaceful efforts to secure the release of the victims and surrender of the perpetrators. I congratulate Dr. Moysey on his deep and meaningful research and his comprehensive and well written account of this hostage taking episode, the style of resolution of which has become a classic example throughout the democratic world for police procedure at such difficult and sensitive incidents.

Lord Peter Imbert, QPM
Her Majesty's Lord-Lieutenant of Greater London
City Hall
Westminster, London
May 30th, 2007

Acknowledgments

The research and writing for this book could not have been completed without the help and support of many different individuals and groups. Firstly, I need to thank my wife Monica for her tireless support and apparently endless patience in dealing with the piles of paper that accumulated around the house and in my office as I worked on the manuscript. I need to also thank The Haworth Press for making the publishing a relatively painless process and especially Dr. Jim Greenstone, of the *Journal of Police Crisis Negotiations*, for being a believer in the book when it was just an idea based on a previous academic paper.

Many former officers from London's Metropolitan Police came forward with their recollections of the IRA terror campaign between 1974 and 1975 and several were critical to reconstructing the events of December 6th 1975 that resulted in the start of what became known as the Balcombe Street siege. I would like to thank Bob Fenton for his dual role as both a voice in the events of that night and as a contact person for the several thousand retired CID officers in his role as Secretary of the Association of Ex CID Officers of the Metropolitan Police. Through Bob, I was able to interview many police participants including Ron Chapman, Derek Wilson, Alec Edwards, David Waghorn and others who have requested that their names would not used in the book. I would also like to thank Alan Hill, FIFireE, formerly of the West Midlands Fire Service, for his excellent first-hand account of the Birmingham pub bombings in 1974.

Other people made a significant impact in the hunt for research material such as the staff at the British Newspaper Library, and big thanks go to Erin O'Connor at the BBC written archives for her tireless help in tracking down tidbits of information, and Kate Parsons of the Press As-

[Haworth co-indexing entry note]: "Acknowledgments." Moysey, Steven P. Co-published simultaneously in *Journal of Police Crisis Negotiations* (The Haworth Press, Inc.) Vol. 8, No. 1, 2008. pp. xxiii-xxiv; and: *The Road to Balcombe Street: The IRA Reign of Terror in London* (Steven P. Moysey) The Haworth Press, Inc., 2008, pp. xv-xvi. Single or multiple copies of this article are available for a fee from The Haworth Document Delivery Service [1-800-HAWORTH, 9:00 a.m. - 5:00 p.m. (EST). E-mail address: docdelivery@haworthpress.com].

sociation and Alan Moss of History by the Yard for their help in researching images for the book. Several members of Scotland Yard's SO15 Counter Terrorism Command deserve a mention for the help and time they extended to me, but because of the nature of their work I cannot name them.

I have enormous thanks for two very special people and the outstanding contribution they have made to the research for this work. Firstly, I have to thank Lord Peter Imbert, QPM JP, along with his staff of Edna Partridge and John Hope. Lord Imbert responded to a request for help from me as a researcher working on a book on Balcombe Street and he did not hesitate in offering his assistance. As someone who has researched and studied the events around the Balcombe Street siege for some time, I still get goose bumps recalling the afternoon of November 14th, 2006, sitting in a car with Lord Imbert and his personal driver Mike outside number 22 Balcombe Street. We were parked on the opposite side of the street to number 22, under the third floor apartment window of 20 Dorset Square where, for six days, Superintendent Peter Imbert and Chief Superintendent Jim Nevill had conducted negotiations with four members of the IRA Active Service Unit holding Mr. and Mrs. John and Sheila Mathews hostage. Almost 31 years later, I was being afforded a privilege by the now Lord Imbert as I sat there and listened to his razor sharp recollections of the events of 1974 and 1975 leading up to the siege.

Final thanks go to John Purnell, GM QPM, for his generous donation of memories around events of the 6th of December 1975. After several phone interviews, John had offered to walk me through the events in person that resulted in the siege. I met John Purnell in London on a bright February morning at the junction of Oxford Street and Portman Street where we retraced the steps taken by John and Sergeant Phil McVeigh, as they gave chase to the IRA team that had eluded capture for well over a year. John's calm recollections of a night filled with both abject terror and remarkable courage helped to put the events into a very clear perspective for the author. I am indebted to John for a quite special morning of recollections and his candid honesty about his own thoughts as he faced the most dangerous moments in his distinguished police career.

This book is therefore dedicated to law enforcement officers everywhere who, behind the scenes, quietly go about the task of combating crime and terrorism in our cities, and to those special people who manage the most delicate and potentially deadly situations in law enforcement: The hostage negotiators.

Introduction

This book is, at its core, about a hostage negotiation episode that occurred in London over six days in December of 1975. The hostage takers were four members of the Provisional Irish Republican Army (IRA) that made up an Active Service Unit (ASU), sent to Britain by the IRA's General Headquarters (GHQ). They had been sent to England, under a cloak of relative anonymity, to wreck havoc on the capital, which they did with some success and notoriety for fourteen months. Their mission was to force the government of Harold Wilson to pull out the British troops from Northern Ireland and allow the six counties of Ulster, controlled by the British, to integrate with the Republic of Ireland. Their mission was part of a struggle that dated back over 200 years. The six days they spent as hostage takers was the direct result of the outstanding work on the part of London's Metropolitan police (the Met) in trapping them in a dragnet operation, designed to entice them one more time onto the streets of London to ply their deadly trade of terror. The six days were the culmination of a fourteen-month collision course the ASU and the Met had been set on since the IRA group became active on the streets of London, with the one side seeking to avoid detection, and the other side desperate to track the terrorists down to stop further death and destruction in the nation's capital. The British had become accustomed to seeing the scenes of carnage and mayhem, on the nightly news broadcasts and in the papers, inflicted on Northern Ireland by the Catholic and Protestant paramilitary groups as they waged a vicious sectarian war. The British public had been exposed on a few occasions to the car and parcel bombs of the IRA, but not since WWII had they been exposed to the concentrated violence the London ASU was to inflict during the

[Haworth co-indexing entry note]: "Introduction." Moysey, Steven P. Co-published simultaneously in *Journal of Police Crisis Negotiations* (The Haworth Press, Inc.) Vol. 8, No. 1, 2008, pp. 1-4; and: *The Road to Balcombe Street: The IRA Reign of Terror in London* (Steven P. Moysey) The Haworth Press, Inc., 2008, pp. 1-4. Single or multiple copies of this article are available for a fee from The Haworth Document Delivery Service [1-800-HAWORTH, 9:00 a.m. - 5:00 p.m. (EST). E-mail address: docdelivery@ haworthpress.com].

campaign of 1974 and 1975. In order to understand the six days of intense pressure, psychological tension, careful maneuvering of the negotiators and the stoic resistance of the hostage takers, we need to trace the steps that both the hunted and the hunters took that drove the ASU to hold John and Sheila Matthews, in their own home, hostages for their cause.

Hostage taking is as old as civilization itself. The spectrum of holding people or possession hostage is very broad, i.e., I have something you want in exchange for something you hold dear or value. Psychologically, we can hold ourselves hostage in jobs or relationships we should have left, or never entered, arguing with ourselves and negotiating a mental truce between the dissonance creating forces so that we can stay in place and accept the situation. We hold others hostage to our own wants and needs, and negotiate to get our own way. We go through life negotiating with bosses, spouses, coworkers, car salesmen, our children and ourselves.

The spectrum of hostage situations, therefore, can be broad and at one end benign and innocent, where at the other end it can be deadly dangerous to the hostages, hostage takers, and those trying to intervene and bring the situation to a hoped for peaceful resolution. At this extreme end of the hostage spectrum, resolution negotiations are never easy and never part of a win-win scenario. By the very nature of the situation it cannot be so, and that is where the skill, intuitive or trained, of the negotiators comes into play. At this deadly end of the spectrum, the hostage situation can take on many forms, each with their own special unique twists. A suicidal ex spouse, high on methamphetamine, holding a family member hostage until he can speak to his former wife. A distraught dismissed employee, holding former coworkers at gunpoint until someone agrees to give her back her job. A group of armed criminals in a botched hold-up, finding themselves trapped in the establishment they were attempting to rob with terrified employees and customers. Each of these situations requires a different, measured response from the law enforcement officers responding to the call for help. And then there are the deliberate, carefully planned and executed hostage episodes, such as the 1980 Iranian Embassy siege, where six armed revolutionaries of the Democratic Revolutionary Movement for the Liberation of Arabistan (DRMLA) seized the Iranian Embassy at No. 16 Princes Gate, London. Such situations can be a negotiator's nightmare, as the motivation to actually come out alive and or release the hostages cannot always be readily established, or assumed to exist. Then there are the "accidental" hostage situations, such as occurred on the night of December 6th, 1975, that involved four highly trained and experienced IRA urban guerillas. These men were not common criminals trapped during a failed bank hold-up. They were determined, disciplined members of the IRA who had absolutely no intention of giving up easily, and for reasons that were best known only to them.

Their opponents were equally skilled and just as determined to secure the safe release of the hostages. Chief Superintendent Jim Nevill and Superintendent Peter Imbert had been searching for the IRA men for the preceding fourteen months, having spent that time repeatedly sifting through the debris of numerous bomb sites and the remains of the human tragedies created by the fiendish handiwork of the four Irishmen. The six days of the siege at Balcombe Street had been almost inevitable, in some respects, with several interconnecting layers, rather like a Russian Matryoshka doll, with elements hidden inside each other. On the macro scale, the IRA were attempting to hold the British Government hostage by the campaign of violence it unleashed on the British mainland, while the British desperately sought a solution to the Troubles that would keep the Protestant parties satisfied and avoid a spiraling escalation to the already horrific sectarian violence in Northern Ireland. Similarly, the British wanted the Irish Government to understand what life could be like in the Republic if they did not assist them in their fight against the IRA. On the micro scale, the ASU were playing a catch-me-if-you-can routine with the Met's bomb squad, who had almost nothing to go on in terms of who they were going after. They had fingerprints that linked one key member of the team to several incidents and locations, but could not establish a recognized identity that connected the prints to any police records in Britain or the Irish Republic. Both the IRA team and the Metropolitan Police Bomb squad were on a collision course that resulted in the six days of the Balcombe Street siege, as a direct result of the fact that the type of investigations the Bomb squad had to conduct were essentially new and different from those they had looked into in the past. The sheer volume of incidents that the ASU unleashed on the capital made the traditional detective work of the Met ineffective in their hunt for the IRA men, forcing the police into uncharted territory in terms of innovative methods of detection and apprehension of terror suspects in a pre-CCD camera London. It was their fate to meet at Balcombe Street.

In this book, we will examine the road that brought the two opposing forces together in Balcombe Street. We will examine the political context of the deliberate campaign of violent terrorist activities perpetrated by the ASU, for without the situational context, we cannot begin to understand the men and their motivation in carrying out the unspeakable acts of violence on the streets, shops, pubs and restaurants of London. We will look at how both sides handled the hostage situation, and then examine the pros and cons of the strategy and tactics used by the Met, and how the lessons from this event apply to other such situations, or if they can be transfer to similar cases. This will give us a framework of how law enforcement and hostage negotiators handle such volatile situations.

doi:10.1300/J173v08n01_01

Chapter 1

Background to the 1974-1975 London ASU Campaign

During December of 1973, Harris Duggan, Sr., received a visit from members of the Provisional IRA at his home in Feakle, County Clare in the Republic of Ireland. They came to Mr. Duggan with heavy hearts and bad news. His son, Harris "Harry" Duggan Jr., was dead, killed on active service with the IRA while on an operation in the North. He had been buried, with honors, in a local cemetery, so Mr. Duggan was told. On receiving the news, Duggan Sr. spent several days searching for his dead son's burial site, but could not find it no matter where he looked. His son had turned twenty-one on his last birthday the previous October. The younger Duggan had been a carpenter, a good trade, and had hoped to go to Canada where he had a job opportunity, but the Canadian authorities had turned down his application for a visa. Rejected, he joined the Provisional IRA. The police on both sides of the border wanted conversations with Harry Duggan regarding certain criminal activities, but now he was dead. Young Harry had been born in Kilburn, London, where he lived with his parents until the age of three, when his father brought him back to Ireland to settle in his native County Clare. The younger Duggan would grow up hearing the tales and exploits of the Republican struggle against the British.

News of Duggan's death reached the Garda, the Irish police force, soon after his father had been told, resulting in Duggan's file being re-

[Haworth co-indexing entry note]: "Background to the 1974-1975 London ASU Campaign." Moysey, Steven P. Co-published simultaneously in *Journal of Police Crisis Negotiations* (The Haworth Press, Inc.) Vol. 8, No. 1, 2008, pp. 5-35; and: *The Road to Balcombe Street: The IRA Reign of Terror in London* (Steven P. Moysey) The Haworth Press, Inc., 2008, pp. 5-35. Single or multiple copies of this article are available for a fee from The Haworth Document Delivery Service [1-800-HAWORTH, 9:00 a.m. - 5:00 p.m. (EST). E-mail address: docdelivery@ haworthpress.com].

Available online at http://jpcn.haworthpress.com
doi:10.1300/J173v08n01_02

moved from the list of active subversives that the Garda maintained on known members of paramilitary organizations, such as the IRA. At around the same time as Harry Duggan's death, another IRA operative disappeared. Eddie Butler, from Castle Connell, County Limerick, had joined the provisional IRA in 1972, a year of increased recruitment for the IRA. He had carried out minor activities for the IRA, such as selling Republican newspapers, but was not wanted for any major operations. He was 24 years old at the time of his disappearance, presumed to be the victim of the sectarian violence between the Republican Nationalist and Unionist Loyalist paramilitary forces, or a victim of the Royal Ulster Constabulary (RUC) and British Army, his body dumped in some remote hedgerow to be picked at by crows.

However, the facts did not match the circumstances. Duggan was not dead, and Butler was not a victim of the sectarian violence either. In preparation for an audacious terror campaign in the heart of the British mainland, the IRA would build them new identities. They had been se-lected, and volunteered, for a mission to strike at the British Govern-ment, through the mechanisms of terror, should the hoped-for truce and changes in the North not materialize. They were being made ready, along with others, through training in explosives, timers and bomb building. Now that they did not exist on record, the IRA could build them new identities and have them operate in England without fear of detection through past misdeeds. The plan was simple, but would prove to be more deadly than previous IRA operations on the British main-land. The Provisionals created sleeper cells, groups of either unknowns or, like Duggan, with new identities. Their job was to blend into the background of British society and keep to themselves. They would avoid neighborhoods traditionally associated with Irish families, and stay clear of pubs and clubs popular with Irish people. They would re-main a tight knit group and stay inactive until they received instructions from the IRA's GHQ to strike at a target or to initiate a string of attacks. The ASU's would be small, between four to six men, and they would re-main unknown to each other, with only GHQ knowing the whereabouts and identities of the units. In this manner, should one group be compro-mised, they would not be able, under interrogation, to give away any de-tails of the other groups. The Provisionals planned to send sleeper cells to London, Birmingham, Manchester, Southampton and Liverpool. The London team had to be their best people, as the scope and range of the mission and the types of targets to be attacked, would require total disci-pline and dedication at what would be a brutally grim campaign of terror on the capital city. The IRA ASU's would be put in place during 1974, a year of bloody violence in both the north and south of Ireland between the warring paramilitary groups and a year of political battling to keep the Westminster goal of a power-sharing assembly, and a link with the Irish Republic, alive in the face of fierce Unionist resistance. But what had led the Provisionals to train and place teams of operatives on the British mainland in waiting for the command to unleash terror on the British public? To understand this, and to contextualize the bloody violence that was to be inflicted on Britain, we need to look at a series of events that occurred during the early 1970's that would result in the IRA London ASU being on a collision course with the London Metropolitan Police that would lead to the siege at Balcombe Street.

The Irish Troubles have been well documented by several expert authors on the subject and therefore this is not intended to be a comprehensive review of the Irish conflict. However there are certain key events that will link us to the placement of the London ASU, and these will be reviewed as they add meaning and context, as stated earlier, to the actions carried out on the British Mainland.

Northern Ireland, a Province of the United Kingdom that during the period of increasing sectarian violence in the 1970's was still governed by the assembly at Stormont Castle, where the elected MPs for the region would meet to govern the Province, as well as having seats in the Westminster government. The partition of the Irish nation, and the establishment of the Stormont assembly, stemmed from the Government of Ireland Act of 1920. The Act recognized that the largely Protestant Unionist population in the northern six counties of the country refused to be governed by the predominantly Catholic free Irish state in the south. The Catholic Nationalist minority in the north became discriminated against by the Protestant majority through control of political power in Stormont and the allocation of housing and state jobs. The Unionists, the Protestant majority, wanted to stay aligned and linked with Great Britain. The way in which the Constitution of Northern Ireland had been constructed, and through the gerrymandering of electoral boundaries in regions where the largely Catholic Nationalist were in the minority, had ensured that the Catholics would be denied political power, and therefore, any vote on the hoped for reunification would never achieve a majority.

In an effort to raise public awareness of the situation in Northern Ireland, and drive to be a catalyst for social change, a group known as the Northern Island Civil Rights Association [NICRA] was established. It had its beginnings in 1968, but held the first official meeting of the group at Belfast's International Hotel on January 28th, 1969. The group

was a cross-section of Nationalists, civil rights activists of several per-
suasions and had the behind-the-scenes presence of the IRA. In fact vocal Unionists, against the whole notion of granting civil rights to
Catholic Republicans, publicly taunted the group arguing that CRA was
"just another way of saying IRA." The leadership was cross denomina-
tional, with Protestant MP Ivan Cooper and Catholic MP John Hulm
prominent members of the group, along with Catholic MP Bernadette
Devlin. The Unionists taunts only helped the NICRA gain in stature, as
no shots were fired during the marches and rallies, and the IRA made a
point of not appearing to look like the IRA when they took part in civil
rights events, blending into the crowds rather than standing out on the
sidelines. The movement was built on the principles of peaceful protest
and passive resistance, reminiscent of the civil rights movement of Dr.
Martin Luther King in the USA during the early part of the 1960's. The
movement was to prove highly successful in raising national and international recognition of the drive for civil rights in the six counties. This
was to be further enhanced after a peaceful civil rights march in Derry
was attacked by the Royal Ulster Constabulary, wielding batons as they
beat marchers in an effort to disperse the crowd, an action that caused a
rapid escalation into pitch battles with stone-throwing youths, degener-
ating into two further days of clashes between the RUC and demonstrators.

Further sectarian violence between the IRA, the Ulster Volunteer
Force (UVF) and other Loyalist paramilitary groups such as the Ulster
Defense Association (UDA), often with the tacit complicity of the
RUC, continued through the remainder of 1970, peaking in August of
that year. The August 12th Protestant Apprentice Boys march, through
Derry and Belfast, triggered three days of intense sectarian violence. By
day two, with the RUC exhausted, Stormont requested that the British
government deploy the Army on the streets of Northern Ireland, and
faced with a mounting crisis the British government agreed, sending
members of the British Army onto the streets of Derry on August 14th.
The Wilson government viewed the move to deploy troops on British
soil as a peacekeeping force, deployed to keep order in a part of the
United Kingdom. Many others in the six counties and beyond viewed
the action as nothing more than a military takeover of the Province. Wilson's Minister of Defense, Roy Hattersley, was to keep a close watch on
day-to-day activities of the Army and insisted that they acted as impartial peace keepers between the warring populations on both sides of the
sectarian divides. The Army presence, and their apparent initial impar-
tiality, did not endear them to either the Unionists, who expected a de-

gree of support from the troops, or the Republicans who felt they bore the brunt of the Army's attentions.

The United Kingdom general election on June 18th, 1970, would have an almost immediate and negative impact on the Republican side. With Harold Wilson's Labour government seen as being responsible for the serious decline in British economic fortunes, with the devaluation of the Pound and the humiliating rebuff from the European Community, denying Britain entry into the Common Market, as European Community was then called, failed to maintain power. The opposition Tory party, led by Edward Heath, won the election with 46.8% share of the seats in the House, and Labour with 43%. This was despite the pre-elections polls and media coverage in Britain all believing that Wilson and the Labour Party would be returned to power. The month-long campaign had coincided with TV coverage of the 1970 soccer World Cup in Mexico, and with England as reigning world champions, soccer proved to be a greater draw for the electorate than politics.

The change in government in the United Kingdom was to have a significant impact on Northern Ireland and on the supposed peacekeeping mission of the British Army. The controls and restraints exerted on the Army by the Wilson government would be relaxed by the new Heath government. The traditional and historical relationship between the Tory party and the Unionists would make it difficult for Westminster not to help with the implementation of Unionist policies and interests. The Army would be seen in action to support the RUC and the Unionist movement, moving them away from the impartial role in the eyes of the Nationalist community. These fears were soon proved by Army action in the Falls Road area, where "streets were barricaded, curfews imposed and streets saturated with troops." For three days the area was pounded with CS gas attacks, with widespread violence, compounded by the use of Scottish Protestant British Army troops in the operation.

The Nationalist communities were outraged at the Falls Road episode, with a flood of money and support flowing into the IRA. The unrest, sporadic violence and rioting continued through into August 1971. During this period, the fiercely Unionists Stormont assembly, led by an equally hard-line Bernard Faulkner as Prime Minister, focused the energies of the assembly on the Catholic paramilitary groups rather than the equally violent and ruthless Protestant bands of militia that openly received the assistance of the RUC, while the British Army often looked the other way. Faulkner was under increasing pressure from Westminster to bring the warring factions under control and prevent the Province from spiraling into all-out anarchy. As a result, on August 9th, 1971,

Stormont, with the full agreement of the Heath government in Westminster, introduced Internment, a policy of arrest and imprisonment without trial and the target population was predominately Catholic, with no Protestants being swept up in the initial mass arrests of suspected Nationalist activists. The sad fact is that the majority of Catholics sent to internment camps in the initial sweep were not members of the Provisional IRA. Despite urgings from Westminster, Faulkner refused to include Protestants on the list of targets to be picked up in the first round, totaling 342 arrested. The bulk of the IRA members picked up came from the Official's and not the Provisionals, because of the supposedly Marxist leanings of the Official's that made them more of a threat in the eyes of the British intelligence service.

As with the Belfast and Derry riots, the anger that resulted from the introduction of Internment drove many more people to actively participate in the IRA or willingly offer shelter and support for its members both north and south of the border. In some respects, Internment helped the Provo's, as the new policy increased support and sympathy for their cause and the ensuing attention overseas, particularly from the United States, resulted in dollars pouring into the IRA's coffers from Republican sympathizers in communities such as South Boston. Even as late as 1993, the author remembers a huge mural on the side of a building in "Southie" depicting an AK47, with the slogan "Support the IRA."

Internment sparked a marked increase in sectarian violence directed at both Protestant and Catholic, reaching such a fever pitch that seven thousand Catholics and two thousand Protestants were driven from their homes by the fighting. Internationally, the Northern Ireland situation was becoming an embarrassment to the Heath government, as it looked as though Stormont was incapable, unwilling, or just plain did not care enough to look for a peaceful resolution to the apparently endless sectarian strife. The situation was compounded by the withdrawal of the Nationalist Social Democratic and Labour Party (SDLP) from the Stormont assembly in protest against the British-backed policy of Internment without trial for Northern Ireland.

As a response to the introduction of Internment, the NICRA started a campaign of civil disobedience, in a nonviolent manner, by encouraging and obtaining a rent and rates strike from those living in public-sector housing. The topic of Internment, an additional burden being faced by the Nationalist population, would become another element of the civil rights movement's protests. Faulkner, in an effort to reduce the impact of the NICRA on the political situation and to undermine the growing public support for the civil rights movement, instituted a ban on public rallies and marches effective from January 18th, 1972, intended to run until the end of the year. But NICRA had planned a large civil rights and anti-Internment rally for Sunday, January 30th, and the organizers, led by Stormont MP Ivan Cooper, wanted the march to go ahead despite the ban, arguing that it was a peaceful march in accordance with the NICRA manifesto. The marchers would be sticking to the passive resistance policy of the civil rights movement, striving for the goals of ending internment without trial, one person one vote in local elections, the introduction of antidiscrimination laws, fair allocation of public housing and the disbanding of the RUC. The organizers pushed ahead with the planned event, despite the misgivings of many involved.

The British Army was under orders conduct mass arrests during the planned NICRA march, to "scoop up" any known troublemakers and arrest any hooligan elements in the crowd. General Ford, commander of land forces in Northern Ireland, placed Andrew McClellan, commander of the Eighth Infantry division, in overall command of the forces involved the containment of the Sunday rally. Fearing a potential powder keg situation could develop between the Army and elements of the IRA, Ivan Cooper sought and received assurances from the IRA they would withdraw from the area during the march. However, the Army expected trouble, especially in the face of the swoop arrest operation they intended to carry out, and so deployed members of the 1st Battalion of the Parachute Regiment to the planned march route. They were members of the Army's crack airborne forces renowned for their toughness and fighting ability. This deployment would add increased tension to an already highly volatile situation, proving Cooper's fears to be well founded.

January 30th was a bright and sunny day, ideal for a peaceful protest march, with people gathering at the start point, the Greggan Estate at around 2:00pm. The intended route was to go from Greggan, through the Brandywell and Bogside and on to Guildhall Square. At Guildhall, the flatbed truck leading the procession would be used as a platform for the speakers to address the gathering crowds. An estimated 10,000 people started the march at approximately 2:50pm that afternoon, with many others joining as the snaking procession made its way through the Brandywell. The Army had no intention of allowing the march to reach Guildhall Square and had erected several barricades to block off the streets leading to Guildhall. Once the marchers had reached the barricades, the Para's planned to start the arrest sweep action as planned.

At 3:50pm to avoid generating any trouble with the police or Army, the organizers, riding on the flatbed truck, led the marchers down

Rossville Street toward Free Derry Corner and away from the Army barricades ahead of them. A splinter group of youths broke away from the main march to head toward the barricades in order to confront and taunt the British soldiers on duty there. They started to throw rocks at the troops, a practice that had become an almost daily scene on the streets of Derry and Belfast. In their usual response, the Army fired rubber bullets and CS gas to disperse the rowdy crowd, which forced many to seek refuge in the Bogside, along with the bulk of the peace marchers heading towards the Rossville flats ahead.

At 4:10pm, under orders to arrest as many civil rights marchers as possible, along with targeted troublemakers and hooligans, the Para's charged down Rossville Street on foot and in armored cars. The troops had been wound-up for the swoop and arrest operational all day, and had also been hyping each other up while waiting to go into action. As they started to make arrests a shot rang out, possibly from a soldier, but subsequently the Army would claim they had come under sustained rifle fire and nail-bomb attack. In response, the Paras started shooting at anyone of "military age" and for twenty-three minutes fired at the fleeing demonstrators trying to take cover from the intense gunfire. Eyewitnesses later described scenes of indiscriminate killing by the Paras.

Raymond Manassas tried to drive a wounded Gerald Donaghy to a nearby hospital in his car. A doctor on the scene told Manassas the young man would die from a serious bullet wound to his lower abdomen if he did not receive emergency treatment. On the way to the hospital his car was stopped at a checkpoint by members of the Army's Royal Anglican Regiment. Manassas was pulled from the car, at gunpoint, and detained for three hours. His passenger, 17-year-old Gerald Donaghy, died while the Army held Manassas for questioning.

The Paras continued to shoot at the marchers, who were desperately trying to get out of line of fire. Outside the Rossville Road flats forecourt, a wounded Paddy Dougherty, age 31, was attempting to crawl to safety. Bernard McGuigan, 41, attempted to reach the man on hearing his cries for help. "If I wave my white hanky," McGuigan told a bystander, "they'll not shoot me." He attempted to reach Dougherty, but was shot in the head and fell dead after taking only a couple of crouched paces. The wounded Dougherty was shot and killed as he lay on the ground.

A local Catholic priest, Father Daley, risked his life to get to the growing number of dead and wounded to administer the last rites. By the time the Paras had ceased firing, thirteen people had been fatally shot and fourteen seriously wounded. Of the wounded, John Johnson,

59, would later die of his wounds, raising the death toll to fourteen. General Ford, later interviewed by the BBC, stated that his men had only fired five to ten rounds in response to incoming fire. It would later be revealed that twenty-one members of the Parachute Regiment had between them fired 108 rounds at the unarmed demonstrators.

Reactions to the shooting were rapid and widespread, with Nationalists and civil rights members outraged at the atrocity. Gerry Adams, the future leader of Sinn Féin, the IRA's political wing, later stated that the operation had been a deliberate attempt by the British Army to "strike terror into the hearts of all Irish Nationalists." The resulting Nationalist outcry would send "money, guns, and recruits" flooding into the IRA, with young men clamoring to join to strike back at the British, as there was a widespread feeling that, on this occasion, the British had gone too far. In the south the following day, tens of thousands of people stopped work to march in protest at the atrocities in the north. Angry crowds besieged the British Embassy in Dublin, throwing petrol bombs that set the building ablaze, burning to the ground.

At Westminster, MP Bernadette Devlin, one of the civil rights marchers who had witnessed for herself the shooting, left her seat in the House to physically assault the Home Secretary Reginald Maudling, hitting him in the face. The shooting incident was making Britain look worse and worse, to the point where it would eventually find itself in violation of international human rights laws. Edward Heath, the Prime Minister, believed it was only his close personal relationship with the United States President, Richard Nixon, that prevented the USA from intervening in the crisis, given the pressure that Nixon was under from powerful Irish-American groups.

Pressure from both inside the country and the growing international concerns over Northern Ireland led Edward Heath to have growing personal doubts about the situation, "The atmosphere had now grown more poisonous than ever," he wrote, "and I feared that we might be on the threshold of complete anarchy." Heath ordered an immediate inquiry into the January 30th shootings, labeled "Bloody Sunday" by the media. He instructed the then the Lord Chief Justice, Lord Widgery, to conduct an investigation and deliver a report in the most expedient timeframe possible. There was outrage in Nationalist circles at having the British Chief Justice investigate acts by the British Army, on British soil, and there was a low expectation for any true sense of justice to be handed out to any involved.

The Official IRA took matters into their own hands. On February 22, 1972, a stolen light blue Ford Cortina was parked outside the officer's mess of the 16th Parachute Brigade in Aldershot, Hampshire. The one-year-old car was packed with high explosives and was detonated by a timing device at lunchtime that day, hoping to catch members of the Parachute Regiment, the unit involved in the Bloody Sunday shooting, while they were at lunch. The detonation was huge and was felt a mile away in Aldershot town center. The blast killed five female kitchen staff and 37-year-old Captain Jerry Weston. Ironically, Captain Weston was a Roman Catholic priest acting as a Padre to the regiment and as a liaison with the Catholic community. The official IRA claimed responsibility for the attack, stating that it was in revenge for the January 30th shootings of innocent Catholics.

Heath had to act. It was becoming increasingly obvious to the Prime Minister that Faulkner and Stormont could not control the security and law and order in the Province, especially since the Nationalist SDLP MP's had withdrawn from the assembly. Heath discussed with his Cabinet the concept of having Direct Rule over the law and order situation in Northern Ireland from Westminster, through the appointment of a Secretary of State for Northern Ireland. Some of Heath's Cabinet pushed back, fearing the problem may be too big to control from a distance. However, an agreement was eventually reached that they would prorogue Stormont, taking control of law and order, leaving the remaining duties of government in the province with Faulkner and his Cabinet. All Heath had to do was to put it to the Northern Ireland Prime Minister, which would not be easy. The prorogue of Stormont would be a temporary measure, while Heath and his Cabinet explored a means of securing a fair and equitable method of power-sharing in the province, something Heath knew the Unionists, such as the Reverend Ian Paisley, would vehemently resist.

Not all of Heath's Cabinet remained comfortable with moving forward with the plan and in a secret and private memo to the Prime Minister, on March 13, 1972, the Foreign Secretary, Sir Alec Douglas-Home, laid out his concerns. He stated he "really disliked" direct rule for Northern Ireland, because, "I do not believe that they are like the Scots or the Welsh and doubt if they ever will be." He believed it would be better to push towards a united Ireland rather than, "tying them closer to the United Kingdom." Home concluded that the government would be left with running the Province indefinitely unless some timetable was put in place for the limitations on the proroguement of the Stormont assembly.

Two days after receiving Home's memo, Heath telephoned Faulkner and invited him to come to Downing Street for a conversation on the current situation. He did not want to ambush Faulkner with the direct rule topic, but at the same time he did not want to tip his hand to the canny Irishman. Faulkner obviously sensed something was amiss, and asked Heath for a written agenda for the meeting, so he could research the issues and be prepared to discuss them. Heath dodged the point with the somewhat vague response, "well, we did consider that," stated the Prime Minister, "we really felt that there was so much from the general points but it is very difficult to put down on a piece of paper." Faulkner agreed to a meeting on March 22nd with Heath in London, but the meeting did not go smoothly. Heath went straight to the point. Faulkner was told of the Westminster government's intentions to take direct control of law and order in the Province, leaving all other duties with the current Stormont Cabinet. Heath also outlined his vision on the timing of talks regarding the Northern Ireland government making a consideration regarding a power-sharing arrangement with the Nationalist parties, in order to give the Catholic minority population a more equitable input into the direction and future of the Province. Faulkner was adamant, telling Heath he would absolutely refuse to do so as he would not have a Nationalist, possibly seeking reunification, serving on his Cabinet. Faulkner also argued that to take away law and order from Stormont and institute direct rule would be akin to neutering his government, rendering it unable to govern effectively. Heath and Faulkner continued discussions the entire day, with Faulkner eventually stating that he would not stay in office under the terms as presented by Heath, and so he would resign along with the rest of his Cabinet and as a result Northern Ireland would be under direct rule from Westminster. Heath appointed William Whitelaw, a long-term political ally of the Prime Minister's, to the post of Secretary of State for Northern Ireland, and introduced direct rule of the Province on March 30th, 1972, to mixed reactions. Gerry Adams described the reaction of the Nationalists as "utter jubilation" as the IRA believed they had pushed the British a step closer to pulling out the troops from Northern Ireland, paving the way for a fair and equitable political process that would, they hoped, result in a populist vote in favor of the reunification of a divided nation.

The Unionists, as Heath would later relate, "responded virulently" with protest marches, demonstrations and very vocal indication of their displeasure at what they viewed as a backdoor way of eventually breaking their stranglehold over the political processes in the Province, processes that had enabled the majority Unionist population to dominate the North and ensure the Nationalist movement would never obtain what the IRA had hoped to gain–a united Ireland. They felt betrayed by the Heath government. On hearing news of the introduction of direct rule, The Ulster Vanguard movement called a two day industrial strike, resulting in power cuts, disruptions in public transportation, and the closure of many shops and business. On the second day of the stoppage, a crowd of approximately one hundred thousand Unionist demonstrators gathered at Stormont Castle to mark the last sitting of the Stormont assembly on March 28th, 1972. The Unionists were not happy with direct rule, and were determined to let the Westminster Government know just how angry they were at the change in status quo in the North.

The IRA would view the fall of Stormont as a tremendous victory, as this had been a declared goal of the Provisionals as one of the steps toward eliminating British rule in the Province. Feeling as though they had the upper hand, the IRA requested a meeting with William Whitelaw in Ireland, and not at Stormont, but the request was turned down. At a June 13th press conference, Whitelaw stated that the British government would not let "part of the United Kingdom default from the rule of law." This comment left the door open for the Nationalist SDLP to meet and talk with Provisional IRA leadership to establish ground rules for a meeting in Ireland between the IRA and representatives of the Westminster government. The results of the conversations between the two groups were related to Whitelaw's office and agreement for a meeting was reached and set up for June 20th.

The location for the meeting was a private country house in Balleyarnet, situated close to the border between Derry and Donegal. The IRA delegation consisted of the Provisionals Chief-of-Staff Daithi O'Connell and a young Gerry Adams of Sinn Fein and the Belfast brigade of the Provisionals. They brought with them a Mr. Paddy McGrory, a lawyer known by the two IRA men. The British government's interests were represented by civil servant Philip Woodfield and Frank Steele of the British Secret Intelligence Service, MI6. Woodfield handed a letter of introduction from William Whitelaw to the lawyer accompanying the IRA delegation. Satisfied as to its authenticity McGrory left the meeting. Woodfield open the conversation with an outline of the Provisionals position, regarding a meeting with Whitelaw, as the Westminster government understood the situation. They were to initiate an immediate cease-fire and put a truce in place, providing the Secretary of State would grant several convicted prisoners political status, cease all harassment of the IRA and grant a meeting with the IRA, providing the truce had held over an agreed period of time. Woodfield's outline triggered three of hours of intense discussion. The Secretary of State, he explained, could not grant special status to prisoners, but would give an assurance that "rights, searches and arrests to look for people wanted for their past activities" would not occur as long as the truce held. The Secretary of State, he stated, was prepared to grant direct talks in London, if the IRA could maintain the truce for a specific period of time. Whitfield suggested fourteen days; O'Connell wanted seven, so middle ground was found in a ten day truce. If the truce was maintained to Whitelaw's satisfaction, then he would grant the meeting the day after the truce period expired. It was important that any meeting arranged would be kept totally secret, both from the rank-and-file IRA members and the British public. O'Connell was unsure as to how best to break the news of the cease-fire and truce without revealing that talks had been held and that the truce was prelude to a full meeting with the British government. Woodfield suggested an approach and dictated a message, which Adams and O'Connell wrote down. The agreed statement would say "we are ordering an indefinite cease-fire to take place effective from, date-to-be-determined, in the confident belief that the Secretary of State will make an exceptional response to this exceptional measure as he has said he will do in his public statements." As the meeting closed, O'Connell requested an effort by the Northern Ireland office to make an introduction for the IRA to the Ulster Defense Association, obviously mindful of the threat posed by the equally violent UDA.

The cease-fire was announced on June 26th, 1972, and held for 10 days as required under the terms of the agreement, so the full-scale meeting with Whitelaw and his representatives was set for July 7th in London. The venue would be at 96 Cheyne Walk in Chelsea, the home of Paul Channon, one of Whitelaw's team of junior ministers. The IRA delegation of Daithi O'Connell, Gerry Adams, Seamus Twomy, Martin McGuiness and Ivor Bell, together with a Dublin lawyer Miles Shemlin, acting as a note taker for the group, flew to Belfast by Army helicopter for a transfer flight to RAF Benson in Oxfordshire. From RAF Benson, the IRA delegation traveled to London in two limousines. The meeting was somewhat historic, as the IRA had, in effect, forced the British government to the negotiation table for only the second time in the history of the Troubles, after fifty-two years of an on-again off-again violent conflict.

Arriving at the meeting location, the IRA delegates were greeted by the civil servants Paul Channon, David Steel and Philip Woodfield. Whitelaw was late, so the Westminster group pushed to start the meeting, however, the IRA delegation would have no part of it–they had come to meet with the Secretary of State and that was who they were going to talk to. Gerry Adams later recalled that Whitelaw appeared flushed and flustered upon his arrival, with damp sweaty hands. From the start of the discussions, it was obvious that the gulf between the two side's positions was huge. The British government wanted a more just and equitable form of power-sharing in the North, with a more representative assembly. The IRA wanted a full-scale independence, not another assembly, the likes of which they had forced into collapse a short time before. Whitelaw was adamant that the only real solution to the situation in the north would be for all sides to have an equal say in how the Province was run, and forge tighter links with the Republic in the south who would help govern the six counties.

The IRA delegation made two key suggestions to the Westminster group that would, they hoped, enable the truce to continue and achieve further meaningful dialogue. They suggested that the British government make a statement that it was for the entire people of Ireland to decide the future of Ireland, and that they should make another declaration, as soon as possible, of the government's intent to withdraw from the North. Whitelaw stated they would consider the suggestions and would return to the IRA with proposals of their own. The meeting ended with little real agreement, other than the satisfaction the IRA delegation had gained from forcing Westminster to talk to them directly. They did, however, agree to maintain the truce until July 14th.

In reality, it would serve no purpose for the IRA to maintain the truce. They were fearful of the British who were simply playing for time, hoping the IRA rank-and-file would get lax and make themselves more exposed publicly than they would have done if the truce had not been in place. Two days after the London meeting, the violence erupted again in Northern Ireland and in doing so the IRA would make a critical tactical error, one that would result in an outcry against the Republican violence from all sides.

In an operation, supposedly planned prior to the London talks, on July 21st the Provisional IRA placed 22 car bombs across the city of Belfast in predominantly Unionist areas. It was a concentrated and coordinated attack, intended to primarily cause financial damage, according to IRA accounts of the episode. Warnings were given to the police and the army, but the IRA vastly underestimated the ability of the authorities to handle such a large amount of incidents in a relatively short time span. In the space of 75 minutes, the 22 car bombs exploded throughout Belfast killing nine people and maiming 130 others. In the attempt to evacuate people from danger, the public were inadvertently moved from one bomb site to another. Two bombs, one in the Oxford

Street bus station and the other outside shops in Cavehill Road, caused the nine deaths. The Oxford street bomb killed four bus company employees and two soldiers. Emergency services personnel reported that some of the victims had literally been blown to pieces, resulting in an initial death toll estimate of 11. Scenes of rescue workers shoveling body parts into plastic bags would capture the horror of that day. At Cavehill Road, a 14-year-old schoolboy was killed along with two female shoppers. The scenes of unbelievable carnage caused by the bombs led the media to label the event "Bloody Friday," and the IRA had handed the Loyalist groups just the type of political ammunition they themselves had gained from Bloody Sunday.

The resulting focus on the IRA from the July bombings also included a greatly increased Army presence. Approximately 4,000 additional troops were poured to Derry and Belfast with the express intention of pulling down the sectarian no-go area barricades and setting up local bases of operation in Republican areas, increasing the surveillance on the IRA. The bombings on Bloody Friday had backfired on the IRA strategically and emotionally. It backfired strategically because their activities and efforts would be hampered by the additional Army presence in their traditional areas of operation. It backfired emotionally, as the droves of recruits that had flocked to the IRA after Bloody Sunday, outraged at the British government for murdering innocent Catholics, would have to look at the actions of the Provisionals and the carnage they had created in a different light. They were just as ruthless and bloody and obviously prepared to perpetrate mass murder on the streets of Northern Ireland in the name of the cause. In an effort to deflect blame away from the IRA for the deaths and destruction, the Provisionals accused the RUC and the Army of deliberately ignoring some of the warnings thereby increasing the number of people left in harms way.

In Westminster, an increased sense of urgency to establish a power-sharing assembly in Northern Ireland took hold, something both the Nationalists and the Unionists were determined to stop as such a setup would give neither of them what they wanted. The Unionists did not want a diluted powerbase that would allow the Catholics to gain greater electoral representation that could, ultimately, result in a potential referendum in favor of unification, meaning they would be governed from Dublin. It was also not what the IRA wanted, as this would represent a step back towards the Stormont type assembly they had fought so hard to bring down. Nevertheless, that was the direction William Whitelaw was driving the Westminster government to adopt and in order to lay the groundwork for such an assembly, and stimulate debate among the interested parties, Whitelaw convened a meeting in Darlington in the North of England. The subject of the meeting was the devolution of Northern Ireland, the establishment of a power-sharing assembly, and a concept around the creation of a complementary Council of Ireland, intended to promote cross-border links and cooperation with the Republican in the south. Predictably, the Unionist groups protested that this would just be a backdoor way of having the Republic involved in the affairs of the Northern Province. Delegates from the Ulster Unionist party (UUP), Northern Ireland Labour Party (NILP) and the Alliance Party of Northern Ireland (APNI) were in attendance at the Darlington meeting, hosted by Whitelaw who had great expectations for the event. SDLP were conspicuous by their absence at the meeting, as they refused to participate in any such discussions regarding power-sharing while Internment was still in force. Somewhat predictably, given the views on the Unionist side, the meeting came to no agreement on a future direction for the Province. The notion of a power-sharing assembly, in a move away from direct rule through Westminster, would become a personal crusade for a determined William Whitelaw, despite all the warning signs that such a policy could be a recipe for continued strife and, ultimately, failure.

When Whitelaw became Secretary of State for Northern Ireland, he made a commitment to hold a referendum for the people to decide the future direction of the Province. Did they want to stay part of the United Kingdom, or unite with the Republic? Given the strong Unionist support in the six counties, and the grip the Unionist parties had on local politics, any such referendum would be unlikely to achieve the goals of the Republican groups. The IRA position, made very clear on several occasions, was that any referendum on reunification should involve the entire Irish people, but again strong historical ties between the Protestant Unionists and the Tory government made that a highly unlikely event. As Whitelaw had promised, on March 8, 1973, in an event that was to become know as the boarder poll, the people of Northern Ireland went to the polls to answer two questions:

1. Do you want Northern Ireland to remain part of the United Kingdom?
2. Do you want Northern Ireland to be joined with the Republic of Ireland, outside the United Kingdom?

The referendum was, by and large, boycotted by the Catholic population with predictable results, as the overall turnout for the vote was 57%

of the eligible electorate. Given that the overwhelming majority of the votes cast were by Protestant Unionists, it was no surprise that 98% of the vote was in favor of question one, wanting to stay with the United Kingdom, while under 2% voted for question two and unification. It was, so the Unionist claimed, a clear indication of what the people wanted, a commentary echoed by the Prime Minister, Edward Heath, who stated that the vote was a "robust endorsement of the existing constitutional arrangements." The boarder poll vote, somewhat misguidedly would help drive an acceptance of the power-sharing agreement the Westminster government were determined, with a dogged support of William Whitelaw, to drive through as soon as reasonably possible in order to end direct rule from Westminster.

The day of the border poll saw six bombs detonated in the city of Belfast, with little reported on the bombs outside of the six counties. However, the IRA had decided to mock the border poll in a more spectacular fashion, one that would provide a vital lesson in politics and public relations for the Republican cause. The Provisionals made a decision to take the border poll to the heart of the British government. To do so, they devised and executed a plan to send a series of car bombs from Dublin to the British capital in readiness for the day of the March 8th referendum. The IRA prepared the vehicles as planned and transported them to the mainland via the Dublin to Liverpool ferry, a route that would become an important link for the London ASU once they became established. Six volunteers were selected to transport the bombs to their intended targets. Among the volunteers were twenty-two-year-old Delours Price and her nineteen-year-old sister Maryon. Their selection triggered a heated debate in the Belfast brigade with regard to their suitability for the mission, but they were eventually allowed to go with the other four volunteers to deliver car bombs to the British capital. After traveling by ferry to Liverpool, the cars were driven to London and put in place on the streets of London early in the morning of the 8th with timing devices set, so the delivery team could make a getaway undetected.

The first of the four bombs exploded outside the Central criminal Court, the Old Bailey, closely followed by the second bomb placed in the heart of the British Government in Whitehall. One person was killed and 180 injured in the explosions. The reported Achilles heel of the operation, leading to the discovery of the remaining two devices, occurred while the car bombs were being prepared in the Republic. The IRA had fitted each car with false British license plates. At the time, each license plate in the UK carried a letter suffix denoting the year the car was registered and each August the letter would increment up one place in the alphabet. Unless the plate was changed, say for a personalized plate, the original plate would stay with the car for the life of the vehicle even when the vehicle was transferred to a new owner, unlike the USA where the plates would be retained by the seller to use on another vehicle. This letter-year suffix became something of a status symbol, as people could tell the year of the vehicle and its age by looking at the plate. The IRA had not taken this into account when creating the false plates, and an obvious mismatch was noticed by an alert police officer who noticed a discrepancy between the age of a vehicle, and the plate on the car parked, in of all places, directly outside the headquarters of the Metropolitan police at Scotland Yard. The fourth car bomb, parked in Whitehall, was also found and both were successfully diffused before they could detonate. The police sealed off the ports after the first bomb, and found and arrested the IRA team at Heathrow Airport waiting for a flight to Dublin. However, Ed Moloney in his excellent work on the history of the IRA, speculated that the police had advanced notification of the bombing attempts, and as such has circulated photographs of the Price sisters prior to March 8th, with instructions to apprehend them on sight. There was also speculation that the Belfast brigade of the IRA had a leak and a source inside the Provisionals had compromised the operation from the outset.

The resulting public outcry at the horrors of the Belfast car bomb being brought to the streets of the English capital would not to go unnoticed by the Provo's leadership. The two car bombs in London received widespread news coverage, while the six bombs in Belfast had received almost no mention in the mainstream British press. The Provisional IRA leadership, at the GHQ level, learned two valuable lessons from the March 8th car bomb attacks on London. Firstly, if there was a leak in one or more of their brigades, they would need a change in tactics if they were to run protracted, undetected campaigns of violence on the British mainland. The March 8th team had been far too easily apprehended. If they were to be successful, they would need to move to a system of compartmentalized independent ASU's, placed in deep cover on the mainland that would stay inactive until given orders to mobilize. The IRA could not afford to have teams picked off so easily, if compromised by intelligence leaks or infiltrations at the brigade level. Secondly, the emotional, tactical and propaganda value of bombing London would far outweigh what they could achieve by bombs in the North. If they were truly to have a chance to bring the British government to its knees, then the target would have to be the British mainland in general, but with a specific focus on London. They needed to make plans to be ready, as the power-sharing moves proposed by British government would not be acceptable to either Protestant or Catholic paramilitary groups. The process of putting in place a power-sharing assembly, if this was the path the Westminster government would follow, could fail with pressure from either side. If that were to be the case, the Provisionals would need to be able to react quickly to inflict their brand of terror on Britain in an effort to force the government to pull out the troops, as a prelude to pulling out of Northern Ireland altogether.

The power-sharing route gained additional impetus with the publication on March 20, 1973, of a Government White Paper, outlining devolution for Northern Ireland and the establishment of a more fair and equitable assembly for Northern Ireland to govern the Province. The White Paper featured three main themes. Firstly, the assembly would be made up of 78 elected members from the various political parties in Northern Ireland. Secondly, there would be the formation of the Council of Ireland, with representation from both the Northern Ireland assembly and the Irish Parliament. Thirdly, and probably most importantly, elections to the assembly would be conducted by proportional representation, which would help counter the gerrymandered electoral boundaries established by the Unionists. On that point, the paper emphasized that the assembly must "seek a much wider consensus than has hitherto existed." The paper went on to acknowledge the previous biases of the Stormont assembly that had favored the Unionist cause at the detriment of the Catholic population in the North. Driving to a more representative assembly was essential and "fundamental," as the problems in the Province were not just driven by Nationalist and Unionist aspirations, but also by the "economic conditions, such as inadequate housing and unemployment" in the Province, factors driven by the political imbalance of the former Stormont assembly that had helped to feed the sectarian violence on both sides. Any future power-sharing arrangement would indeed have to be truly "shared," if it were to avoid the self-sustaining cycles of bias and violence. The final recommendations of the paper, which would form the basis of a Bill to be presented to Parliament, concluded that the Province of Northern Ireland would remain a part of the United Kingdom "for as long as that is the wish of a majority of the people."

The White Paper on the Northern Ireland assembly was presented to the House of Parliament in April 1973. One important element of the bill, pushed by Heath and Whitehall, related to the formation of the Council of Ireland. After elections to the power-sharing assembly, the bill outlined that Westminster would arrange a meeting of the elected representatives of the assembly with members of the government of the Irish Republic, in order to determine the most effective way of creating a joint membership council. The Nationalists opposed the notion of any power-sharing deal as did the Unionists, but the concept of having the Republic in the south involved with any of the management of the North would remain a major sticking point for the Reverend Ian Paisley and the Unionists, who viewed any such move as a sneaky backhanded way of moving toward eventual unification. The Council of Ireland concept would be a hard sell for Heath and Whitehall.

Elections for the new assembly took place on June 28, 1973. Faulkner's UUP won twenty two seats, the SDLP nineteen seats, the hard-line Unionists led by Ian Paisley won eighteen seats, Unionists with no outward or professed affiliations gained ten seats, the Alliance Party eight seats and the NILP one seat. The elections were relatively straightforward, but Heath and Whitehall would be faced with a possible lengthy delay in getting all the elected members to work out who was to lead the assembly, how the assembly would function and when they could take over the running of the Province. The Royal assent of the Northern Ireland assembly Bill passed into law on July 18, 1973, finally abolishing the old Stormont assembly, and starting a political stopwatch on the whole power-sharing process. The elected representatives would have until March of 1974 to work out the details of the assembly, otherwise the law would lapse and the Heath government would be back to square one on the entire process.

The first meeting of the newly elected assembly took place on July 31, 1973. The intent of the session was to elect a presiding official and obtain nominations for members of the committees required to draw up procedural rules by which the assembly would govern. The meeting was, as Heath later put it, "frankly farcical, thanks to Paisley going on the rampage again." Paisley's Democratic Unionist party, DUP, created an alliance with the other hard-line Unionists in the assembly, creating a 27 strong alliance to protest against the power-sharing assembly. This new Unionist alliance had issued statements the day before the meeting rejecting Westminster's plans for the assembly. During the rowdy session, Paisley said, "I should like those members of the British government who are here and the Westminster members who are skulking in the galleries to know that Ulstermen are free people and are not going to be bullied!" Gerry Fitt, veteran leader of the main Catholic opposition party, the SDLP, attempted to calm the situation, "we have come here today," he said, "with a clear commitment to make this assembly a fair and just system of administration for the people of Northern Ireland."

The meeting was adjourned after two hours of heckling, with Paisley and his Unionist alliance staying in the chamber, with the lights turned off, as they continued their protest against the British government's position. The assembly had not had a very auspicious beginning.

Many in the Heath government worried that the assembly would not be able to function as intended, given Paisley's open and vociferous protests against the concept of the assembly and the notion of power sharing with the Catholic SDLP. Shadow Foreign Secretary James Callahan warned the House of Commons that Britain may need to reconsider its position with regard to Northern Ireland if, through sectarian maneuvering, the assembly became undermined and unable to reach a consensus. Harold Wilson, leader of the opposition party, echoed Callahan's views, stating that if the principles as outlined in the White Paper on the power-sharing assembly were rejected, Britain may have to pull out of Northern Ireland completely. It was not in the best interest of the Heath government to allow the Northern Ireland assembly to be hijacked into failure. Through sheer determination, William Whitelaw worked diligently to pull the parties together and construct a meaningful dialogue about the makeup and selection of the power-sharing executive. Through a series of meetings over several weeks, Whitelaw would strive to drive the different viewpoints of the parties involved towards a unified position. After a lot of effort and political maneuvering, he was finally rewarded with a breakthrough agreement, with all of the parties involved agreeing on a final formula for the assembly. There would be an 11 person core executive team, made up of six Unionists, four SDLP members and one alliance party member. Faulkner, from the UPP, would be the Chief Executive, with his Unionist allegiance balanced by the appointment of the SDLP's Gerry Fitt as his deputy. There would also be an additional four non-voting members, made up of two from the SDLP and one each from the Unionists and the alliance party. The major hurdle faced by Whitelaw, in pulling off the final assembly agreement, was the vehement rejection by the Unionists of the Council of Ireland proposal. They viewed the move as an attempt at unification, a notion they would fight tooth and nail to defeat. After weeks of fruitless negotiation on the Council of Ireland proposal, Heath and Whitelaw convened a four-day series of meetings at the civil service college at Sunningdale, England, with the intention of hammering out an agreement all parties could support regarding the involvement of the Republic in the affairs of the northern six counties. The meeting would be somewhat historic in nature, as it would be the first time since 1925 that the acting Prime Minister of the United Kingdom, Edward Heath, the

Prime Minister of the Republic of Ireland, at that time Liam Cosgrove, and the government of Northern Ireland in the form of the Northern Ireland assembly executive, had met for talks on the future direction of the Province. The Irish Prime Minister, the Northern Ireland executive, Heath and Whitelaw spent the four days hammering out the-who-and-the-how of an agreement on the controversial Council of Ireland. The final format of the agreement, proudly announced to the nation as the Sunningdale agreement, would be on thin ice as the Heath government attempted to keep all sides on the same page. The agreed format for the council consisted of seven members of the Northern Ireland assembly and seven members of the Irish Parliament, forming the primary Council. A second, larger, consultative counsel would be made up of an equal number of the Northern Ireland assembly and the Irish Parliament. The primary role of the council would give the Republic jurisdiction on matters of joint concerns to both the South and the North. Sunningdale was hailed as a major breakthrough in the Northern Ireland story, with the Westminster government of Edward Heath convinced it was a step in the right direction for the Province to govern independently from Westminster. Heath, obviously blinded by the political achievement of Sunningdale rather than the overarching practicality of the implementation and longevity of the agreement, commented that the "historic accord was one of the proudest moments of my premiership." Heath and Whitelaw had not looked beyond the polite table manners of the Sunningdale attendees in their assessment of the genuineness of the agreement. Sunningdale would be a sticking plaster used on a wound that needed a tourniquet. In a manner similar to the IRA car bombs in London, the agreement reached at Sunningdale would remain a ticking time bomb waiting to go off, rip apart the Province and drag the British mainland into the maelstrom of the Northern Ireland Troubles in a way that Heath, and Whitelaw, could only imagine in their worst nightmares. The hard-line Unionists viewed the whole thing as a secret plot to destroy Northern Ireland and so bitterly resented the agreement. There was also widespread dislike of the agreement among the Provisional IRA, believing that they needed to "kill off Sunningdale, before Sunningdale killed it." The much lauded agreement that Heath was so proud of would end up on borrowed time.

The Northern Ireland assembly executive officially took office on January 1st, 1974. The meetings that followed this event saw a significant amount of Unionist protest against power-sharing and the Sunningdale agreement, to the point where Ian Paisley and 18 other staunch Unionists had to be bodily removed from Stormont for being a disruptive element in the official proceedings of the assembly. The Unionists were apparently determined to do all they could to undermine the hard earned power-sharing and dismantle everything that the Sunningdale agreement stood for. The really contentious issue remained the Council of Ireland, which the Unionists still viewed as a shortcut to a united Ireland. The Ulster Unionist Council (UUC), the governing body of the UUP, held a vote on January 4th against the concept of the Sunningdale agreement, where the members voted 427 to 374 to reject the agreement. Infuriated at the about face of the UUC, Faulkner resigned as leader of the UUP three days later.

Back in London, the Heath government faced increasing Unionist rebellion in the North of Ireland, together with rising domestic industrial strife. The mine workers Union, stirred up by the radical leadership of Arthur Scargill, had rejected an offer of a 13% pay increase. To step up pressure on the government, the mine workers union banned all overtime work, seriously impacting industrial capacity. Britain in the 1970's was a nation highly dependent on coal for the generation of electricity, for steelmaking and domestic heating. The mineworkers, realizing they had a significant bargaining position, used their collective power to leverage the government to up the pay raise offer. But Heath would have nothing to do with it. Rather than deal with the unions, Heath put the country on a state of emergency with a mandatory three-day workweek for all nonessential industries and business to conserve energy supplies. The mineworkers countered with a vote on a national strike, which was carried by 81% of the members being in favor of the action.

The mineworker's decision to take industrial action through a national strike broke Heath's patience. Against the better judgment of his cabinet, Heath called for a snap general election for Great Britain to gain, in his opinion, a much-needed mandate from the nation to answer the question in his mind as to who ran the country, the government or the unions. The cabinet tried to reason with Heath, as they still had 18 months more in office before they were required to call a general election, by which time the mineworker's situation would be ancient history, and the Northern Ireland position clearer. They argued to no avail and the date for the election was set for February 28, 1974. Heath and the Conservatives would campaign behind the "Firm Action for Fair Britain" manifesto. Harold Wilson, leader of the opposition Labour Party, had a different strategy. Wilson and The Labour Party, traditionally the party of the unions, had to tread a fine line. Wilson, a very canny and able politician, could not openly support or condone the strike action of the mineworkers, but then again he could not afford to alienate the unions by distancing himself from their cause, the bedrock of support for his political party. In a very astute move, Wilson positioned Labour as a mediating force in the country, driving for a social contract with the unions, seeking partnership rather than confrontation. It was a smart move, as while the unions would be only too happy to topple the Tory government of Edward Heath, they would not want to undermine a future government of their own party. There would be a quid pro quo on the social contract, for the mineworkers would expect something in return from Wilson if they helped to elect his party, but that was a price deemed worthy of payment in order to win the election.

The decision to go to the country would backfire on Heath in several ways. In the most basic sense he lost the election to the Labour Party, failing to gain the much lauded mandate from the country in the process. The loss to Labour resulted in the first hung parliament since 1929, for while Labour had received fewer votes than the Conservatives, they had won more seats, 301 to 297. With the Conservatives unable to hold a majority, or persuade the much smaller Liberal party to form a coalition government, Heath was forced to resign after four days of behind closed doors dealings with the Liberals. Remarkably, what Heath failed to realize was that a snap election fell right into the trap waiting for him set by the Unionists in Northern Ireland. With the increasingly rabid resistance to Heath's precious and much lauded Sunningdale agreement, the Unionists took the general election and used it to their own advantage. They did so by forming a highly effective coalition of Unionist forces behind the newly formed United Ulster Unionist Council (UUUC), bringing together Paisley's DUP with the Ulster Vanguard and Official Unionists, in a move that totally blindsided the Nationalists. The Unionists capitalized on the Protestant fear and loathing of any notion of sharing control of Northern Ireland with the Irish Republic, and used that boogieman image for all it was worth, campaigning behind the fear and dread provoking slogan of "Dublin is just a Sunningdale away." The UUUC put forward one candidate in each of the Northern Ireland constituencies and swept the election, with the UUUC scooping up eleven of the twelve available parliamentary seats, with the SDP left desperately clinging to West Belfast with the one remaining seat.

The election result in Northern Ireland sent a clear message to the Westminster government and the Nationalists. It demonstrated that the unionist opposition was real, organized and a force to be reckoned with. While the election results did not immediately signal the end of the Northern Ireland assembly, power-sharing and the Sunningdale agreement, it would signal the entire concept was at risk and potentially on borrowed time. The message was not lost on Heath who, in a somewhat bitter fashion, commented on the situation in Northern Ireland in his autobiography, "ultimately it was the people of Northern Ireland themselves who threw away the best chance for peace in the blood-soaked province of the six counties." Heath, so proud of the Sunningdale achievement, realized that Paisley and his Unionists had sent a message across the nation that they would not, under the proposed agreement, cooperate with the British government or the Irish Republic in any way, shape or form.

To capitalize on their resounding victory in the general election, the UUUC organized demonstration marches to the doors of Stormont, demanding the assembly be suspended. Inside the assembly, Unionists argued that the Sunningdale agreement should not be ratified, which was counted by the SDLP arguing that the Sunningdale agreement was a roadmap for the future of the province and should not, under, any circumstances, be "watered down." The Unionists kept up the pressure and announced the formation of a new organization, a labor union; the Ulster Workers Union (UWC) intended to represent the best interests of the Protestant workforce in the six counties, but in reality the organization was a politically contrived vehicle to push the Unionist agenda through the Protestant workforce of the North. The agenda of this new group would soon be revealed to the British government, as in March 1974, the UWC made a statement demanding a fresh set of elections to the Northern Ireland assembly, with the obvious objective of increasing the Unionists hold on the power-sharing assembly, further capitalizing on the electoral success in the February general election. The UWC threatened to unleash civil disobedience on the Province if the British government did not comply with their demands, forcing the new Secretary of State Merlyn Rees to basically ignore their saber rattling. However, Rees did eventually agree to a meeting with the UWC leadership in April, where they made it clear to the Secretary precisely what they meant by civil disobedience. They threatened to bring the Province to a painful grinding halt via a massive general strike, stopping all industry, power generation, petrol supplies, and food distribution and totally disrupting the very fabric of life in Northern Ireland. Rees and the Wilson government ignored the threats as pure chest thumping and posturing by the UWC, as other labor unions in the province had threatened such a strike in the past and had not managed to muster sufficient support to make any significant impact. The UWC would be viewed no differently by the government than other Unionist labor groups that had gone before them, a decision that would turn out to be a grave miscalculation on the part of Westminster. Rees and Wilson would quickly realize the mistake they had made when they started to question the degree of support the UWC was receiving from the UDA paramilitary group. The UDA had publicly announced its support in backing the UUUC in their opposition to the Sunningdale agreement. The storm clouds were gathering, with many indicators of the serious problem that was about to be unleashed in the North visible to those who cared to look hard enough.

On May 14th, 1974, during a very stormy meeting of the Northern Ireland assembly, a motion to condemn the power-sharing Sunningdale agreement was defeated 44 to 28. The failure of the Unionists to win the motion triggered a chain of events that was to spin out of control quite rapidly. On the evening of the 14th, the Unionists announced there would be a general strike across Northern Ireland to commence the following day. This was the civil disobedience the UWC had promised the Wilson government if they did not meet their demands for new assembly elections. The strike started with sporadic support, though the UWC, aided by the visible support of the UDA, pressured, cajoled and intimidated massive numbers of workers to stay away from their places of employment. The UWC controlled power stations, food distribution and even disrupted the delivery of mail in the province. The UWC published a list of "essential services" that would be allowed to continue without disruption as they steadily took over the administration of the Province, creating much misery and suffering in the process. The people in the Irish Republic would also be on the receiving end of the Unionist fervor gripping their neighbor in the North, with catastrophic results.

On May 17th, the UVF embarked on a spree of car hijacking in the North. The first car, a green Hillman Avenger, was taken from the owner in the Old Bank area at 10:00am by three masked gunmen, with two of the gunmen holding owner captive until he was released at 4:00pm that afternoon. A blue Austin 1800 taxicab was hijacked in Belfast at 9:00am. The driver was held until 2:00pm, but told to wait one hour until reporting the theft of his vehicle to the police. A third vehicle, a blue Ford Escort, was stolen from the parking lot of a Belfast haulage contractor between the hours of 8:0am and 10:30pm. The final vehicle in this particular episode was stolen from the Portadown District of Belfast, while the owner was shopping, at sometime during the morning. The stolen green Hillman Minx, along with the other three vehicles, were driven to a UVF hideout somewhere in the North. At this location the vehicles were all packed with a powerful homemade explosive called ANFO, used by both Protestant and Catholic paramilitary groups. ANFO (Ammonium Nitrate Fuel Oil) can be made by mixing agricultural grade fertilizer with diesel oil, materials readily found on most farms. When mixed and stabilized, it has, at best, eight-tenths the explosive power of TNT and so would be capable of causing extensive damage. The explosives were primed with timed detonation devices, transforming the passenger vehicles into lethal car bombs. The UVF team set out for their target destinations in the South, the Hillman Minx to Monaghan, the other three cars to Dublin. On the way to its target, and driving at speed, the Hillman Avenger narrowly missed colliding with a tractor backing out all of a farm entrance. The three Dublin car bombs were parked and left, one each in Parnell Street, Talbot Street and Leinster Street. The Monaghan device was parked outside a popular public house in the center of the town. With the UVF team safely back across the border, the unsuspecting citizens of Dublin and Monaghan went about their business on that Friday afternoon in May. At 5:30pm, at the peak of the rush-hour on the busiest day of the week, the first car bomb exploded without any prior warning being given by the UVF to the Irish authorities. The second of the bombs was also detonated, with all three exploding within 90 seconds of each other, a degree of precision unheard of in the previous paramilitary activities of either side. The area of Dublin impacted was totally devastated by the three bombs and, in total, twenty-six people were killed by the blasts in Dublin that day. Near the Talbot Street bomb, one eyewitness stated that "there were bodies and bits of bodies around the rubble . . . we went back and lifted a woman outside O'Neill's. She was still alive and moaning. As we lifted her, her body simply disintegrated in our arms. We placed her down again." Another eyewitness was entering a Talbot Street hotel when the second device exploded, "a newspaper stand was blown into the air beside me and the newsboy next to it just disappeared before my eyes."

At 6:58pm, the car bomb in the center of Monaghan exploded, killing a further seven innocent people. As with the Dublin bombs, no warnings were given by the UVF before the attack, ensuring maximum death and injury from the blast. A total of thirty-three people were killed by the four bombs that day and hundreds more wounded. The victims included an entire family of four, and a pregnant woman and her unborn child. It would remain the deadliest attack by either Paramilitary group for the entire duration of the hostilities.

There has been intense speculation regarding the UVF and its level of technical sophistication in 1975. Some have argued that they did not have the technical skills to carry out such a raid, and were aided in the attack by British intelligence and elements of the SAS. This assertion was not disputed by the later inquiry into the attacks driven by Ireland's Justice Barron in 2004. The report generated by the enquiry that stated that, "suggestion that members of the security forces in Northern Ireland could have been involved in the bombings is in Mr. Justice Barron's own words 'neither fanciful nor absurd.'" That the UVF could have conducted the attacks unaided was also questioned by one of the forensic scientists to give evidence to the Justice Barron report. Dr. James Donovan stated that "from what I have heard about the UVF at the time, it would have needed direction of some sort to assemble the bomb, know where to place it for maximum effect, detonate it and get away."

There can really only be two reasons for the British forces support the UVF, if in fact this is the case. Firstly, they would have wanted to demonstrate to the IRA and Republican forces, increasingly disturbed and off balance by the events orchestrated by the Unionists in the North, that the UVF was a force to be reckoned with and were being supported by British intelligence. Secondly, the British would be sending a message to the Irish government, giving them a taste of what life would be like if the Troubles spread to the south, something more likely to happen if the Republic did not help the British in their fight against the IRA.

The bombings created an outrage in the Nationalist groups because of the savagery of the attacks, of the huge loss of life, made all the more deadly by the timing of the explosions on a busy Friday and the lack of any warning. The bombs were not intended to just cause material damage to property in the towns, as they were designed and placed to kill and maim. The Republican anger was further fueled by comments from Sammy Smith, press officer for both the UDA and the UWC, when he told the press that "I am very happy about the bombings in Dublin. There is a war with the Free State and now we are laughing at them." The statement, directed at the Republicans, only served to increase the anger and frustration felt by the Catholic population in the North as they endured the continuing suffering inflicted by the deprivations of the general strike.

The bombings further increase the pressure on the UWC-driven strike, with an upsurge of sectarian violence breaking out across the region. The UWC criticized the Wilson government for not negotiating with them on their basic need to call off strike—an agreement to hold fresh elections in the Northern Ireland assembly. As the strike continued and Northern Ireland was brought to its knees, Merlyn Rees ordered a state of emergency across the North—he had no choice as the UWC, with the support of UDA, had taken control of the Province and the British government in Westminster was almost powerless to stop the ensuing anarchy.

By May 24th, 1974, day ten of the strike, a crash meeting was held at Chequers, the Prime Ministers country home, between Faulkner, Fitt and Wilson to go over the deteriorating situation in Northern Ireland. Faulkner stated that if nothing was done "a condition of anarchy would spread . . . constitute a threat to government elsewhere in the UK." Wilson pressed Faulkner on how far he thought the UWC would go, to which Faulkner replied that he thought they would avoid a direct confrontation with the British Army, but with "every hour that passed" it became "increasingly evident that the administration of the country was in fact in the hands of the Ulster Workers Council." Faulkner added that the situation was out of the control of Ian Paisley and passed onto "other, more dangerous hands." The objective of these more sinister forces, stated Faulkner, was the creation of a "neo-fascist Northern Ireland," controlled by extreme Unionists elements.

In a May 27th top-secret memo from Wilson to his cabinet, the Prime Minister discussed, and chillingly foretold, the rein of terror that was soon to be unleashed on the British mainland. He talked about drafting "doomsday scenarios" that would pull Britain out of Northern Ireland, despite the still public adherence to the existing policy and belief in power-sharing. Wilson argued this may be necessary because "the press and an increasing number of MP's will soon be telling us that the emperor has no clothes," with regard to the government's strategy on Northern Ireland. Wilson acknowledged the risks of a complete British pullout and the domestic and international ramifications of such an action, and the spectrum of possible scenarios, ". . . outbreak of violence and bloodshed, possible unacceptability to moderate Catholics, ditto to the Republic, the United Nations *and the possible spread of trouble across the water* [to the UK, emphasis added], to name but a few."

In a follow-up to Wilson's memo, Secretary of State for Northern Ireland, Merlyn Rees, told the Prime Minister that it would be in the government's best interest if the Executive of the Northern Ireland assembly were to "go of their own accord." He said they could not have any "plausible complaint that they have not received the full support of Her Majesty's Government." Rees continued to state that with the Northern Ireland Executive out of the picture, the government would be free to do a number of things under the Constitution Act, such as reinstituting direct rule from Westminster.

Given the almost impossible task the Wilson government had on its hands to deal with the chaos in Northern Ireland, compounded by the Unionist strike, having the assembly collapse in on itself was an acceptable strategy to allow the Wilson government to work its way out of the jam it was in. Rees clearly wanted Faulkner and the executive of the Northern Ireland assembly to resign. Faulkner had been urging Rees to go to the bargaining table and meet with the UWC, in an effort to bring the strike to a close and save the power-sharing assembly. To do so, Rees would have appeared to have allowed the Unionists to blackmail the Wilson government into making a deal. It was a no-win situation for Rees. If he made a deal with the UWC and agreed to fresh elections in the North, he would have been accused by the Republicans of selling them out. The option that would allow Rees to wash his hands of the situation would be to have the assembly collapse under the weight of the actions of its own Executive. If they went, the assembly would fall, and the Wilson government would be able to point the finger of blame at the people of Northern Ireland for bringing about the collapse of the assembly and the tearing up of the Sunningdale agreement, throwing away a chance to reach a lasting peace in the Province. The blame would not be laid at the government's door, as they could conveniently point out the extraordinary effort of the previous administration in reaching the historic Sunningdale agreement that all parties had signed. Wilson and Rees were not the architects of the strife they faced, but they were the caretakers of the situation they had inherited.

The following day, May 28th, Rees again refused to meet with the UWC leadership and have any discussion regarding their demands for new elections to the assembly. This refusal pushed Faulkner to the edge, forcing the veteran Northern Ireland politician to resign as Chief Executive of the Northern Ireland assembly. In a likewise fashion, many of Faulkner's colleagues on the Executive also resigned, resulting in a rapid collapse of the power-sharing agreement and an end to the new assembly at Stormont. News of the collapse of the Northern Ireland assembly spread rapidly to Protestant areas of the Province, sparking off jubilant celebrations. Any faint hope the Wilson government may have had about keeping a working power-sharing assembly vanished in the smoke of the Unionist bonfires. The Protestants of Northern Ireland, all British citizens, had staged a rebellion against the British government and its policy on power-sharing and won. With the collapse of the assembly, the UWC victoriously called an end to the strike that had destroyed the British government's hopes for a more integrated and equitable rule of law in the Province. The Unionists had won a significant victory and would fiercely resist any further attempt at creating a power-sharing governing body for the North.

The Provisionals had watched the UWC and UDA as they gained a stranglehold on the Province. They would blame the Wilson government for the collapse of the assembly, because despite their dislike for the Council of Ireland, the power-sharing assembly had at least given them a hope of working out a Republican agenda in the North. With the inevitable reintroduction of direct rule from Westminster, the Provisionals put the Active Service Unit plan into place, as a prelude to unleashing an unprecedented reign of terror on the British mainland in a desperate effort to re-establish a balance of power between Westminster, the Unionists, and the Republican Nationalist cause. The phase one campaign against London was about to start in earnest, pitting the London ASU against the Metropolitan Police Bomb Squad in a deadly game of cat-and-mouse that would culminate in the six-day standoff at Balcombe Street.

doi:10.1300/J173v08n01_02

Chapter 2

Phase One

The Provisional IRA was going to take the fight to the mainland and would focus its efforts on the capital, London. Other areas of England would also be targets, but the capital was where the Provo's expected to gain the greatest psychological impact from their particular brand of terror on the people of England. The London ASU set up operations in August, after careful preparations had been made to establish the supply links and logistics for the five-man team.

The IRA did not want to wait until its full time team was in place, and so started operations against the British using other IRA operatives sent over for a specific mission and then returned to Ireland. On the morning of July 17, 1974, one or more IRA operatives entered the Houses of Parliament by mingling with a group of building workers carrying out construction work on the underground parking garage under the building. Over 100 workers were employed in the construction effort. The Metropolitan police stated that each of the workers was supposed to be issued with a security past to get in through the site entrance, separate from the main entrance, but the site agent claimed that not all of them had a pass. Many were casual Irish laborers who would sign on for a few days work and then move on. Once in through the entrance, the IRA operatives placed a 20 pound device in the canteen and left the building. At 8:22am, the Press Association received a phone call from a man with an Irish accent giving a warning about a bomb in the House of Commons, using a recognized IRA codeword to confirm the authenticity of the

[Haworth co-indexing entry note]: "Phase One." Moysey, Steven P. Co-published simultaneously in *Journal of Police Crisis Negotiations* (The Haworth Press, Inc.) Vol. 8, No. 1, 2008, pp. 37-87; and: *The Road to Balcombe Street: The IRA Reign of Terror in London* (Steven P. Moysey) The Haworth Press, Inc., 2008, pp. 37-87. Single or multiple copies of this article are available for a fee from The Haworth Document Delivery Service [1-800-HAWORTH, 9:00 a.m. - 5:00 p.m. (EST). E-mail address: docdelivery@haworthpress.com].

Available online at http://jpcn.haworthpress.com
doi:10.1300/J173v08n01_03

call. Six minutes later the bomb exploded and although the police had been unable to completely clear the building before the explosion, those who were caught in the blast were not seriously hurt. The building was badly damaged, with a fire from ruptured gas main caused by the blast contributing to the problem faced by the emergency services. One Member of Parliament, Mr. David Steel, told the BBC News that the whole of Westminster Hall had been filled with dust from the blast. Security in the building was described as "casual" by one former MP, as no one expected the House of Commons would be a target of a terrorist attack, a quite remarkably naïve approach to the safety of the seat of government. That would all change after the blast of June 17th. The Provisional IRA had sent a message to the Wilson government, at their place of business that would shake the British out of their complacency. The Northern Ireland Troubles were knocking at the door of the British Government and the knocking would only become louder and more deadly for the British people.

Exactly one month later, the IRA hit another target, again without warning. The Tower of London is a very popular tourist spot and historical building. A magnet for overseas visitors, the Tower of London is also a site regularly visited by groups of schoolchildren in England as a history class outing. Such was the case on Wednesday, July 17th at 2:00pm when a device concealed under a cannon in the Mortar Room, an exhibit hall in the building's basement, exploded with devastating effect. The explosion, contained within the thick stone walls of the room, was channeled out through the doorway blowing apart a heavy oak door leading to an outer passageway. Forty-seven-year-old Dorothy Household, a librarian and Sunday school teacher, was killed instantly in the blast with 41 others, including a group of schoolchildren, seriously wounded. Many of the victims had lost limbs and some had received terrible facial injuries, while others had been impaled by pieces of the oak door as it fragmented in the blast. The attack was an indiscriminate strike at innocent tourists and schoolchildren, to which the public was justifiably outraged. No warning had been given and the bomber obviously knew the victims would be tourist families and schoolchildren on outings. It was a meaningless and cruel attack. The Metropolitan police Bomb Squad, in an effort to find something that could help in the investigation, collected undeveloped film from people at the scene so that they could print the photographs and look for any known subversives or suspicious looking people. No paramilitary group ever claimed responsibility for the horrific attack, but it is widely viewed to have been the handiwork of the IRA.

The setup of the phase one IRA campaign in England began with the arrival in London of two key operatives, Joe O'Connell and Brendan Dowd. O'Connell was the commander of the eventual five-man group. Twenty-three-years-old at the time, he was a thin featured man with a shock of black hair. It would be O'Connell's responsibility to pull the ASU together and make tactical plans for the forthcoming bombing campaign. The ASU were to be given occasional strategic direction from GHQ, but would be given a wide-ranging brief from their commanders back in Ireland to use their initiative in the selection of targets, providing they did so in order to pursue the overall focus of the mission, which was to create fear and destruction on the streets of London.

O'Connell and Dowd moved into a flat at 22 Waldemar Avenue in Fulham. The location was carefully selected, as it was a relatively quiet neighborhood with little in the way of an established Irish community, something GHQ had instructed them to avoid. They were also under orders to avoid frequenting pubs and clubs popular with Irish people in London, so as to not be seen associating with any suspected IRA member potentially under surveillance by British intelligence or Special Branch. The adoption of these isolation tactics would work well for the ASU as they engaged in their deadly mission, enabling them to stay off the police radar and keep the Bomb Squad leadership guessing as to their whereabouts.

The ASU would be kept supplied via couriers, mostly female, who would bring explosives, weapons, money and instructions to them from Ireland using the Dublin-to-Liverpool ferry route. The couriers would then make the drive to London to deliver supplies and then return, undetected, to the Irish Republic. From a financial perspective, the ASU were not overly well-funded. Eddie Butler would later tell Chief Superintendent Jim Nevill that the couriers brought the ASU cash in the amount of £1,000 every two months. This worked out to £25 weekly for each of the team, when at full strength of five men, which was less than the average gross weekly wage in the UK in 1974 of £41. Cynics might argue that the ASU were not paying taxes or National Insurance to the British government.

O'Connell and Dowd would spend a period of time, after settling into the new flat, planning the first phase of the ASU campaign. They would draw up a list of potential targets from resources such as their growing collection of press clippings, the Army List, Whitakers Almanac, the civil-service yearbook and The Daily Mail yearbook. The planning for the first phase of their attacks would focus on striking military personnel, and so would see the IRA men research the most effective way of carrying out their plan and getting at military targets. As the nation prepared for the second general election that year, announced on September 18th and scheduled to be held October 10th, O'Connell and Dowd were getting ready to carry out their first attack, timed to send the British government a message prior to the election that the issue of Northern Ireland was still to be resolved and was not about to go away.

With the upcoming general election, O'Connell needed to make a plan and strike at the military as instructed GHQ. The question that remaining for O'Connell and Dowd was how best to strike and where? The county of Surrey, just south of greater London, is home to several garrisons and military training schools. Attacking these directly would mean getting past Army security guards at the base entrance, which would be risky. What did young soldiers like to do when they were off-duty? Where did they gather to meet other young soldiers? Could the IRA men find a location to catch a large number of military personnel while they were off base and off guard? O'Connell and Dowd formulated a plan to make the first strike against a military target. They researched the gathering places of young army recruits and selected two targets that met their criteria of being both easily accessible by road and popular, thereby ensuring they would be targeting a large group of people. The best time for their first attack, in order to inflict the highest number of casualties, so they reasoned, would be a Saturday night when young trainees from the army camps around Surrey streamed off base for a night on the town to blow off steam and spend their pay. O'Connell and Dowd constructed two explosive devices from gelignite using approximately six pounds of explosives in each bomb. The gelignite was primed and set with Westclox pocket watches used as timing devices to detonate the bombs. They placed the bombs into two small carrying bags, plain and innocuous enough that they would not arouse much suspicion. Besides, the British public had yet to have a reason to fear bags or packages left unattended.

On Friday, October 4th, Dowd rented a white Hillman Avenger from the Swan National car rental office at Victoria Station in London. The car was rented to Dowd under the assumed name of Martin Moffat, one of his aliases. The following evening, Saturday October 5th, O'Connell and Dowd, accompanied by two of their female Irish couriers and one unidentified man as cover, set off with the two bombs to the town of Guilford in Surrey, covering the 26 miles in approximately 45 minutes. They arrived in Guilford at approximately 8:0pm and made their way to Epsom Road. Here O'Connell, his female escort and the unknown man were dropped off at the Seven Stars pub, with Dowd and his companion traveling a couple of hundred yards further to the Horse and Groom. Both pubs were very popular with the young "squadies" as the trainee soldiers were collectively called. Both pubs were doing a lively trade and steadily filling up as the night progressed. In the Seven Stars, O'Connell brought drinks for himself and his two companions, and they found a corner table to sit and enjoy their beverages, with O'Connell casually pushing the carrier bag bomb under his chair where it would remain undetected. At the Horse and Groom, the scene was replayed with Dowd placing his bomb under a chair situated at a table in a corner alcove. Finishing their drinks at a leisurely pace, to avoid drawing any unwanted attention, the two groups met up in the parking lot of the Seven Stars, got into the rented car and started the drive back to London, leaving the time bombs ticking toward detonation in the two totally unsuspecting pubs filling with the vital exuberance of youth.

By around 9:00pm, the Horse and Groom was packed, primarily with young off duty soldiers. A group of seven trainee Scots guards, who had joined the Army three weeks before, chatted with a group of Women's Royal Army Corps recruits from the nearby Queen Elizabeth barracks. One of the women, Ann Hamilton, age 19, also in the Army for only three weeks, had recently told her concerned parents of her desire to join the military police, which would send her to the conflict-torn city of Belfast. She had told her parents not to worry. At a nearby table Paul Craig, a 22-year-old plasterer, was celebrating a double birthday with his soldier girlfriend, Carol Burns, who had also turned 19 that day. Three young trainee Scots guardsmen had sat down earlier at the table vacated by Dowd and his companion. They had finished a round of drinks and, teased by his two friends, 20-year-old Jimmy Cooper got up to go to the bar to get another round as it was his turn, his friends reminded him. Squeezing his way through the crowd to the bar, he was served three pints of lager by 21-year-old Maureen Sullivan who had taken a job at the pub four months earlier after arriving from County Kerry, Ireland. Cooper was about to return to his friends at the table when the bomb exploded. The blast blew Cooper out through the front window of the pub and set his hair on fire. His two friends, sitting directly over the bomb, Bill Forsyth, 18, and John Hunter, 17, were both killed instantly. Ann Hamilton and fellow WRAC recruit 17-year-old Carolyn Slater were also killed along with Paul Craig. Over 60 people were wounded, with 30 of the wounded receiving life-threatening injuries. The building was shattered in the blast, the sound which caused the landlord of the Seven Stars pub, Owen O'Brien, to run outside to see what had happened. On seeing the devastation of the neighboring Horse and Groom, O'Brien ran back into his pub and immediately ordered everyone out of the building. The pub emptied quickly as the emergency services and police started to descend on the scene. O'Brien, somewhat foolishly, searched his pub for a suspicious looking package, and was caught in the blast as the second device went off. He sustained a fractured skull, with the blast also breaking his wife's leg and injuring five bar staff employees and a teenage customer who had just left the building. The Surrey police, concerned there could be more bombs undetected, evacuated all of the pubs in Guilford. They also evacuated and closed two cinemas in the town. There had been no warnings given by the IRA prior to the attack.

As with all bomb events and crime scenes, a methodical examination of the physical evidence at the scene was conducted by the Surrey police and two forensic scientists, Douglas Hayes and Donald Linston. They would sift through the rubble and debris of the two Guilford pubs, looking for telltale signs of the explosives employed, searching for any remains of timing devices and detonation circuits, collecting and collating any physical evidence that could eventually lead to a link with other events. It was painstaking work.

The subsequent outpouring of anger, shock, and grief from the British public was understandable and justified. There had been no warning of the attack that cut down five young people, four teenage army trainees and civilians in their early twenties. Predictably, under such circumstances, there was immediate outcry for the reintroduction of the death penalty for crimes involving murder caused by terrorism. Sir Michael Havers, Tory candidate in the upcoming general election stated, "The sense of outrage and horror in the minds of the public deserves to be recognized." Although a longtime opponent of capital punishment, Sir Michael indicated a change of heart, ". . . the time has come for urgent reconsideration of capital punishment for terrorist offenses." The death penalty, long abolished in Britain was still on the books for treason and "violent piracy." Many argued that the IRA terrorism was treason, and therefore covered by the statute that would allow convicted terrorists, guilty of murder, to be hung. That was all well and good, but first the Surrey police, as this was outside the jurisdiction of the Met, would first have to find their terror suspects and get a conviction. They would be under considerable public pressure to bring the perpetrators of the horrific bombings in Guilford to book as quickly as possible, and that pressure would have serious future consequences for the British judicial system as the Surrey police went about their investigations.

One unfortunate red herring the investigating officers would come up against was the expounded theory that they were looking for a pair of female bombers. While it is true O'Connell and Dowd did in fact have a female companion each as they planted the two devices, it is not noted that the two couriers acted together without the IRA men being present. One of the group of Scots guardsman present in the Horse and Groom claimed to have brought drinks for two young women, who also claimed to have visited the Seven Stars that evening. Brian Scanlan, aged 20, said "they seemed like a couple of nice birds."

What outraged the British public was the unannounced violence against such young people. A comment, made by a neighbor of Ann Hamilton, one of the female victims of the bomb, summed up the national sentiment, "they were just wee lads," she stated. While they were "wee lads" to the British public, to the embryonic ASU, led by O'Connell, waging a war against the British, they were a legitimate military target as active service personnel of Her Majesty's armed forces. The ASU would also shrug off the whole matter of issuing a warning before bombing attack. The 33 victims of the Dublin and Monaghan bombs had not been given the benefit of a warning, so why should they issue prior notice? As Eddie Butler would later allegedly tell Jim Nevill, "we weren't going to warn people we were trying to kill."

Harry Duggan, resurrected from the dead in the new identity of Michael Wilson, traveled to London from his hiding place in the Irish Republic with fellow ASU member Eddie Butler. Butler, aged 25, was one of four brothers born in Castle Conner in Limerick, had also been off the radar since his disappearance in December of 1973. The pair arrived at 21 Waldemar Avenue and took another flat in the building already occupied by O'Connell and Dowd. Duggan had made one earlier "appearance" from his period of training in preparation for the London campaign. Along with the Oxford educated British heiress turned IRA sympathizer, Dr. Bridget Rose Dugdale, her boyfriend Eddie Gallagher and one other IRA operative, Duggan had helped carried out the largest art robbery in British history. The four-member IRA group raided the country house of Sir Alfred Beit's in County Wicklow on the night of April 26th, 1974. The gang, armed with an assortment of weapons including an AK-47, entered the house and held the staff at gunpoint and bundled Sir Alfred and his wife into the basement. One of the gang was somewhat apologetic for the rough stuff handed out to the couple and their staff, as the others gathered paintings estimated to be worth £8 million in 1974 pounds. They left the Beit's bound and gagged, but they managed to struggle free of their bonds and raise the alarm. Subsequent to the raid, Dugdale rented a small cottage on a farm, posing as a French tourist complete with false French accent! She was discovered by Garda police before the paintings, intended to be used as ransom for several IRA operatives held in British prisons, could be collected by the IRA. Having split up from Dugdale and Gallagher after the raid, Harry Duggan and the other unidentified IRA operative had holed up in a deserted farmhouse in Charleston County Mayo. After a tip off, Garda police surrounded the building, but after a brief shootout Duggan and his accomplice managed to escape without capture. However, the Irish police managed to obtain fingerprints from the house, but failed to make a match with any known active subversive from their database. The records of Harry Duggan, deceased, were not checked against the unidentified prints lifted from the farmhouse. Why would they have been? He was dead, after all.

With Butler and Duggan in place the ASU was almost a full operational strength. The final member to arrive in London in October of 1974 was 25-year-old Hugh Dougherty, who had been born and raised in Glasgow, Scotland, of Irish parents. Dougherty had bounced around the British Isles in his trade as a joiner, working on construction projects in London during 1970 and after the six month contract he been working on expired he returned to the Irish Republic. Like his colleagues, he was picked for the ASU by the IRA command. He was regarded as a solid soldier by superiors and would help provide "muscle" for the group.

A second attack had been planned for the evening of October 11th, 1974. In the strike, the ASU would be targeting a different demographic than that of the Guilford bombing, but still targeting military personnel. As with the Guilford attack, two gelignite devices were constructed and placed bags. The ASU had made a change in tactics for this attack. The bombs were not timed devices, but fitted with combustible safety fuses that would require one of the ASU men to light before throwing the bomb at the target. Driving out to the West End of London that evening the ASU first target was the plush Army and Navy club in Pall Mall, the second target was the Victory Club in Seymour Street. On this attack, the targets were veterans of the British armed forces and not young trainees.

In the Victory club approximate 700 people, all veterans from the two world wars were celebrating with wives or husbands at a reunion function. After a night of eating and drinking, the party was in full swing when the ASU lobbed a bomb outside the billiard room where it exploded, destroying the billiard room and sending a shower of broken glass into the club.

Within minutes, the ASU had reached the Army and Navy club where the second bomb was thrown at the building, exploding beneath a room where seventy-eight members of the West African frontier force celebrated their annual reunion. Both blasts caused considerable damage to buildings, but no one had been seriously hurt. The crusty former soldiers took the blasts in their stride, complaining more about the inconvenience than anything else. One retired Colonel present at the Army and Navy club commented that, "it really irritates me no end when some character lets off a bomb as I'm about to have some more drink!" Another retired officer stated, "that ruined my dinner. It didn't disturb me, I was more annoyed!"

Now that they had conducted a bombing in London, the ASU were fair game for Commander Roy Habershon's men in the Met Bomb Squad. There would be an all-out effort to get the unknown bombers before they could pull off a Greenwich style attack in the heart of the capital. Detective Chief Superintendent Jim Nevill and 41-year-old Detective Superintendent Peter Imbert would be two of the officers from the Bomb Squad in the vanguard of the investigation to track down and arrest the IRA men before they could create a wave of terror-driven anxiety and damage across the city. As the Bomb Squad would note, there had again been no warning in an attack on off-duty, in this case retired, military personnel received from the IRA. They need warnings to evacuate the scene before any devices detonated. They also needed the opportunity to let their expert bomb disposal officers, many of whom had come from the Army, such as Captain Roger Goad, defuse a device and go over the construction so they could look for fingerprints and examine how the bomb had been constructed. There could be a pattern of consistency in the types of explosives used and in the means to set off the bombs, almost like the bomb maker's signature on the device as it was carefully assembled.

The first out-of-town attack carried out by the ASU, in Guilford, involved a rented vehicle from Swan National. That was a risky practice, as there was always the chance of something going badly wrong on a mission and the rented car traced back to its point of origin, where a staff member might remember a Mr. Martin Moffatt, leading to an artist's impression of the man appearing in the newspapers. Stealing cars carried its own risks, but would afford the ASU a large selection from around London to choose from. The ASU would use the term "borrowing" cars, rather than stealing them, as the latter implied that a car had to be broken into and the ignition hot wired to drive the car away. They had a better solution. The Ford Cortina and Granada were highly popular vehicles in the 1970's, with several variants of each model available on the market. One security defect Ford's suffered from at the time concerned the door and ignition key for the vehicles. It was quite possible that a key intended for one car would allow access to another car of the same make and model.[1] By having a large enough collection of keys it was possible, by trial and error, to find a key that would work with the vehicle the ASU wanted to "borrow." The trial and error could be reduced with practice and it may have been practice that found O'Connell and Dowd, on the night of October 18th, on the fourth floor of the multistory Semley Place car park near Victoria Station. They were observed tampering with several vehicles by two off-duty police officers who were on their way home after working their shift. Twenty-four-year-old PC David Lloyd and PC Joseph Nichols, age 21, were both based at the nearby Gerald Road police station. The two officers entered the car park just before midnight and observed the two IRA men acting suspiciously in the dim light of the building. As they approached the IRA men to inquire as to what they were doing, Dowd pulled out .45 caliber semiautomatic handgun and aimed it at the two officer. PC Nichols managed to escape without being shot, but PC Lloyd was overpowered by the two men, had his hands bound behind his back, and was unceremoniously shoved in the back of a stolen Ford Cortina. Knowing the other officer would raise the alarm, O'Connell and Dowd decided to beat a hasty retreat to avoid being caught in the area. PC Nichols did indeed call for backup and armed units of the Met's Special Patrol Group [SPG] rapidly arrived at the parking lot and cordoned off the area. Fearing that explosive devices may have been placed in the parking garage, occupants of the nearby Semley house apartment building were instructed by the police, using loudhailers, to "open your windows and doors and lie down flat!" Over 100 officers surrounded the flat block and the immediate area around it, but the ASU had already slipped through the ring of officers and escaped. O'Connell and Dowd, having driven a quarter-mile from Semley Place to Lower Sloane Street, had no further use for the young officer who obviously feared for his life at the hands of the two armed men. The two IRA men dumped PC Lloyd at the rear of the Gauroche restaurant, but not before Dowd had stolen the officer's wristwatch and O'Connell taken his warrant card [Police ID] and credit card. PC Lloyd, hands bound behind his back, ran to the backdoor of the restaurant and kicked it to attract attention. One of the restaurant dishwashers opened the door to find Lloyd pleading, "help me, help me!" After being freed from his bonds, PC Lloyd used a restaurant phone to call in the incident and within minutes squad cars surrounded the building. Fearing yet another device may have been planted in the area, the police went door-to-door in the vicinity in order to evacuate hundreds of occupants as a precaution. After an extensive search of both the area around the restaurant and the Semley Place car park, nothing suspect was found and the Met allowed the very nervous residents to return to their homes and their beds.

The tactics employed against the Victory club and the Army and Navy club were viewed as a success by the ASU and carried less risk than placing timed devices inside target buildings, as this meant that the ASU could be identified, or the device noticed and defused, which would place one of their bombs in the hands of the Met's forensic scientists. The use of short fused throwing bombs gave little warning and afforded the ASU a quick and probably unimpeded get away. O'Connell would later tell Jim Nevill that they regard the lit fuse "throwers" as being "safer" than the timed electrical circuits. They would use the "throwers" again.

The first attack attacks made by the ASU had been against military personnel and the places of entertainment they frequented. The ASU were also to demonstrate that they were intending to target the ordinary citizens and the upper elements of the British establishment. On Tuesday, October 23rd, the ASU paid a visit to Brooks Club, the second oldest gentleman's club in London, founded in 1764. The club, situated in St. James Street, was only 400 yards from the Army and Navy club the ASU attack two weeks prior. Just before 10:00pm, Mr. Michael Plank, senior wine steward for Brooks Club restaurant, was sitting eating a late dinner in the servery after having seen the last of the evening's diners out of the dining room. Two apprentice wine waiters, Michael Phillips aged eighteen, and Jeffrey Backhoff, seventeen, were washing dishes in the kitchen behind Plank, and twenty-one year old waiter Joseph Caravellio chatted to the two apprentices as they worked. The anteroom next to the restaurant, used for lunch during the day and by members and ladies in the evening for coffee and liquors, was closed, and empty, on Tuesdays.

O'Connell and Dowd pulled up outside Brooks in a stolen Ford Cortina. Both men got out of the vehicle, one to throw the five-pound gelignite bomb and the other to cover the throwing with a handgun. The bomb's short fuse was lit and the device lobbed at the bay window of the anteroom. Plank, eating his meal, recalled hearing what sounded like "the smashing of crockery" coming from the anteroom of the main dining room, as the bomb crashed through the window. The light also went out in the anteroom, as the bomb apparently hit the main light fixture as it flew into the room and landed on the floor. Hearing the crashing of glass, Phillips and Backhoff, closely followed by Caravellio, raced into the anteroom. Phillips and Backhoff were furthest into the room when the fuse burned down to the detonator and the bomb exploded. The two young apprentices took the brunt of the blast partially shielding Caravellio in the process, but the blast also knocked him off his feet and slammed him into the back wall of the anteroom. Plank, following Caravellio into the room was also knocked off his feet. Backhoff, closest to the bomb when it exploded, had his left leg partially amputated by the blast and Phillips had a piece of metal from a fixture in the room blown into his left leg. A private party of 25, in a room above the anteroom, were unaffected by the blast.

Butler and Dowd were noticed by passersby as they drove off at speed from the scene. Detective Superintendent Peter Imbert, in charge of the crime scene investigation, speculated on whether the bomb had been placed in the room earlier in the evening, or if it had been thrown from the street. The bomb blew a hole in the floor roughly in the middle of the room, but Imbert was unsure if the bomb been thrown, as it would have had to clear the railings at the front of the club. Imbert and his team went about their methodical examination of the crime scene. They interviewed staff members and the people who witnessed the ASU making a hasty getaway. The observant bystanders had taken down the license plate number of the Ford Cortina, but the vehicle stolen earlier that evening had been abandoned long before the ASU got anywhere near their base of operations. The wounded Backhoff received a "massive" blood transfusion at Westminster Hospital where surgeons managed to save his leg from amputation. One hour after the blast, the Home Secretary Roy Jenkins visited the scene to be briefed by Detective Superintendent Imbert on the situation.

The following day, members of the Bomb Squad and officers from the SPG raided several hippie communes focusing on the ones that bordered London parks. They had received a tip-off that a group of young Irishmen had been staying in a commune in London and naturally wondered if these could be the IRA men responsible for the recent bombings. No arrests were made, but information relevant to the search was obtained and passed onto the Surrey police detectives investigating the Guilford pub bombs. Scotland Yard also issued a warning to all West End clubs to increase their level of security and be vigilant, as it appeared to the Bomb Squad that the ASU had switched tactics, and rather than going after military personnel they had switched to establishment targets. There had been no security in place at Brooks, the Army and Navy club, or the Victory Club. The Bomb Squad was concerned that the clubs of the West End would be easy targets for the bombers if they continued with their apparent current strategy. The ASU's intent was to keep their adversaries in the Met guessing. To that point they had committed four "no warning" raids on two different types of target. They were about to shift tactics again.

The Met had several growing security worries. There was mounting public resistance in England to the policy of keeping troops in Northern Ireland. They reasoned that the IRA campaign in London was leveraging this concern, and they expected the bombing to continue until they either caught the crew responsible or some political compromise was reached. Any political compromise would be highly undesirable to the Wilson government, particularly if it involved any public announcement that they had been forced into making a withdrawal of troops due to the pressure in London from the Provisionals activities. The Met also had to worry about the state opening of Parliament scheduled for Tuesday, October 28th following the earlier October general election. The event was sure to draw a crowd to watch the Queen arrive at the Houses of Parliament from Buckingham Palace. Security at Parliament had been greatly increased since the previous bombing of the building, with daily searches of the entire building made inside by the police, but they worried that the state opening of Parliament would be a highly symbolic event for the ASU to attack.

However, the Houses of Parliament did not feature in the future plans of the ASU. Instead, in what can only be described as a somewhat interesting change of tactics, the ASU's next target was one of Britain's most famous private schools, Harrow school, situated on Harrow on the Hill in northwest London. The school, founded in 1572, was the boarding school of choice for the upper strata of British society with many of the pupils being signed up at birth for a place at the prestigious establishment. The school was most probably targeted due to its elite nature, and as such would have fitted with the establishment category of targets. But attacking a school, where children could be injured, was a highly risky decision. To mitigate the risk, the ASU made a change in strategy. They placed a five-pound gelignite device timed with a Westclox pocket watch outside Peterborough Cottage, a three-story cottage in Peterborough Lane in the grounds of Harrow school on the night of October 24th. O'Connell called the Press Association at 11:30pm, and using a recognized IRA codeword, told the listening journalist that "there is a bomb at Harrow school. There is a warning this time but if nothing is done there won't be one any more. If you don't move the kids, they will be okay." Ten minutes after the telephone warning the bomb exploded outside the bedroom of one of the school's masters, Mr. Jeremy Gates, who was asleep with his wife at the time of the blast. Two other couples, who occupied the flats above Mr. and Mrs. Gates, were also rudely awakened by the explosion. Despite damage to the rear of the house, there were mercifully no injuries to any of the people in the building, including Mr. and Mrs. Gates whose room the bomb exploded outside. The ASU had issued their first warning of a bombing, but the target made little sense other than as a symbolic strike an establishment school. The warning was a political move by the IRA men, as with only a ten-minute warning to the Press Association, who would have had to pass the details along to Scotland Yard, there would have been little time for the police to react. The bomb had been deliberately placed so as to avoid any real risk of casualties among the pupils and was really only for effect.

Meanwhile in Northern Ireland, the sectarian violence between the paramilitary units on both sides continued, with the Protestant UVF stepping up pressure on the government to release 17 of its members held in internment. In Dublin, Liam Cosgrove the Irish Prime Minister stated that the formation of any new Northern Ireland executive must include a true power-sharing arrangement. In retaliation to this remark, Ian Paisley gained the support of two of the three loyalist parties to back his call for a trade boycott with the Republic.

In a coordinated effort to find the IRA active service unit cells, the police conducted a series of dawn raids on the morning of October 25th in London, Birmingham, Liverpool and Bristol. Over 50 people were questioned and their homes searched, but no arrests were made. The targets were people of Irish origin who were known sympathizers of Irish republican groups. The ASU, safely anonymous in Fulham, were not among those called on by the police that morning as their strategy of staying out of the Irish community started to pay off. The following day, over 100 officers from the Bomb Squad and Special Branch raided a north London pub after a tip off that it was being used to store explosives. The police surrounded the Lord Palmerstone pub in Kilburn High road, an area popular with Irish expatriates, at around 9:30pm, and detained twelve people for questioning at West Hampstead police station. The pub landlord, Michael Book from Ireland stated that, "members of Sinn Féin use my pub but as far as I know the IRA themselves don't come in." The police failed to find any evidence of explosives in Book's pub, and did not extract any useful information from the people they detained. The Bomb Squad, as a result, found themselves no closer to finding ASU, and they had a growing concern regarding the upcoming the Christmas shopping season that would find London packed with people doing their holiday shopping. With a large concentration of department stores in the center of London, the crowds of shoppers would be a highly vulnerable target to any IRA bombs placed in cars, post boxes or trash bins. They needed to apprehend the ASU before further carnage was inflicted on the people of London, but this was all new to the Met. They were using conventional police techniques of investigation against a group of urban guerilla and their techniques were not getting them close to catching the men.

The throwers, as the ASU referred to their hand-launched-bombs, had proved effective against London clubs in three of their four past actions and the ASU commander thought it was time to bring some of the additions to the unit into the next attack. Hugh Dougherty, primarily responsible in the unit for skilled reconnaissance, had scoped out another target where the ASU could attack off duty service personnel. O'Connell constructed another thrower for the attack, planned for the evening of November 6th, 1974. It would take Butler and O'Connell approximately 35 minutes to drive from Waldemar Avenue to Francis Street in Woolwich by the river Thames. Wednesday evening and trade was slow at the Kings Arms pub, a popular watering hole for soldiers from the Woolwich barracks just 50 yards down the road. In fact the trade was slow enough for two ASU men to abort the planned attack on the pub. There were not enough targets in the pub to make their attack worthwhile, they reasoned in their cold-blooded calculus, so they drove back to Fulham with the bomb still in the bag they had planned to throw through the window of the pub. Before heading back to Fulham, the two men noticed a sign outside the pub. It stated that it was forbidden to take any bags or parcels into the pub, mindful of the two Guilford bombs planted in squadie pubs the previous month. The ASU had no intention of carrying a bag into the Kings Arms.

Thursday, November 7th was payday for many of the young soldiers from the Woolwich barracks, and what better way to spend their hard-earned money than in the local pub, such a short walk away. Inside the Kings Arms, a group of WRAC women soldiers were laughing and playing a game of darts as they enjoyed their night out. By 10:15pm, the business in the pub was reaching a peak. The landlord, Mr. Gerry Nash, had gone out for the evening leaving his wife Margaret in charge of the busy pub. Her three children, aged seven, five, and four were asleep in the family living quarters above the pub.

Butler and O'Connell, in a white Triumph Dolomite, stolen from the Wembley area of London earlier that night, pulled up near the Kings arms. Both out of the vehicle, Butler covered O'Connell as the bomb was thrown at the pub. The bomb, placed in a satchel, arced through the air and crashed through the front window of the pub. Inside, a soldier sitting enjoying a drink with his friends recalled the event " . . . the window smashed in and the bag exploded almost immediately, a pal of mine was thrown off his feet. Everything went black." Given the close proximity of the soldiers in the pub to the bomb as it exploded, it is nothing short of a miracle that only one young soldier lost his life in the attack. Twenty others were wounded; seven seriously, with the injured rushed to Brook Hospital in Shooters Hill. All four operating theaters in the hospital were put into use and eight off-duty surgeons were called back in to assist with the wounded. The wounds were horrific, as the bomb had exploded at a table height, inflicting chest and stomach wounds to those in the immediate area of the blast. Many of the wounded were trapped in the rubble of the collapsed room, and soldiers, police and firefighters clawed at the debris with their bare hands to free the victims. The sign forbidding the carrying of bags or parcels into the pub lay wrecked in the road outside the building it had been intended to protect.

The Army placed a cordon of soldiers in battle dress in a ring around the apartment buildings in Artillery Place, just off Frances Street where the shattered Kings Arms stood, where they stopped people and checked their ID. It was noticed that at least two of the soldiers were carrying heavy wooden staves, possibly looking for suspects in the third attack on pubs frequented by soldiers.

Once again, the Bomb Squad team, accompanied by the forensic scientists, would have to sift through the aftermath of the ASU's deadly handiwork. They had now attacked a soldier's pub on their patch, not in Surrey this time but on their ground. They were grimly determined to find the ASU before they could strike again. But who were they looking for? Where were they operating from? At that time, they had no clear leads to the identity of their quarry, but their counterparts in Surrey felt they were getting close to an answer. The Met would have to see how the Surrey leads played out and how they, in turn, may end up helping the Met in their own investigation.

The bombings were taking a toll on the British psyche. People were angry at the apparent inability of the police to protect them in their everyday activities, such as going for a drink in a local pub. The political environment was also under pressure because of the bombings. Edward Heath, the embattled leader of the defeated Conservative party, faced a backbench revolt over the reintroduction of the death penalty, with some MP's threatening to break party ranks and demand a debate, and vote, on the issue of capital punishment. Heath also faced a threat to his leadership of the party with one of his cabinet ministers, Margaret Thatcher, mounting a rear guard action to oust Heath from the top slot and take his place. There were also increasing rumblings, led by the senior leadership of the Metropolitan police, to grant the police greater powers of search, detention of suspects and sanctions against IRA membership. The Home Secretary, Roy Jenkins, would struggle with the opposing needs of maintaining civil liberties and the need to fight a new, hidden enemy on the streets of mainland Britain. This was not Northern Ireland and the people of England were becoming increasingly angry, afraid, and impatient at the apparent inability of the police to trap the bombers and put them behind bars.

With the police making dawn raids, the ASU determined, quite correctly, that having all five men in the same location was a strategic liability. They decided to split up, with Butler and O'Connell moving to 34 Dunloe Avenue in Tottenham, north London under the assumed names of Tony Clark (Butler) and Joseph Powell. Duggan and Dougherty moved two miles from Waldemar Avenue to 39 Fairholme Road under the names of Michael Wilson (Duggan) and John Anderson. Dowd elected to stay on at Waldemar Avenue. The Fairholme Road address would become the main base of operations for the storage and preparations of the ASU's explosives.

The ASU had been watching the TV news coverage of the bombing campaign, and collecting press clippings from the newspapers. Several of the Bomb Squad leadership, such as Roy Habershon, Jim Nevill and Peter Imbert had been getting coverage in the media. They would make ideal targets for the London ASU, if they could find a way to get at them. Their home addresses were a closely guarded secret, for obvious reasons, but there had to be a way, so the ASU team reasoned, for them to be able to strike at the police officers. O'Connell, the primary mapmaker for the group along with Dougherty the reconnaissance man, would spend several evenings in the vicinity of St. James Park underground station, just a stone's throw from the Metropolitan police headquarters at New Scotland Yard on Broadway. At the junction of Broadway and Tothill Street is a pub called the Old Star.[2] Peter Imbert recalled that after some members of the Bomb Squad had finished their work for the day, they would visit the pub as a group for a quick drink before going home. As a rail commuter, the pub would be convenient for Imbert as it was right next to the St. James Park underground station. The Met team had been spotted by the ASU on one of these trips to the pub, and their patient waiting and watching had paid off for O'Connell. He had watched known members of the Bomb Squad leave Scotland Yard, walk down Broadway and into the Old Star for their quick drink. Drawing a map of the area, O'Connell laid out the route taken to the pub by the police officers as a dotted line, and wrote next to the line that ended at the pub, "this is the way they go." The police had become targets of the very people they were attempting to run to ground. It would be a question of time to see who would get in the first strike, the ASU or the Bomb Squad.

The ASU based in Birmingham, in the industrial Midlands of the country, had made attempts at placing booby trap bombs under the cars of two magistrates, but they had been detected and disarmed. They had also targeted Denis Howell, the government's sports Minister whose home was near Birmingham. A bomb placed under his car detonated when his wife attempted to drive it away from their house. Both Mrs. Howell and her son were miraculously unhurt in the explosion. The Birmingham ASU's timing was off as Mr. Howells was in London at the time. However, the Birmingham team would continue their efforts in the attack on the mainland. On the night of November 21st, 1974, the Birmingham ASU placed time bombs, in holdalls, inside two Birmingham city center pubs. The Thursday evening drinkers in the Mulberry Bush in the rotunda building, and the basement pub The Tavern in The Town were totally unaware of the imminent danger they faced, despite the fact that a man with an Irish accent called the Birmingham Post with a warning that there were bombs placed in the pubs. By the time the newspaper had called the police, there was precious little time for them to get to the pubs and evacuate the customers.

Twelve minutes after the phone warning, the bomb in the Mulberry Bush exploded in the first floor pub with devastating effect. People rushed into the streets from surrounding buildings with a crowd of around 100 people gathering outside the TV shop above the Tavern in The Town. Traffic ground to a halt in the city center due to the explosion at the Mulberry Bush, preventing some essential emergency services from getting to the scene as quickly as needed. The second bomb exploded seconds before one fire engine, dispatched to the Mulberry Bush, reached the site of the Tavern. Alan Hill, one of the firemen on the engine, recalled how many of the crowd in the street had been knocked off their feet by the blast. The explosion blew out intact a plate glass window from a shop above the Tavern and sent it sailing across the road, smashing to pieces as it struck parked cars in the street opposite. Alan Hill and his three colleagues, who had been heading for the Mulberry Bush, made a radio call to the central control; the first notification there had been a second bomb. The traffic gridlock was delaying the arrival of fleet of ambulances to ferry the critically wounded to hospital. Hill asked for able bodied volunteers to help in the extraction of wounded from the basement, which would be a grim task. With the explosion contained in the basement pub, the blast had sent people and furniture flying around the room with horrific effect. Many people stepped forward to help despite the potential danger of further explosive devices being in the building.

The significant number of walking wounded, and people requiring hospital treatment, had the potential to overwhelm the ambulance crews on their arrival. Alan Hill found himself approached by a cab driver who recognized him, and the cab driver told Hill he had been asked by an injured couple to drive them to hospital and inquired if he was allowed to do this, and Hill told him that it was fine and to carry on. It then suddenly occurred to Hill that the Birmingham Taxi Owners Association had an excellent radio system and other cabs could still be in the city center area. Alan Hill called out after the cab driver and asked him to send out a distress call for help at the Tavern. Within seconds the cab driver gave Hill the thumbs-up that help was on the way. Alan Hill later recalled that because of the bombs, all trains into Birmingham's New Street Station had been stopped, causing an unusually large number of cabs to build up in the station's taxi rank. The call from the cab driver at the Tavern resulted in a stream of cabs turning up at the scene in an orderly line to ferry the wounded to one of two hospitals in the area. Many cabs made multiple trips to and fro, and one eyewitness later recalled how a cab driver had apologized for blood in the back of his taxi, as he had been ferrying the wounded to hospital. Within a short time the large crowd of wounded people had dwindled to just the critically injured, allowing the arriving ambulance crews unimpeded access to the seriously injured people. Alan Hill's quick thinking in using the cabs probably saved many lives that night.

The fire crews had the grisly task of extracting bodies and body parts from the basement, where they were transferred to the street and covered with sheets. By the time the incident was under control, Hill and his fellow emergency service personnel had spent 11 hours at the scene.

Alan Hill reflected that the £10 he was paid for the 15 hour night shift had certainly "been well-earned."

The attack was the single most brutal loss of life in Britain as a result of bombings since the Second World War. In total twenty-two people were killed by the two bombs and almost 200 seriously wounded. There was outrage in Britain at the bloody carnage unleashed on the youth of Birmingham, with some citizens taking the law into their own hands, firebombing several Irish pubs and clubs in the city in retaliation. The Birmingham CID were determined to act, and to be seen acting swiftly to bring the guilty to justice. The day after the bombs, Birmingham CID arrested six men. Five were arrested on the Belfast ferry at Haysham, the sixth at his home in Birmingham. All of the men were originally from Northern Ireland but lived in England for over 11 years. Taken back to Birmingham, the men were interrogated over the weekend and confessed to the attacks. They were formally charged with the offenses on November 24th, 1974, three days after the attacks. This rapid rush to apprehend the offenders was aided, so Birmingham police stated, by the fact that the men were under suspicion of being IRA members before the bombs in Birmingham. Assistant Chief Constable Morris Buck, leading the investigation stated that "we are satisfied that we have found the men primarily responsible." The people of Guilford and London would wonder why their respective police forces had not been able to respond as rapidly as the Birmingham team in the apprehension of the IRA team in the south.

The events in Birmingham reverberated around the halls of Westminster. Under pressure in the House of Commons the day after the Birmingham car bombs, the Home Secretary Roy Jenkins made a promise to the House that he would make a statement on Thursday the 25th regarding emergency measures to deal with the mainland terror campaign. Jenkins struggled with the implications of what he was going to present to the house. In consultation with the Met leadership team, Jenkins and the Home Office had created the basis for what would become The Prevention of Terrorism Act. This would involve several changes to the way the police could act in situations of terrorism or, more importantly, suspected terrorism. Firstly, it would make the IRA a proscribed organization, making it an offense to be a member, publicly display insignia, or raise funds for the organization. Secondly, the new act would allow, on suspicion of involvement with terrorist groups or terrorist acts, the immediate expulsion of such individuals providing they had not been resident in Great Britain for more than twenty years. The greatest change would impact the powers of arrest and detention granted to the police. In a secret memo to the Cabinet on November 24th, Jenkins outlined the proposal. He stated that after discussions with the police they had told him that "the feature of the present arrangements which they find inhibiting is that they cannot lawfully detain people for long enough to check their identity against other evidence available to them as a result of earlier incidents." Jenkins proposal was to grant greater powers of search and detention allowing the police to hold terror suspects for 48 hours and for up to seven days, with Home Office approval, without charges being made. The powers the new act would give the police were significant. Under regular British law, the police could arrest a person on suspicion that they had committed a specific arrestable offense and hold them for a short time before either placing charges or releasing them. The Prevention of Terrorism Act would give the police the power to detain someone they "reasonably suspected" of being concerned in the "commission, preparation, or instigation of acts of terror." The new powers, as Jenkins described them were "unprecedented in peacetime Great Britain." Jenkins was concerned with being criticized for doing too little, rather than too much, in dealing with the terror campaign. While the changes were viewed as unprecedented, Jenkins was also mindful of the societal impact of allowing the erosion of civil liberties in Britain; "we must guard against the danger of being driven to more and more extreme measures involving unwarranted infringement of personal liberties." The bill would also increase border controls at ports and airports to monitor and govern the flow of people to and from Ireland. After spirited debate in the House of Commons, the bill came into law on November 29th, 1974.

The Prevention of Terrorism Act would allow Surrey police arrest and hold Paul Hill, originally from Belfast, on suspicion of being involved in the Guilford bombing attack. He was arrested in Southampton on November 28th and signed a full confession statement the following day admitting his involvement with the Guilford events. Under intense interrogation, Hill readily gave up the names of his supposed accomplices in the Guilford pub bombings. Subsequently, Gerry Conlon, Patrick Armstrong, both originally from Belfast, and Armstrong's girlfriend Carol Richardson, were arrested and taken in for questioning. After lengthy interrogations, they too signed statements of their involvement in the bombing attacks. Surprising as it may seem to us today, in 1974 there were no tape recorded interviews with suspects and the police could have the detainees sign a blank statement and fill in the details, to their satisfaction, over the suspect's signature. News of the arrest of the Guilford four, as they would become known, would cause the London

ASU considerable amusement as according to O'Connell, the IRA had been "after" Hill and Conlon for about 18 months on suspicion of passing information to the British Army. It was ironic, therefore, to hear of the arrest and formal charging of four people not involved in the Guilford bombs in any way.

The Prevention of Terrorism Act and associated crackdown on the IRA gave the police the long-awaited chance to swoop on known IRA sympathizers. However, the police were somewhat critical of the new law, as there was still no provision for the overall coordination of investigations, under a national police force such as in the USA with the FBI. Each regional police force would still be responsible for the coordination of investigations on the terrorists and rely on an ad hoc cooperation between the regional divisions to bring the bombers to justice. One unintended consequence of this somewhat disjointed system was that information, vital to one regional investigation, could sit for a long time in the notes of a different regional crime squad, delaying the detection and eventual apprehension of suspects.

As the Home Secretary Roy Jenkins had announced to the press the new measures would be presented to the House of Commons on November 25th, the ASU prepared to send a message of defiance back to the government. Three small gelignite bombs, with pocket watch timing devices, were concealed in packets small enough to fit through the slot of the standard cast-iron post box, the cylindrical bright red colored boxes so common throughout London. With the devices armed, Eddie Butler went out to mail the explosive packages to three locations. One package was placed in a post box in Piccadilly Circus, the second in a box on the Pentonville Road near Kings Cross and the third in a box in Victoria, outside the Metropole Cinema. Timed to go off at the peak of the London rush-hour, the three post box bombs exploded, injuring a total of twenty people, with sixteen of the injured being caught in the blast at Piccadilly Circus. The three explosions, combined with false alarms at Charring Cross and Euston stations and in Kingsbridge, Mayfair and Hammersmith, created traffic chaos in the capital. The Met called in teams from the Army Bomb Squad for the enormous task of physically checking all post boxes in the W1 and N1 postal areas. Many collections were halted in these districts until the Army gave the all clear.

Commander Robert Huntley of the Mets Bomb Squad called the explosions "classic IRA tactics to cause chaos." The bombs would also have a wide reaching impact on the capital's Postal Service. The Post Office, as part of its usual run up to Christmas, encouraged people to mail letters, cards and parcels early for the holiday. The day after the three post box bombs, many postal workers refused to empty Central London mailboxes, fearing there could be more bombs. When told by their supervisors to open the boxes, the post workers, in so many words, told their supervisors to go and open the boxes themselves! It is not noted if the supervisors did actually go and empty any boxes. However, hundreds of boxes slowly clogged up across the city, with the post office urging customers to bring their mail to a post office rather than use a postbox that may not get emptied.

The ASU had not finished with post boxes, but the next employment of Post Office property would send a chilling warning to the likes of Jim Nevill and Peter Imbert. The Bomb Squad was already a target for the ASU, and the IRA men had studied their movements and worked out where the members of the Bomb Squad went for a drink after work and mapped it accordingly. Planting a bomb in a London pub, just literally yards from the Met's headquarters, could have been achieved but would have involved a lot of time just watching and waiting for the Bomb Squad officers to show up. That would be both time-consuming and risky, as to closely monitor the Old Star pub, with a made-up bomb so close to Scotland Yard would be inviting trouble. The most efficient way to get at the Bomb Squad would be on the streets of London, doing their job, rather than in the cozy confines of the public bar of the Old Star. Several months down the road, a young Detective Sergeant in the Bomb Squad would have a similar thought regarding the ASU, believing it would be easier to catch the IRA team "on the job" rather than looking for them in their homes.

The IRA had already perfected a technique to entrap the Bomb Squad as the ASU wanted, and they went about their plans to pull this off. On the evening of November 27th, 1974, Eddie Butler and Joe O'Connell took two timed explosive devices to Tite Street in fashionable Chelsea. They selected a postbox and inserted the armed bomb packet into the mail slot. They then carefully concealed a larger device under a bush behind a railing directly behind the postbox, and headed out of the area.

At 8:30pm, the postbox bomb exploded, wrecking a Ford Escort parked in front of the box in the blast. Within minutes, the area was swarming with police officers from the uniformed branch, the Bomb Squad and several bomb disposal experts. Tom Smith, a Daily Express news photographer, snapped the scene, with the police milling around the wrecked car, looking for clues. A police officer took a firm grip of Smith by the arm and escorted him back behind a barrier used to cordon off the crime scene. Seconds after Smith had been moved out of the street, at 8:50pm the second concealed device exploded. Fortunately no one was killed, but four officers, a bomb disposal expert and three support staff were injured in the blast. Tom Smith, safely behind a barrier, avoided being caught in the past by virtue of the actions of the police constable who had moved him out of the area. The ASU had trapped the police in what the IRA called a "come on" bomb. Brought to the scene by the first, smaller explosion, the police were then targets for the second bomb. It was a callous and calculated means of inflicting potential casualties on the law enforcement and emergency services teams, who would be attending to the impact of the first bomb. The only reason for the second blast was to maim or kill those on the scene. Detective Chief Superintendent Jim Nevill would later ask Eddie Butler about the Tite Street bombs, while Butler sat in a cell in Paddington Green police station under interrogation. Nevill asked Butler the reason for the second device, to which Butler replied that it was to get the Bomb Squad. Surprised, Nevill enquired if there were orders from GHQ to try and kill members of the Bomb Squad. Butler allegedly responded "not exactly, but you are targets." Nevill asked if they were targets for bombings or shootings, to which Butler chillingly responded that it really didn't matter. "Either way, as long as we are dead, eh?" asked Nevill. Butler did not respond, but just shrugged his shoulders and smiled back at Nevill.

The ASU campaign had created a hyper-vigilant state in the population of London, with the Post Office workers nervous about emptying post boxes and members of the general public calling the police at the merest sight of a hastily discarded bag or suspicious looking package that looked out of place. Bomb scares had become a way of life for Londoners, and one such bomb scare episode was recalled by Inspector John Purnell of Paddington Green police station. John Purnell had joined the Metropolitan Police as a cadet in 1963 at the age of 17. He was made a police constable in 1965 and was subsequently selected for the accelerated fast track promotion program at the Police College at Bramshill. This opportunity allowed Purnell to move through the ranks quickly, and by the age of 25 he was an Inspector at Paddington Green police station in London, supervising a uniformed branch shift. Inspector Purnell was 28-years-old in November of 1974.

A suspicious looking cardboard box, outside a shop doorway, had been called into the police and officers from the nearby Paddington Green responded to the call. The officers cordoned off the area, keeping the crowd of morbidly interested onlookers at a safe distance from the suspect package. Inspector Purnell, arriving on the scene, took a closer look at the box and cautiously lifting the top flap of the box, Purnell quickly realized the contents were, in fact, harmless. However, the police had something of a show on their hands, with all the blue flashing lights, barriers and bomb disposal teams all observed by the increasingly curious crowd. So, the police would go through the motions of dealing with the "bomb" more as a public relations exercise than anything else. The bomb disposal team carefully lifted the cardboard box and gently placed it into a large metal container, which in turn was placed in the back of a police transit van to be transported back to Paddington Green, lights flashing and siren wailing. Show over, the police removed the barriers and returned the scene to normal, with the spectators all marveling at how smoothly the police had handled the situation. Back at Paddington Green police station, the cardboard box was removed from the bomb proof container and taken to the staff canteen, where the large cake contained in the box was sliced up and enjoyed by the offices with mugs of tea! Not every bomb scare, it turned out, was a waste of police time!

With the Prevention of Terrorism Act in Place, the Met wasted no time in increasing their surveillance of passengers arriving from Ireland at Heathrow Airport's terminal one, examining all baggage and carry-on luggage of each passenger. Additional security measures were also taken in terminal one, with the removal of old doors from the public telephone boxes and the sealing up of mailboxes. Passengers would have to hand mail into the airport post office instead. The Met were speculating if the IRA men they were looking for had already left the country to avoid any potential seizure under the new law. Maybe they had been scared off? They could hope, but the ASU were still in town and ready to inflict further mayhem.

The Talbot Arms pub is situated in Little Chester Street in the upscale district of Belgravia. It is a large pub, popular with local families as a place to relax and unwind over a drink and a pub meal. Eddie Butler and Joe O'Connell decided to pay the Talbot Arms a visit on the evening of Saturday, November 30th. Each man had a 2 1/2 pound throwing bomb fitted with a short fuse. The Talbot Arms, tucked away off a small mews, was ideally situated for thrown bomb attack, as there would be little or no passing traffic to observe the ASU men as they carried out their plan. Both ASU men were on foot, having left their stolen car parked ready for their getaway. Facing the front window of the pub, Butler threw his bomb first, but his aim was off. The bomb hit the window frame, not the glass, and bounced back onto the pavement outside the pub.[3] O'Connell's aim was better, sending his bomb crashing through the window into the saloon bar of the pub. The first bomb exploded, shattering the front window and sending a shower of broken glass into the pub. This was the first bomb the ASU had laced with shrapnel, using steel nuts packed around the gelignite core of the bomb, adding to the destructive nature of the blast and intended to increase the bomb's lethality. The second bomb, inside the pub, failed to go off although O'Connell would later tell Jim Nevill it was deliberately made as a dud and was not intended to explode, which is somewhat hard to believe. Five customers inside the pub were injured by flying glass caused by Butler's badly thrown bomb. Had the bomb actually passed through the window, rather than striking the window frame, the shrapnel device would have created carnage inside the crowded bar. Butler and O'Connell made their getaway unimpeded.

The Talbot Arms pub bombings would mark the first time the Bomb Squad would recover one of the ASU's explosive devices intact. The forensic science teams from both the Met and the Royal Armaments Research and Development Establishment (RARDE), based at Fort Halsted in Kent, would carefully examine the bomb for evidence. The unexploded device would also be carefully deconstructed to see what its structure revealed to the two science teams.

By the beginning of December, the British police had been populating an exclusion list of IRA and Sinn Fein suspects and had obtained the home office approval on the documents to deport or exclude them from mainland Britain. Three of the targeted men were in Ireland at the time, two were missing from their homes in England and one had been taken into custody. One of the men in Ireland, Brendan McGill, the senior most Sinn Fein man in England, had been resident in England for 21 years which theoretically put him over the 20 year exclusion limit. His wife Francis told news reporters "he's not a bomber, and never has been. His aims are political only." The Prevention of Terrorism Act had a lot of political, and not so political, supporters of the Republican movement running for cover to avoid the possibility of being shipped back to Ireland. The ASU, safe in their anonymity, had no such concern as they calmly carried out their well laid plans of terror on the streets of the capital, and more was to come. Daithi O'Connell, Chief of Staff of the Provisional IRA, gave a grim warning of what the British public could expect from the IRA on mainland Britain. In interview with the news media, Daithi O'Connell stated that due to the "total indifference" of the British public towards "the terrible war in Ireland," the British would suffer the consequences. The IRA, said Daithi O'Connell, would strike at "economic, military, political and judicial targets." He did not state that the IRA may have to kill, maim and injure innocent civilians in the process, such as at two Birmingham pubs.

The run-up to the Christmas holiday would see an increased level of activity from the ASU, all intended to strike more fear into the hearts of the people of London, as they went about their business, while increasing the pressure on the Wilson government for meaningful dialogue on the Irish situation. During the month of December 1974, the IRA team would again attack military clubs, and add to their target list communication networks and Christmas shoppers.

The ASU's next foray onto the streets of London was to be a somewhat audacious simultaneous attack on two military clubs less than a mile apart. The first would be on the Navy and Military Club, primarily for serving officers of the armed forces, situated on the exclusive St. James Square in Westminster. The second was the Cavalry and Guards Club, eight-tenths of a mile away at 127 Piccadilly, facing Green Park. The ASU's plan was to have a coordinated strike on both buildings, with the intent to confuse and split the Bomb Squad's attention between two targets. On the night of December 11th, traveling on foot to the front of the Navy and Military Club, known to its members as the "in and out" because of the two separate gateways to the driveway, O'Connell and Duggan prepared to lob another of their shrapnel-loaded thrown bombs. As they readied for the attack, a line of three taxi cabs drove toward their location. The driver in the second cab described the scene, "I saw two young men throw something into the club. They walked off a few yards, stopped and waited." The bomb had been thrown into the famous long bar of the club, where several members were relaxing. The club receptionist recalled the bomb exploded almost as soon as it crashed through the window of the bar, injuring a steward slightly as it detonated.

Back in St. James's Square outside, the cab drivers were shocked to see an explosion erupt from the club. O'Connell and Duggan ran off, but the posse of cabdrivers where not about to let them get away unchallenged. All three cabs set off after two ASU men. The cabbie in the second vehicle had two passengers, the cab in front and behind him had passengers bail out of the cabs prior to the drivers giving chase. Realizing they had been seen and were about to be chased by three taxi cabs, both ASU men pulled out .357 Astra magnum pistols. The two ASU men turned to face the approaching line of cabs and each fired a round at the lead cab. The first round thudded into the vehicle's radiator, the powerful .357 bullet stopped by the engine block, and the second round penetrated the windshield and exited through the roof. The two shots provided enough incentive to convince the cab drivers that discretion was, in fact, the better part of valor, so they radioed in for police assistance. Jim Nevill later asked O'Connell about the shooting, wondering where they lost the cabbies, and O'Connell allegedly replied that "we lost them just there, where we fired the shots. We got up to the top [of the street] and there was nobody after us." The two ASU men made their escape toward Park Lane.

While the bomb attack had being going on, Eddie Butler and the other two ASU members were cruising up to the Cavalry Club in a stolen car. Butler was armed with a World War II era mark II Sten submachine gun, which he planned to use to rake the front of the club with a prolonged burst of fire. The Sten gun, a product of a national wartime need to mass-produce a cheap automatic weapon for British troops and resistance units in Europe, had a notorious reputation for misfeeds from its 32-round magazine. British troops had dubbed the weapon the "plumber's nightmare" because of the weapons welded tubular construction. A misfeed would result in a round jamming in the breach that stopped the gun from firing, and were typically caused by the magazine. Made from stamped and welded sheet-metal, the magazine suffered from two basic defects. Firstly, the sheet-metal feed lips that controlled the transfer of a new cartridge into the firing mechanism could be easily deformed, thereby creating a misfeed. Secondly, the magazine was sensitive to dirt, and once debris got into a magazine it was very difficult to get it out again, and any debris in a magazine could cause the gun to jam. The use of the Sten gun was an interesting choice for the ASU, given the other weapons available to them. The Sten gun could have advantage in that it was compact and easy to conceal, and easily stored away, once the horizontally fitting magazine had been removed.

As the other members of the ASU were attacking the Navy and Military Club and fending off cabdrivers, Butler and the rest of the group approach the cavalry club. There were several people outside the club, including Terry Lethan, visiting London from his native Devon, and a young Irish couple getting out of their parked van outside the Cavalry club. Butler prepared to fire the Sten gun, which under normal operating conditions, would discharge its 32 rounds of 9mm ammunition in approximately four seconds. Aiming at the front of the club, and by default at anyone outside the building, Butler intended to fire a lengthy burst. He pulled the trigger and the Sten briefly spat out bullets until the gun jammed. Following the standard procedure for clearing a jam, Butler quickly tilted to the weapon to the right, bringing the magazine to the vertical, while the same time cycling the cocking lever to the rear, allowing the jammed cartridge to fall out of the ejector port. Butler fired the gun again, and again the Sten jammed. It would jam three times on

Butler as he fired at the club. On the receiving end of the shooting, Terry Lethan recalled how the first burst of fire slammed into the red Commer van, just as the young Irish couple was getting out of the vehicle. Lethan threw himself down on the ground as the second burst ricocheted off the wall of the club behind him. The third volley of shots kept everyone down, avoiding any further gunfire, as ASU made their escape. One eyewitness in a hotel near the shooting claimed to see the shots coming from just behind the railings of the park opposite the cavalry club, a report which was later passed on to the police

The two attacks created a traffic nightmare in the surrounding areas. A total of 40 detectives and 100 uniformed officers, some with dogs, descended on the vicinity, some having to make the final part of the journey on foot because of the traffic snarl up. Houses, clubs and restaurants near the bomb attack site were evacuated as a precaution in case additional bombs had been planted and had yet to be detected. An intense manhunt ensued, with police using floodlights in Green Park to help the officers with dogs track down the IRA men, who by that point were safely out of the dragnet area and heading back to their base of operations. Once again they had made a strike, two in this case, and escaped before police could encircle them. Their tactics of throwing bombs, and hit-and-run shootings, without any prior warnings, would keep them ahead of the time it took the police to react to calls from the scene of the crime, and the Met knew that. Commander Robert Huntley of the Bomb Squad praised the actions of the cabdrivers who had attempted to chase down the two ASU men at the Navy and Military Club. It was the first time in London that someone had "had a go" at the bombers, and Huntley described it as "marvelous public spiritedness." But, he added, that if "members of the public wish to have a go, it is up to them. I am not advocating it."

The Irish young couple and the three cab drivers were taken to Vine Street Police station near Piccadilly Circus to assist police in piecing together the events of the night. They also helped police artists pull together impressions of the IRA men, from which a picture emerged of the two men involved in the bomb attack. Both were estimated to be in their mid-to-late 20's, with one around 5'7" with a slight build and fair hair. The other was around 5'10" with black hair. The information was sketchy at best, but captured the basic descriptions of Duggan and O'Connell.

Despite the escape of the ASU, and the wounding of a steward in the first club attacked that night, the Met were making progress, as they had solid eyewitness accounts of both events and a description of the two suspects who threw the bomb. Good police work is about the patient collection and collation of facts, gently shaken with a dash of luck, to produce a lead that just might result in some bigger clue that, in turn, may lead to something even more substantial. It was about keeping eyes and ears open, grabbing any snippet of intelligence that on its own may have been meaningless, but highly valuable when integrated into the overall big picture. The tools the Met had to track down the ASU did not include the ubiquitous desktop and laptop computers of the late 20th century. They relied on good solid work of the traditional police techniques of watching, listening and lifting rocks to see what crawled out from underneath. Only later would the Met realize that maybe the techniques they were using would prove too slow in the fast moving and evolving world of urban terrorism.

Ironically, as the ASU were carrying out their own attacks on military club land, the House of Commons had been locked in a sometimes overly emotional debate on the reintroduction of the death penalty for crimes of terrorism. The threat, made by Edward Heath's back benchers, to drive such debate had been carried out. The bombings of the IRA in London and Birmingham had enraged the constituents of many MP's, but the Home Secretary, Roy Jenkins, remained firmly and vocally opposed to any such backward slide towards executions. Some of the more right-leaning Tory politicians, such as Margaret Thatcher, demanded that the will of the people be heard and that guilty terrorists pay the ultimate price for their villainous misdeeds. The motion was defeated in a free vote 369 to 217, a majority of 152. This would not be the last time the House would debate the topic, for the longer and more bloody the ASU's campaign became without interruption by the powers of law enforcement, the greater the outcry from the British public would become.

The ASU were building up to an attack on the Christmas shoppers in London, but carried out another drive-by shooting on the evening of December 14th against the Churchill hotel in Portman Square near Marylebone station. Using a stolen Ford Cortina as the transportation, a team of the ASU drove up Portman Street towards the hotel, where Eddie Butler opened fire with the Sten gun, firing approximately sixteen rounds at the front of the hotel and the crowd emerging from the main door. They had picked the Churchill as it was an "exclusive" establishment, as they would later tell their police interrogators. An American couple staying at the hotel was taken to hospital with slight gunshot wounds, while a Scandinavian couple received treatment for shock and cuts from flying glass. The attacks seemed to have no motive to the police, however, the forensic evidence gathered from the Churchill shooting would firmly link it to the attack on the Cavalry Club. Butler, later asked if he had been intending to hit people standing outside the hotel, reportedly replied that "if you're going shooting at someone, we shoot to kill." Fortunately, so it would appear, Butler's aim with the Sten was less than deadly.

The same cannot be said for the ASU's bombings. In a pre-Christmas attack on the capital's telecommunication system, on December 17th, the ASU placed three powerful devices outside telephone exchanges. One bomb was placed on the back of a parked motorcycle in Draycott Avenue, a second device was left in a parked car in New Compton Street, and the third was left in tartan holdall in the entrance of the Museum telephone exchange in Chenies Street, near Tottenham Court Road. O'Connell made a telephone call to the Daily Mirror newspaper at 9:05pm, warning of impending explosions. The first bomb went off at 9:15pm as police were evacuating the area, blowing out windows of buildings up to a mile from the explosion. The Compton Street device detonated at 9:35pm, sending wrecked cars scattered across the road. The bomb at the Museum exchange was discovered by a telephone operator who, somewhat foolishly, peeked inside the bag to see wires coming out of a battery. The operator beat a hasty retreat, but before the police arrived the bomb exploded, killing a telephone exchange worker. Eddie Butler would later tell Jim Nevill he had covered O'Connell while he planted the bombs in the Museum exchange and in New Compton Street, acknowledging the death of the telephone exchange worker.

The Met could only watch and wonder where and when the ASU would strike again. They continued to gather forensic evidence from the bomb scenes, but were frankly no closer to apprehending the unknown perpetrators. December 19th, 1974, with five shopping days to go before Christmas, the Met could only encourage a state of vigilance from both their officers and the general public. Any tidbit of information, no matter how insignificant, could be just the breakthrough they needed in the race to stop the bombers.

At 8:20pm on the evening of the 19th, a light blue Ford Cortina, borrowed in Fulham by the ASU, pulled into a bus stop bay on Oxford Street almost opposites Selfridges department store. The car had been loaded with 100 pounds of gelignite, stowed in the trunk, and fitted with a pocket watch timing device making it the largest bomb the ASU had constructed to that point. Unfortunately for the driver of the stolen Cortina, the awkward angle he had pulled into the bus bay prevented the parked in front from pulling back out into the street. The bus *as* less than impressed, so he climbed out of the bus and, ac-ing to the police "had words with the driver of the Cortina, and as a *it* the car was moved." The ASU moved off from their preferred parking spot and drove a few yards west down Oxford Street past Selfridges, then took a right and navigated around the one-way system, taking them behind their target, parallel to Oxford street traveling east until they could take a right turn that put them pack into Oxford Street. Traveling west again as they approached the store, they took a right into Duke Street and parked the stolen car at the side of the Selfridges building. The time was 8:30pm. Inside the store, the chief executive, a Mr. French, and several of his directors were participating in a Christmas function on the top floor of the building. At 8:40pm, O'Connell telephoned a national newspaper based in London with a warning of a bomb in Selfridges. Once the police received the warning from the newspaper they reacted immediately, with squad cars racing to the scene to block off the area and get the Thursday evening shoppers out of the streets. Oxford Street was full of people gift shopping, window shopping or just soaking up the Christmas atmosphere looking at the decorative lights and festive shop window displays, such as the Dickens Christmas display in the front window of Selfridges. Having received a warning from the police, chief of store security for Selfridges, Gordon Rose, was in the process of clearing the shop staff from the building. In a nearby Oxford Street pub, The Henry Holland, the publican packed 200 customers into the cellar bar where they stood "like packed sardines," as they awaited the all-clear from the police. Trade was brisk, the publican later noted.

The bomb exploded at 9:0pm in what was described by Commander Robert Huntley as "a very big blast," shattering shop windows for hundreds of yards in both directions on Oxford Street, knocking down masonry and blowing in doors. Because of the advanced warning, there were remarkably few casualties, none of them serious. However, it was later estimated that the blast had caused £1.5 million worth of damage, in 1974 money. The damage was so extensive, the Met shutdown Oxford street between Bond Street and Marble Arch underground stations, a stretch of 600 yards of prime shopping, until 12 noon the following day to allow cleanup crews to do their work and to allow repairs to be made to make it safe for the public to return. Selfridges, refusing to accept any lost business because of the IRA, was ready for business at 9:0am the following day thanks to the efforts of many staff members who worked through the night to clear up the damage and make good as best they could. The shop workers mood was defiant of the IRA and their bombing campaign on London, and that mood was spreading. London was adopting a blitz mentality, the German Luftwaffe had not broken their spirit during World War II, so who did these Irish upstarts think they were dealing with!

The bus driver, who had argued with the driver of the stolen Cortina, reportedly gave police a detailed description of the man in the car, adding more data for the investigation. But the Met needed more, more eyewitness accounts, more fingerprints, more evidence of the ASU's technical prowess, and maybe more luck.

The ASU were not the only ones looking to profit from the use of sticks of gelignite as the Christmas holiday approached. On the day after the Oxford Street car bomb, a man carrying a briefcase filled with sticks of "dynamite" failed to convince the manager of the Newmarket branch of Midland bank to part with £30,000. The would-be robber handed Mr. Ted Kell a note, explaining the bomb and outlining his demands regarding the cash. Unconvinced, Mr. Kell sounded the alarm, trapping the robber in the bank. The street outside the bank was evacuated, as the bungling robber explained that the briefcase would go off if pulled away from him. After some discussion, he was eventually persuaded to hand over the case, and bomb disposal officers later blew open the locks with a controlled explosion. The "dynamite" turned out to be a number of 12-inch-long sticks of rock candy, pink on the outside, with a white mint core on which was printed the name of an English seaside town. The hapless would-be bank robber was taken away into custody and later charged with attempted robbery. It is also possible that somebody later consumed the evidence. It was a "sweet" end to that particular "bomb" episode and the Met probably wished they could get the same result in their pursuit of the ASU.

The day of the stick-of-rock attempted robbery, Friday 20th December, was also a day when many service personnel would have been heading home for the Christmas break, to be with family and friends for a few days before going back to barracks. Aldershot, home to the Parachute Regiment, would see a significant number of army personnel passing through the town's rail station on that day, making it a prime target for the ASU. They placed a timed explosive device containing 44 pounds of gelignite, hidden on one platform of the station, and placed a telephone warning to a national newspaper. The police swung into action, located the bomb and defused the device before it could go off. The Met was thrilled, as they had received a Christmas gift from the ASU in the shape of a completely intact timed device. They could check for prints, pick at the modified Westclox timers that used adapted drawing pins as electrical contacts, and pass the device over to the scientists at RADRE for further examination. They also prevented a potentially murderous bombing attack on service personnel right before the holiday. Merry Christmas ASU! The news that the device had been defused with apparent ease would be a concern to O'Connell. As the chief bomb architect for the team, it would be up to him to construct some form of effective anti-handling device, because if the warnings they issued resulted in bomb disposal experts handling and defusing their bombs, it presented yet another opportunity to strike at the Bomb Squad. O'Connell would raise the stakes for future bomb disposal crews, but that would be for later.

Behind the scenes in Northern Ireland, members of the IRA had met in secret with the group of a Protestant clergyman from Northern Ireland, led by Dr. Arthur Butler. The IRA delegation, led by Daithi O'Connell, was presented with a policy document, previously cleared by the British government, which outlined a move towards a negotiated truce and eventual settlement. The Protestant clergyman would engage in shuttle diplomacy between the IRA and representatives of the British government in an effort to stop the shootings and bombings. As a result of the talks between the IRA and the Protestant clergyman, the IRA announced a temporary cease-fire on December 2nd, 1974, to go into effect at midnight on the 22nd, and last until January 2nd, 1975. The cease-fire was intended to give the British government time to respond to proposals made by the IRA via the Protestant clergyman, and relayed to Merlyn Rees, the Northern Ireland Secretary. In a press statement on the cease-fire, the IRA praised the actions of the Protestant clergyman, stating that their approach "unlike that of others, was frank and constructive at all times." The Army Council of the IRA made it clear they expected that "a positive response would be forthcoming from the British government." The statement went on to say the Republican leadership awaited a reply from the British government to the proposals for a cease-fire and added "if there is not a satisfactory answer by midnight on January 2nd, then the Irish Republican Army will have no option but to resume hostilities." The IRA's proposals to the British government contained nothing new: A commitment by the British to withdraw troops from Northern Ireland, the release of political prisoners, and the right of the people of Ireland to determine their own future. One of the lead Protestant clergymen responsible for brokering the cease-fire, Dr. Butler, stated that he was "delighted we shall have this chance of a cease-fire, but there is a long way to go." Predictably, the reaction from

Dr. Ian Paisley, leader of the Democratic Unionist Party, was less than enthusiastic. "The terms of the truce are terms of capitulation and surrender," he said, "the only reason the IRA are having a truce is because they have got what they wanted." The fact that it was unclear precisely what the IRA had agreed to, or what the British government had signed up for, did not stop the Reverend Paisley from pouring water on the notion of a halt in hostilities. Brian Faulkner, the former Chief Executive of the assembly of Northern Ireland, and leader of the Ulster Unionist party of Northern Ireland stated that "no temporary cease-fire can justify negotiations with the IRA." It appeared the Ulster Unionists would not support any negotiations with the IRA. The truce would be tenuous, pulled at by Unionists and vulnerable to sudden changes of heart by either the IRA or the British government. But, reminiscent of some World War I and World War II Christmas truces at the front line, the shootings and bombings would stop for the holiday, while the protagonist's celebrated the birth of Christ and proclaimed peace and goodwill to all men, as they cleaned their Armalite rifles and their AK47's. With the cease fire announced, the ASU were on a deadline, and with hostilities due to stop at midnight on the 22nd, they still had two pre-Christmas deliveries to make.

Harrods in Knightsbridge is a shopping institution, famous for his many departments from the lush food hall on the first floor, to furs, fine china, even paints and hardware. At peak times it is like a small city block, with 6,000 employees all hustling and bustling to deal with the floods of customers coming into the store. The run-up to Christmas is one of the busiest times of the year for the store, with people from all over London and other parts of the country, together with a significant tourist presence, all looking for gifts to carry home in triumph in the distinctive green and gold bags, a trademark of the top drawer store. Harrods sits like a majestic island, surrounded by Brompton Road to its northwest, Hans Road to its southwest with Basil Street and Hans Crescent completing the baseball-diamond like layout of the surrounding streets. There are twenty doors into the store, so security in 1974 was a headache of no small proportions. To their credit, the store recognized its value as a potential terrorist target, and as such had devised and practiced a very "stringent evacuation drill," as the store's managing director of the time, Robert Midgley, explained.

Mingling with the Christmas shoppers, Butler and O'Connell entered the store on Saturday, December 21st, the last big shopping day before the Christmas holiday. Butler carried 10 pounds of gelignite into the store in a carrier bag and met up with O'Connell at a prearranged meeting place in one of the men's restrooms on the second floor, near the hardware department. O'Connell took the explosives and inserted a detonator, and set the Westclox timing device for the delay required in order to escape the store in good time before the explosion. The timing device had been modified so that the hands of the clock accepted adapted drawing pins. The pins were placed through the clock hands with the heads facing in opposite direction. The detonation circuit wires were soldered to the shaft of the drawing pins that protruded out from the hands of the clock. The wires, connected to an HP7 battery and to the detonator, would carry the current to the explosive charge of the detonator when the two drawing pins heads made contact after a predetermined delay. A mention of drawing pins to O'Connell, by Jim Nevill during the IRA man's interrogation, had elicited a wry smile from the Irishman.

With the bomb "made up" as the ASU referred to the arming process, the device was surreptitiously placed in the hardware department near the household paint. The location was deliberately chosen, as the paint would cause a fire after the bomb had gone off, creating more damage. Butler and O'Connell made their exit and headed for a pay phone to call in a warning. Butler called a national newspaper and claimed there were in fact three bombs in Harrods and that they had 30 minutes before the bombs went off. However, before the warning had been passed on to the police, the hardware department buyer, Mr. Jack Butler, spotted the suspicious package and called store security staff. With military precision, the entire store was evacuated in 12 minutes flat, with people pouring out of the exits in an orderly fashion.

The bomb ripped through the hardware department, smashing windows and bringing down parts of the ceiling. The paint, as planned, started a fire, but Harrods meticulous planning had anticipated the risk that fire posed to the whole building and so had installed steel fire shutters that would seal off any department to prevent the spread of fire. The fire sprinkler system also helped prevent greater damage from the blaze, although water from the sprinklers leaked through the floor into the fur department below, damaging some of the coats on display. Mr. Midgley, talking to the press the day after the explosion, thought the damage could run into "hundreds of thousands of pounds."

Interrogating O'Connell later about the Harrods attack, Jim Nevill would shake his head and state, in utter disbelief, "I can't believe how you could just take that [the explosives] in in a bag."

With the deadline to the truce approaching, the ASU had one remaining target for 1974. At the urging of GHQ, who provided the address of the target, ASU planned to assassinate a prominent political figure. The attack was justified, in the opinion of their superiors back in Ireland, as Edward Heath had been Prime Minister when the hated practice of internment had been introduced. His death, at the hands of the IRA, would be a dramatic end to the 1974 campaign and send a chilling message to the political leadership of the country: we can get to you if we want to.

Edward Heath, an accomplished musician and conductor had a life-long affectionate attachment to his childhood village of Broadstairs in Kent, and he had a tradition of conducting the annual carol concert in the village each Christmas. Sunday, December 22nd was the day of the carol concert and Heath had driven down to the village in his Rover car for the event. The ASU had been provided with vital intelligence on Heath and his address of 17 Wilton Street, only 200 yards from the previously attacked Talbot Arms, was an important part of the intelligence, but the key element was the knowledge that Heath liked to work at his desk of an evening. The desk faced a first floor window with a small balcony outside, a target vulnerable to a thrown bomb, something the ASU had gained plenty of practice with over the previous series of attacks. Heath had moved into the leased premises in July of 1974 after losing his official London Prime Ministerial residence of 10 Downing Street following the February election defeat.

Using a stolen Ford Cortina, a three-man team of the ASU drove to Wilton Street. They stopped the car to allow the bomb to be thrown onto the small first floor balcony of the house, believing Heath was in the room and at his desk behind the window. Two police officers in Wilton Street saw the bomb being thrown and gave chase to the group who, urging the bomb thrower to quickly get back in the car, escaped as the bomb exploded. At the Talbot Arms Pub, Mr. Neal Denton had been drinking with friends and had just stepped outside on his way home when the bomb went off at 8:55pm. The sound of the bomb made him think the IRA had attacked the nearby Pig and Whistle pub, and so he . hurried to Wilton Street just in time to see the stolen Cortina speed past at about 60 mph. Denton ran to his sports car with the intention of giving chase, but the car failed to start. The Cortina's speed and skidding turns were noticed by two officers in a patrol car, as Peter Imbert later recalled, "there were some of our traffic officers nearby and they saw this car skidding along through traffic lights and they gave chase. They got as far as Hyde Park Corner when it came through on the radio that there had been a bomb in Westminster. So, our lads abandoned what they thought was a traffic offence and went to where the bomb had gone off, not realizing they were chasing the people responsible for this attack!"

Heath recalled hearing of the explosion as he neared his home, on a radio news flash, where it was reported that a bomb had gone off in Chelsea. He found out it was actually at his home as he pulled into Wilton Street and found the road blocked off and a search going on for any other devices. The ASU had missed Heath by ten minutes, as he had decided on the spur of the moment to stay and have tea with friends after the carol concert had finished. The snap decision saved his life, as he would have almost certainly been at his desk when the ASU came to call. Asked if he believed the attack was an attempted assassination, Heath replied "I can't tell what they were doing. Obviously they wanted to damage the house or injure the people in it."

Driving quickly to get out of the area, the stolen Cortina collided with a white Volkswagen Beetle in Lower Sloan Street, where the three-man ASU team abandoned the vehicle and made off on foot, leaving the Bomb Squad with very welcome forensic evidence they would gather from the stolen vehicle, and a somewhat shaken and irate owner of the damaged Beetle. The ASU had completed their final planned mission, but had failed to kill their intended target, and they would have to wait for another attempt as at midnight on the 22nd, the IRA cease fire commenced. The question was would it last, and who would be the first to break it?

The Christmas truce between the IRA and the British government would prove to be a very tenuous and temporary peace, with both sides being less than truthful to each other. The British hinted to the IRA Army Council that they did, in fact, want to pull out of Northern Ireland but were fearful of a potential Unionist backlash. The veiled hints gave the IRA some false hope that the cease-fire could yield some eventual benefit, but there was a marked lack of trust toward the British government. In truth, both sides were playing for time. The Wilson government, terrified of a very real threat of an ultra-violent Unionist reaction to any public concessions made to the IRA, would not pull out the troops, despite the veiled promises whispered into the ears of the Army Council. The Government had plenty of evidence as to the capability, and willingness, of the Unionists to create bloody anarchy in the six counties, as the Ulster Workers Council strike of 1974 demonstrated. The IRA needed to draw breath, rearm some of its units with supplies from American-backed Republican organizations, and get ready for anticipated all-out fight with Loyalist paramilitary units in the north. But the Christmas truce gave some rank-and-file Provisional IRA members the impression that the Army Council was weakening in its resolve to carry the fight to the British and achieve the Republican objectives so long striven for in the north. Keeping the truce going would need work on both sides, and both sides knew that would require public statements of good intentions to keep the peace. So, in such an effort to keep the cease-fire going, and dangle a carrot in front of the Army Council, Merlyn Rees stated three days before the truce expired, that in the event of a "genuine and sustained cessation of violence, the British government would not be found wanting in its response." The following day, January 1st, 1975, the Provisional IRA extended the truce for an additional two weeks, moving the deadline out to January 16th. In reality, the British government was stringing the IRA along in an effort to keep the truce going. The longer the truce went on, the more opportunity the government had to gather intelligence on IRA operatives, some of whom had become lax in their discipline under the cease-fire. Having extended the Prevention of Terrorism Act to Northern Ireland, the practice of internment would eventually become obsolete in some respects, with the new act giving the government better options to deal with suspected IRA activists. The truce allowed the government to begin to lay the groundwork for a new security setup that would use the Prevention of Terrorism Act as the principal weapon in the British government's fight against the IRA.

Some of the IRA senior ranks were becoming concerned that maybe the Army Council had been tricked into calling a truce and taking part in negotiations the British had no intention of bringing to fruition. There were also concerns about the rapid escalation of violence from Loyalist paramilitary groups, who were fearful of an unpredictable outcome from any IRA talks with the Wilson government. There were also signs of dissent in the IRA leadership, with the hardliners wanting to break off the truce and recommence hostilities, fearing they were being trapped into a cycle of negotiation that would only weaken their position and make it less likely the British would agree to terms down the road. This was becoming apparent in the manner in which the British publicly addressed the IRA's five-point set of demands, trying to make the IRA look unreasonable in the eyes of the public. The IRA had required the release of 100 internees by the middle January. The government's position indicated that such a release was indeed possible, but they would not be dictated to over the timing. The IRA wanted meaningful talks between the British government and its political wing Sinn Féin, to which the government's response was that the door was wide open for discussions, and all the IRA had to do was ask! Their third demand was a complete withdrawal of troops to their barracks in Northern Ireland, to which the Government replied that Mr. Rees was totally prepared to do so. But the IRA's final two demands were serious sticking points for the Wilson government. The IRA wanted a declaration of intent that the government would withdrawal from Northern Ireland in the near future, and amnesty for all Republican political prisoners held in jails in the United Kingdom and Republic of Ireland. On the first point, the British government would not comply as Northern Ireland was a part of the United Kingdom, and as such, they had every right to have troops present in the Province. It would also not grant any amnesty to convicted prisoners, as this would undermine the British judicial system. Any release from prison of convicted Republicans would have to be through the normal process of law. The two sides were still far apart and despite several attempts to reach a compromise, neither side would shift position.

In a move that was almost inevitable, by January 16th, the hawkish hardliners in the Provisionals senior leadership had prevailed over the members of the Army Council who had agreed to the truce in the first place. In a statement to the press, the IRA stated they "could not in all conscience renew the cease-fire principally because of the total lack of response from the British government." The IRA claimed that in the week prior to the cease-fire expiring, there had been no comment from Merlyn Rees regarding the IRA's proposals for ending the war. The British government had only released a handful of internees, the IRA stated, which represented an "insult to every member of the Irish race." The cease-fire was over.

Merlyn Rees responded to the cancellation of the cease-fire with a counter statement. "I share the feelings of outrage and disappointment of the people of Northern Ireland," he stated, "that the provisional IRA have today showed a total lack of concern for the people's clear call for an end to violence." Rees concluded his statement, "I will not be influenced by any causes which are backed with threats of the bomb and the bullet." Ulster Catholic leader Gerry Fitt stated, "it will be an absolutely insane person who orders the resumption of hostilities." Fitt accused the IRA of using "brinkmanship" with the British government in an effort to get them to agree with their terms. He was wrong. The IRA had already gone over the brink and was prepared to put the British mainland firmly back in its sights with the resumption of the terrorist campaign in London. The ASU were told to prepare for further engagements with the "enemy," and once again the Bomb Squad would be facing the actions of Joe O'Connell and his team of determined urban guerrillas. The IRA would step up attacks in Northern Ireland and activate other sleeper cells in Great Britain. They would use the bomb and the bullet to back their position, and despite Mr. Rees's comments to the contrary, they would push home their campaign to the British government.

With the resumption of hostilities in Northern Ireland, the ASU would go back to work on the streets of London. On the night of January 19th, two shooting teams headed out for their respective targets, one group, including Eddie Butler armed with the Sten gun, drove to the Portman hotel in Portman Square. In the hotel, a group of 500 teenagers were dancing in a disco on the first floor, while several people settled down to eat in the dining room. Outside, the doorman, Tony Willis, was helping guests with taxis. Willis spotted the ASU's car as it approached the hotel, and stated, "I saw this big car come along as it passed the coffee shop." The car slowed down as it closed on the hotel, and Butler fired the Sten gun at the front of the hotel, getting off approximately 20 rounds of 9 mm ammunition. Willis stated that "I saw lots of flashes and heard the rattle of machine gun fire. The whole thing was over in seconds!" Bullets ripped through the dining room window and through the front of the coffee shop, narrowly missing Willis and several guests eating in the dining room. One round smashed into a dining room mirror, as one eyewitness stated, "a split second after a waiter had walked past." Several diners were injured by flying glass from the shattered window, but remarkably no one was hit by the extended bursts of gunfire.

Two hours after the attack on the Portman hotel, a second team fired on the Carlton Towers hotel in Belgravia. The Carlton duty manager stated that there had been very little damage, with only a few bullet holes through the front window, most probably from one of the two World War II era American M1 carbines the ASU had at their disposal. As a semiautomatic weapon, the M1 could not deliver a sustained burst of fire like the Sten gun, but it could deliver individual shots in rapid succession. The ASU would use the weapon again in subsequent attacks.

In Northern Ireland, support for the IRA was becoming somewhat strained. There had been widespread revulsion at the horrendous attacks in Birmingham, despite the IRA's vocal denials of responsibility. Despite what they said publicly, the attack had all the hallmarks of the IRA and people in the north were becoming war weary. The prospect of a cease-fire had been appealing to many, and a lot of people on both the Unionist and Nationalist sides had enjoyed a few weeks of relative normalcy in the Province over the Christmas holiday. The IRA would face increasing pressure and resistance among Nationalist supporters regarding the resumption of hostilities. That pressure would grow toward the end of January, forcing both the Wilson government and the Provisional IRA to examine their relative positions regarding the London campaign and the possibility of an extended cease fire. Some cynics accused the Provisionals of having lost control of the London ASU and that they were, in actuality, rogue operatives acting on their own initiative. As a retort, the IRA promised a display in London of their control over the group. People would have to wait and see as to when and where, but there would be multiple explosions in one night toward the end of the month, the IRA promised.

The ASU carried out an attack on London's infrastructure, with the bombing of the Metropolitan water board pumping station at Woodford. The explosion at 10:50pm followed a telephone warning about the device delivered 20 minutes earlier. The blast slightly injured four people, and created major traffic issues as water from the pumping station flooded roads in the vicinity. The attack did little to impact the supply of water to the capital, but did send a signal to the country that the bombers were back in business.

By way of a response to the peace marchers who demonstrated on both sides of the border in Ireland on January 26th, and as part of the promised display of control the IRA had over the London ASU, the group undertook the largest series of coordinated attacks in London since they had become active in 1974. A total of seven time bombs were placed across London on the night of January 27th. Individual phone warnings, regarding the seven devices, were called into national newspapers, giving the police time to respond to the mammoth task of attending each of the locations. Five of the bombs exploded with the first at Grieve's military tailors in Old Bond Street. Two bombs were successfully defused, one in the doorway of a shoe shop at 139 Putney High Street, with the second device being diffused in the doorway of the Charco Grill restaurant on Heath Road, Hempstead. The four other devices exploded, the detonations of all five bombs timed over a four-hour period between 6:50pm and 10:50pm in an apparent effort to give police time to deal with each situation and avoid a repeat of a Bloody Friday type debacle on the streets of London. In a parallel attack in Manchester, in the North of England, a bomb attack on the Lewis department store injured nineteen people, raising the total number of casualties for the evening to twenty-six.

The campaign of violence was becoming all too much for many people to bear in Great Britain and Northern Ireland. There appeared to be no end in sight to the continuous cycle of destruction and killing, and the police appeared to be no closer to stopping the violence in London. The peace marchers continued their opposition to the continued violence, driving the IRA and the Wilson government to make contact again in late January 1975 for further talks on introducing an extended cease-fire, so that they could explore options to reach a peaceful settlement.

At the beginning of February, the IRA rotated Brendan Dowd out of London, sending him back to Dublin for reassignment to head up a new ASU, intended to be based in the North of England. Dowd would stay in the Republic for several months as he made preparations for a new campaign. He was replaced with a young American from San Francisco by the name of William Joseph Quinn, whose nickname within the IRA was "Yankee Joe." Quinn, raised in the USA as a devoted supporter of the Republican cause, had thoroughly immersed himself in all things Irish, including adopting an Irish accent. With Dowd gone, the ASU gave up the Waldemar Avenue flat and Quinn moved in with Duggan and Dougherty at 39 Fairholme Road, the ASU's principal bomb making facility in London.

With the IRA and the Wilson government talking again about a cease-fire, a term the IRA did not like as it implied the process was all too one-sided, i.e., the IRA were to halt hostilities, whereas the term "truce" was more bilateral and implied both sides were combatants, a notion about which the Wilson government would squirm with discomfort. Likewise, the British government did not like the term "truce" as it gave the appearance of legitimizing the IRA's "military" actions. The fact that the two sides could argue over the terminology of a cessation of hostilities indicated they had a long way to go, and the efforts would not be helped by the rabid sideline sniping of the Reverend Ian Paisley. Dr. Paisley made a "call to the Protestants of Ulster," in a sermon at his Martyr's Memorial Church in Belfast. His call was for the Protestants to preserve their country in the face of "perfidious British government." He lambasted the Protestant clergy who had helped broker the Christmas cease-fire with the IRA. Paisley earnestly urged his flock to "protect and defend their fields, homes, fire sides, graves of their fathers, their cities and churches, wives and families." Paisley would stop shy of describing just how such a defense should be conducted, but people would fill in the gaps for themselves, figuring that the Loyalist paramilitary groups would stand firm and protect the Unionist beliefs in a strong link to Britain, absolutely no dealing with the Republic and a continued effort to sink any further talks regarding a power-sharing arrangement in the Province.

On February 11, 1975, the Provisional IRA declared an indefinite truce with the British government, to allow the exploration of talks on concepts for the future of the Province. The London ASU would be able to stand down for the foreseeable future, but the IRA would not pull them out of London, as they needed the ability to ramp up hostilities again if the hopes and aspirations behind the truce failed to materialize. There would be a powerful sense of déjà vu for many political commentators at the reinstatement of the cease-fire, as both sides were still a long way from agreeing across the board on the future of Northern Ireland, and the Unionists would doggedly refused to entertain any notion of a cooperative system of government that had anything to do with the Republic, or the Republicans. The situation appeared to be one of hope for hopes sake, with both the Wilson government and the IRA clutching at political straws that the Unionists had a very firm grip on and they would be very reluctant to let go of their end. For a time, the bombings and shootings would stop and the paramilitary forces of the IRA in Northern Ireland would be turned, for a while, toward a more political role in the province. Conversely the Bomb Squad would not stop and would continue to determinedly work toward getting closer to the ASU and bring them to justice, to answer for the crimes they had committed on the streets of London. The Bomb Squad had a clearer picture of the bombings the ASU had perpetrated. A report issued by the scientists at RADRE made a forensic link between the bombs at Woolwich, Guilford and others carried out in London. The report would cause some consternation among the police, given that Surrey CID had already arrested and charged four people with the Guilford and Woolwich bombings, but the report clearly indicated a link with bombs beyond the initial two attacks, and this would prove problematic for the police and the British court system at a future point.

The Met would keep pushing, hoping the ASU would make a mistake, but with the cease-fire in place and the ASU out of action for the foreseeable future, they were unlikely to see that occur on the streets where they operated. Maybe the Met would get lucky, as police work on one crime sometimes paid off on another investigation totally unrelated to the original case. Maybe, just maybe, they would get a break, and maybe that break would lead Imbert and the Bomb Squad one step closer to apprehending O'Connell and his team.

On the morning of February 25th, 20-year-old Kathryn Tibble got ready to head out to her job as a bank clerk at a branch in Brentford, five miles from the flat she shared with her husband of two years Stephen in Auriol Road, West Kensington. Stephen, 21 years old, had been a Metropolitan police officer for three months after graduating from training at the Police College in Hendon, where he was regarded as the most promising recruit in his class. Stephen Tibble was still asleep as his wife quietly left the flat, so as not to disturb him as he slept after working a night shift. As a probationary officer, Stephen Tibble would spend his first two years as a Constable under the watchful eyes of his more experienced colleagues, who described the young copper as being "as keen as mustard!" Tibble, based at a local police station in Fulham, was a familiar sight to his neighbors as he went to and fro on his blue Honda 125cc motorbike, always with his white crash helmet firmly in place. While Tibble slept, a one-minute motorbike ride away four unarmed plainclothes police officers, Temporary Detective Constable's [TDC] Derek Wilson and Kenneth Mathews and PC's Adrian Blackledge and Les White, all from Hammersmith police station, began a day of surveillance in the West Kensington area, on the lookout for burglary suspects after a spate of house breaking around the neighborhood. The four officers were split into two teams and issued with radios to keep in touch with the communications officer at Hammersmith Police station. It was going to be a long day for the four men who, unbeknown to them, were literally on the doorstep of the ASU's bomb factory in Fairholme Road.

Steven Tibble would leave later that morning to head out from his flat on errands, after feeding Scampi, his black cat, waving to his neighbor's children Paul and Christopher Stewart as he rode off, calling out to them, "hello boys . . . I'll see you later tonight!"

By mid morning, the four officers decided to take a break for a cup of tea, after which they returned to their observation duties, with Derek Wilson and his partner covering Charleville Road and with Blackledge and White working in the Fairholme Road area. As the two officers got closer to number 39, Blackledge spotted Quinn acting suspiciously outside the entrance to the basement flat at number 39, and as Derek Wilson later recalled, "they must have thought there was something dodgy about this guy because they decided to hang around to see what he was up to."

Lunchtime arrived and PC White wanted to go and get fish and chips, but Blackledge wanted to see if the suspect emerged again, so White went off for lunch on his own, leaving Blackledge alone to wait for Quinn to make another appearance. Derek Wilson added, "that should have never happened. You either work as a team or you don't." Blackledge saw Quinn leave number 39 and decided to follow him as he walked toward North End Road, where Quinn waited at a bus stop. Blackledge approached the suspect and introduced himself as a police officer and requested that Quinn empty out his pockets. Blackledge noticed that Quinn was carrying a lot of Irish money on him, and so told Quinn he wanted to escort him back to the address he had been seen leaving in Fairholme Road to see what he had been up to. With that, Quinn made a break for it, running west down Charleville Road, pursued by Blackledge, heading toward where Derek Wilson and his partner were sitting on a bench. "First thing I recall," said Wilson, "was seeing a man running along Charleville Road followed closely by Adrian Blackledge. Both Ken and I wondered, 'what's he up to now?' Ken and I joined in the chase and I was going along Charleville Road when I heard a motorbike enter the street from the North End Road end." Stephen Tibble, on the motor bike, was approximately half a mile from his home, riding down Charleville Road, where he saw three men, apparently police officers, giving chase to a young man with collar length hair. Derek Wilson flagged down Tibble, "I was on the pavement, so I stepped into the road, held up my police ID and asked the rider if he would give me a lift," said Wilson, "intending to go on the back of his motorbike. But just that week the law had changed introducing motorcycle helmet regulations, so that everyone on a motorbike had to wear a helmet, sods law really. He didn't really respond to me, although he paused and then drove off and followed after Quinn and Blackledge along Charleville Road."

Tibble rode past the three officers, past the running Quinn, and pulled to a stop at the Junction of Charleville Road and Gledstanes Road. Getting off his Honda, Tibble crouched down on the sidewalk, spreading out his arms to block the path of the fugitive and catch hold of him. Quinn, being chased down by three police officers, now faced an additional threat from what appeared to be a member of the public. Still running, Quinn pulled out a .38 revolver and shot the unarmed Stephen Tibble twice in the chest at close range. The gunshots startled Tania Lee, working in the study of her apartment with the window open, as it was a relatively mild day for February. "I heard the shots ring out, dashed to the window and saw a young man in jeans and anorak and a white crash helmet," she stated, "crumple over. I saw him fall face first onto the pavement."

Derek Wilson recalled the events as they unfolded, "we heard the shots ring out in rapid succession, two shots. We also heard other shots ring out and I later formed the opinion that these rounds were intended for Adrian Blackledge and myself, although I wasn't conscious of that at the time. Tibble fell and the gunman ran past him. Blackledge stopped by Tibble and I was the next one there. Blackledge had frozen to the spot, so I crouched down to Tibble and removed his helmet and unzipped his jacket. Tibble then spoke to me and said he was a police Constable and that was the first time I realized he was a police officer. He was wearing a pale tan sweater and all I saw was a slight discoloration, there was no blood visible, no bullet holes, just a discoloration on his sweater. There was nothing more to do, as I couldn't see what was wrong with him other than I had heard the shots and he had gone down, I knew he had been shot but there was no visible wound for me to tend."

Mrs. Lee called for the police and ambulance service, grabbed a blanket and ran down the stairs and into the street, where she rolled the blanket up and placed under Stephen Tibble's head, noticing that the wounded officer was barely conscious. Derek Wilson put out a call for assistance for the wounded officer and reported the direction the gunman had headed. Quinn, with quite a head start on the three officers, continue to run north on Gledstanes Road, heading for a possible escape from pursuit in the nearby Barons Court underground station, but Wilson was determined to run down the gunman and arrest him, "PC Tibble was on the ground, Blackledge had frozen, and then Ken Mathews caught up with us. I went across the road and jumped on PC Tibble's bike, started up the engine and set off after the gunman, giving a running commentary on my radio as I headed into Gledstanes Road, where he turned left and onto Comeragh Road and then onto Palliser Road." Wilson, a keen motorcyclist, owned a British Matchless motorbike, but he was not accustomed to the layout of the Japanese machine borrowed from the wounded Tibble, as he would later explain, "you would think a motorbike could catch up with a running person, but as I was riding along I thought to myself 'I'm going to have a word with that guy as this bike is crap.' I'm anxiously trying to catch the guy, but every time I wound the throttle back, the engine cut out. I was use to British bikes not Japanese ones, and the gear pedal and the brake pedal were on opposite sides to what I was used to, so I would come to a junction, push down on what I thought was the brake and changed gears instead! Equally, when I went to change gears, I was stamping on the brake. As it turned out it may have saved my life, but that was not the idea, I was trying to catch the guy."

Detective Chief Superintendent Robert Wilson, commander of the Hammersmith District CID, was driving near the scene when Derek Wilson's radio call for help went out. Arriving at the site of the shooting, Wilson was shocked by what he saw. PC Stephen Tibble had, by that point, slipped into unconsciousness and had lost a lot of blood. Ambulances arrived and one rushed Tibble to New Charing Cross Hospital on Fulham Palace Road for emergency surgery. The police sent a car to pick up his wife Kathryn from her bank in Brentford and dashed back to the hospital so that the young woman could be by the side of her badly wounded husband.

Derek Wilson continued to follow Quinn as he approached Barons Court underground station, still giving a running commentary to the communications officer at Hammersmith Police station, but things were not going smoothly as the regular communications officer was on a refreshment break and another, less experienced officer, was manning the radio. The increasing radio traffic, with officers asking for directions and more details of the events, was overloading the stand-in. Derek Wilson recalled the chase, "I followed him onto Talgarth Road, with Barons Court underground station on my left. I said on the radio 'now heading towards Barons Court station' but nobody took control of the radio traffic, resulting in confusion. Someone needed to say 'all units wait, commentary in progress.' They didn't do that, so the last thing people heard was a reference to Barons Court tube station. I went over Talgarth Road and saw a patrol car coming toward me with five officers on board. They passed me and the suspect."

The confused radio traffic resulted in the police descending on Barons Court underground station, believing that the gunman had, in fact, entered having been chased there by Derek Wilson, where they cordoned off the station, disconnect the power to the rails, and went about searching for Quinn, the SPG officers in the group with their service revolvers drawn. A shot rang out from outside the tube station, sending officers there diving for cover. Unfortunately, Constable Gavin Cheeseman's .38 revolver had slipped out of its holster and discharged a round as it hit the ground, with the bullet wounding Cheeseman in the lower leg.

Despite extensive search of the station area and the train tunnels, the police failed to find William Quinn, because he was never there. Derek Wilson had pursued the gunman until he ran into a block of flats and then out through the other side, giving the police officer the slip. Wilson recalls, "I spent the next hour riding around looking for the suspect, getting dirty looks from traffic cops as I was not wearing a crash helmet."

Two hours after arriving at New Charing Cross Hospital, with his wife at his side, PC Stephen Tibble died from his wounds. He was 21 years old.

Returning to the scene of the shooting, Derek Wilson was told that the young officer had died and was ordered to take the motorbike to Hammersmith Police station as evidence. Not apprehending Quinn would weigh heavily on Derek Wilson, as he would later say, "for ten years I felt pangs of guilt for having allowed the suspect to get away," he said, "I didn't actually get hold of him. I was later told the gun he used was found at Balcombe Street." Detective chief Superintendent Robert Wilson would later tell Derek Wilson that he regretted not taking command of the radio communication, as the confusion directly impacted Quinn's ability to slip by the police and escape.

Several years later, Derek Wilson was on a police First Aid course where one of the instructors announced to the class, oblivious of the fact that Wilson had been involved, that if the officers on the scene had administered First Aid to PC Tibble, he would have survived. "That was so shocking to me," said Wilson, "I actually went to see the coroner who conducted the inquest into PC Tibble's murder and told him what I had heard. He said it was complete and utter rubbish. The bullets had apparently gone into Tibble and ricocheted around inside his chest, severing his aorta."

William Quinn was now a wanted murderer, as well as a possible terror suspect. The Met obtained a search warrant and went into 39 Fairholme Rd, where the landlord Mr. David Ahmed, told police that there were flats in the building rented to a Michael Wilson (Duggan) and a John Anderson (Dougherty), both young Irishmen who had recently been joined by a third young man by the name of William Rogers, an interesting alias for American-born IRA operative.[4] The basement flat, rented to Michael Wilson, was found to be a treasure trove to the men of the Bomb Squad when they arrived at the premises. After a search of the flat, they realized they had discovered the principal bomb making facility for the London ASU. In the flat they found explosives, wires, timers, detonators and another bomb making paraphernalia. Under the basement floor linoleum, they discovered hidden maps and plans for attacks on other parts of London. They found numerous books and documents, all of which would yield vital forensic evidence that would help them track down the ASU. One key document discovered in the flat was a letter, addressed, "Dear Joe," and was signed "Grannie." The letter was a thinly-veiled set of instructions to the ASU leader, explaining how he could get a copy of the Army List from a "Spotter Murphy" and how other intelligence could be obtained by going to a certain pub and asking for someone nicknamed "Damage." The discovery of 39 Fairholme Road, by sheer happenstance, had temporarily put the London ASU out of business, cease-fire or no cease-fire, so the Met reasoned. They had gained highly valuable intelligence and forensic evidence and they had two names, Wilson and Anderson and they would gather prints from the flats to add to their alphabetical terror suspect register. They also realized they had forced the other IRA occupants of the flats at the address to flee in order to avoid being picked up by the police. The tragedy of PC Stephen Tibble's murder would not be in vain. His selfless bravery in attempting to stop a fleeing suspect resulted in the Met finding the ASU's "house of death," as one newspaper described the address of 39 Fairholme Road, London W4. Tibble was a hero who had sacrificed his young life in the pursuit of his duty and, in doing so, had exposed the IRA's London team in the process. The Bomb Squad had a principle name for the ASU member who had rented the apartment that had produced a cargo of death and destruction: Michael Wilson, code name Z.

Phase one of the ASU's campaign of terror was over. The remaining members of the ASU had to scatter, their base at Fairholme Road compromised and its contents in the hands of the Metropolitan police Bomb Squad. Eddie Butler found a flat in Hackney at 103 Wilberforce Road, but moved after one week as the place was "not suitable." Butler, along with Hugh Dougherty, settled on 61 Crouch Hill in Islington, North London, under the names of John Farley and John Anderson. Duggan and O'Connell found a suitable flat at 99 Milton Grove, three miles from the other two men, in Hackney N16. They had to regroup, reequip and create new plans for their expected phase two campaign. The cease-fire, so they reasoned, would probably not hold and GHQ would want them ready to strike as soon as possible once the truce fell apart. Taking their reign of terror back to the streets of London was just a question of time. Nothing positive would emerge from the cease-fire and so they would wait for the call from GHQ to start their murderous activities again. The question remained as to what would be their new orders? What targets would GHQ instruct them to attack in the capital city of England?

NOTES

1. A family friend related a story to the author some years ago on this very subject. As the owner of a dark blue Cortina, this person had parked in a large parking lot and gone out for a few drinks with friends. Arriving back to the lot after dark, and somewhat well refreshed, he found what he thought was his Ford, opened the door, started

the car and drove home. He realized the next day he had driven home in the wrong car, and alerted the police!

2. The pub was previously called The Old Star and Crown and was later renamed as it changed ownership. There is some chance the pub was called The Horse and Groom back in 1974, but this has not been verified.

3. In Britain, pavement refers to the sidewalk

4. Will Rogers was a famous American cowboy entertainer of the 1930s

doi:10.1300/J173v08n01_03

Chapter 3

Phase Two

The British objectives for the February cease fire were based on the belief that they could politicize the Provisional IRA, even without the group realizing that it was happening. They also wanted to sap the strength of the Provisionals through constant intelligence surveillance, infiltrations into the various brigades and through the exploitation of informants. The politicization would occur through the checks and balances the British government would use with the IRA to ensure the cease-fire/truce was maintained.

In order for both sides to help maintain the cease-fire, a three-layer communications chain became established between the IRA and the British government. At the low-level, a chain of incident centers became established across the North that linked Sinn Féin, the Provisionals' political wing, to the British government monitors based in Belfast. The objective of the incident centers was to ensure that minor problems or incidents did not escalate into large truce-breaking issues through misunderstandings or miscommunications, putting the Provisionals in the role of a quasi-police force in Republican areas. The middle tier to the communications chain was a series of regular meetings between members of the IRA's executive and British officials held in a British government property in County Down. The top-level talks occurred between delegates from the IRA's Army Council and senior officials in the Northern Ireland office. Having the Provisionals act as political go-betweens and as a Republican stronghold police force

[Haworth co-indexing entry note]: "Phase Two." Moysey, Steven P. Co-published simultaneously in *Journal of Police Crisis Negotiations* (The Haworth Press, Inc.) Vol. 8, No. 1, 2008, pp. 89-127; and: *The Road to Balcombe Street: The IRA Reign of Terror in London* (Steven P. Moysey) The Haworth Press, Inc., 2008, pp. 89-127. Single or multiple copies of this article are available for a fee from The Haworth Document Delivery Service [1-800-HAWORTH, 9:00 a.m. - 5:00 p.m. (EST). E-mail address: docdelivery@haworthpress.com].

Available online at http://jpcn.haworthpress.com
doi:10.1300/J173v08n01_04

would give the IRA a level of prominence and exposure it had not previously enjoyed, much to the chagrin of the Unionist movement in Northern Ireland.

One other reason the British government was so keen on the notion of a cease-fire was to establish the introduction of what they had dubbed the Constitutional Convention Initiative. This was basically a resuscitated Sunningdale with slight nuances, power-sharing was still power-sharing no matter how it was dressed up and spoon fed to the Nationalists and the Unionists. The process was all too painfully like the Sunningdale attempt to establish a fair and equitable means of governing the Province, complete with proportional representation elections, which would return a given number of elected representatives to propose assembly. In order to move forward with the proposed Constitutional convention initiative, elections were called for May 1st, 1975, resulting in a very predictable outcome. The Provisional Sinn Féin, unsurprisingly, demanded a Catholic boycott of the elections as per the border poll of the previous year. The UUUC won 54% of the overall vote, formed a coalition with other Unionist parties and then attempted to ram through its own plan for a return to a pre Sunningdale Stormont assembly setup, complete with the absence of power-sharing in any shape or form. Predictably, the British government choked on all of the Unionist proposals and, magnanimously, offered the fledgling convention one more chance to come up with a plan they could stomach. It was an exercise in futility, and with the Unionist bluntly refusing to give "not an inch," the convention failed before it even really started. It is reported that the Heath Government had given the IRA assurances, somewhat rashly, that if the Council failed they would pull out troops from Northern Ireland. The Wilson government had no intention of doing any such thing, and the IRA came to realize this was the case. Feeling the British were about to renege on the supposed pull out deal, the Army Council gave the London ASU, in August, in advance of the eventual official collapse of the cease-fire, the green light to recommence hostilities. O'Connell and his men were ready for the new call to arms.

The start of the ASU's phase two campaign would be a direct copy of the early stages of their first acts of terror against British military personnel. The ASU had spent the time during the cease-fire scoping out new targets with a view to hostilities starting again sometime in 1975, and by August of that year the British public had become socially less vigilant than at the height of the ASU's phase one campaign. Five months without bombings and shootings on the streets of London had lulled people into a sense of false security, hoping the bombers had in fact gone away. While pubs such as the Talbot Arms had been the targ of the ASU's thrown bombs, a timed device had not been left in a pub since the attack on the Kings Arms in Woolwich during November of 1974. The ASU would go back to the tactic as they started the next phase of their work.

August 27th, 1975, was a Wednesday and payday for hundreds of soldiers of the 1st Battalion of the Welsh Guards based at Caterham in the county of Surrey. The Caterham Arms pub, in Coulsden Road, was just a quarter of a mile from the Guards barracks and proved to be a popular place with the young soldiers, as on Wednesday nights the pub had a disco in a room attached to the main bar. Two members of the ASU paid a visit to the Caterham Arms on the evening of the 27th and concealed a five-pound timed gelignite bomb in a small bag under a bench seat in the disco room. It was not the first visit of the ASU to a pub in Surrey: they were, in effect, re-creating the first attack of their British campaign on the pubs in Guilford. Finishing their drinks in a leisurely manner, the two men left the pub and headed back to London, leaving the bomb to tick towards detonation. Trade in the pub that evening was brisk, and 36-year-old barmaid Kitty Stone was pulling pints behind the bar of the disco as fast as she could to keep the thirsty revelers satisfied. Mrs. Jean King, 46, was in the bar drinking with friends when the bomb exploded at 9:20pm without warning. "There was just a split second of noise," said Jean King, "then I found myself lying on my back." The blast was devastating, blowing limbs off of three people in the confined space of the disco and flung people through the room, blowing the roof off the pub in the process. Kitty Stone, behind the bar, recalled that "glass was flying all around me," and yet the biggest wound she received was a gash to her right leg. Thirty-three people were wounded in the attack, many maimed for life losing limbs and eyes in the explosion. Twenty-year-old Guardsman Paul Thomas had both legs and one arm amputated as a result of his injuries in the blast, with two other guardsmen each losing a leg.

In a move all too gruesomely akin to Guilford and Woolwich, the ASU had attacked another pub in Surrey in almost grisly signal to the Surrey police that the people going to trial and charged with the Guilford bombings were not the people responsible. There was also speculation in the media that the latest pub bombing was a protest at the sentencing of the six men found guilty of the Birmingham bombs. However the bombing of the Caterham Arms was to be interpreted, to the officers of the Metropolitan police Bomb Squad the meaning was crystal clear: the London ASU were back and they meant business.

ald continue their efforts against London in a rapid suc-
cks, but with a new, deadly twist. They had, on occasion,
ed warnings for time bombs placed in store or shop door-
result, they had seen several of their devices defused by the
alled bomb disposal officers who worked with Bomb Squad.
ell, in consultation with GHQ, intended to up the stakes with
disposal teams. With the addition of ball-bearings, steel nuts and coach
bolts, the ASU's bombs had become increasingly lethal in their nature,
but remained relatively simple from a timing circuit perspective, making the work of the disposal officers, while highly risky, reasonably
straightforward. That would all change. O'Connell employed a technique that gave a bomb two arming circuits, one false circuit, on the ex-
terior of the bomb, and one live circuit concealed inside the bomb itself
in a section hollowed out in the explosives, making it extremely difficult for any bomb disposal personnel working on the device to find,
without moving the bomb to get a better look. That was the trap, as
O'Connell would fit a microswitch on the underside of the bomb and
while the spring-loaded plunger of the switch was pushed in by the
weight of the bomb, the device would explode only by the activation of
the timing circuit. If the bomb was lifted, even slightly, the pressure
would be removed from the microswitch plunger, closing the circuit
and causing the bomb to explode. All bombs are designed to kill, but
booby-trapped bombs are designed to kill the people attempting to disarm the device, in a battle of wits between the bomb-builders and the
bomb disposal officers.

The ASU planted their first bomb with a microswitch anti-handling
device in an office of the Prudential Assurance Company on Oxford
Street on August 28th, 1975, over the Peter Brown's men's clothing
store near the junction of Tottenham Court Road. One of the ASU telephoned a national newspaper with a warning about the bomb and added,
"they're in London now." There was very little time between the warning and the bomb going off. Police managed to clear the immediate area,
but the evening crowds in the city appeared unusually curious about
the imminent explosion. The manager of a nearby club stated that,
"sightseers were lined up 10 deep across Oxford Street." The blast
showered the crowd with broken glass and debris, but remarkably only
seven people, including three police officers, were slightly injured in
the explosion. Detective Chief Superintendent Jim Nevill, in charge of
the scene, ordered bomb sniffing dogs in to search the area as there were
concerns about another "come on" device as the police had found in the
Tite Street bombing of the previous year.

The following night, August 29th, O'Connell and Butler parked their stolen Ford Cortina approximately 100 yards from the K shoe shop in Kensington Church Street. The two men walked the remainder of the distance to the shop, and with Butler acting as armed cover man and look out, O'Connell placed the booby-trapped bomb in the shop doorway, ensuring the microswitch was depressed before arming the device. With the bomb in place and armed, the two men made their way back to the stolen car and drove off to find a public phone box. A national newspaper received a call from a man with a "pronounced Irish accent" who said, "listen carefully. A bomb has been placed in the K shoe shop in Church Street, Kensington," and then hung up the phone.

Two officers from Kensington police station were the first on the scene after receiving the warning. They described the device as looking like "sticks of explosives attached to a wristwatch." Fortunately, they did not touch the bomb. The local police cordoned off the area and evacuated a nearby pub as a precaution while they waited for the Bomb Squad disposal team to arrive. 40-year-old Captain Roger Goad, a former Army officer, was the senior bomb disposal expert on the scene. Captain Goad, a married man with two children, had been decorated for gallantry while serving in the Army, and was no stranger to dangerous and stressful situations. The local police officers took cover as Captain Goad moved in to examine the device in preparation for the delicate task of disarming the bomb. Mr. Monty Butler, observing the scene from his nearby apartment, watched as Captain Goad crossed the road and cautiously entered the shop doorway. Mr. Butler describes how Captain Goad appeared to bend down, as if to pick up something, and then, "suddenly there was a flash and the man flew backwards through the air. My eardrums rang and I was thrown to one side." Monty Butler ran to check on Captain Goad, but the bomb disposal officer had died instantly in the blast. A police officer gently covered Captain Goad's body with a red blanket, as his lifeless form lay on the ground surrounded by broken plate glass from the shattered shop windows blown out by the explosion.

We cannot be sure if device went off through the anti-handling device or if the timer triggered the blast. Either by coincidence or design the time of the explosion was almost identical to the Oxford street device of the previous day, with the bomb in the K shoe shop exploding at 10:13pm. It is highly unlikely that an officer of Captain Goad's experienced would have triggered the anti-handling device, but it could be possible he was not expecting a device of that degree of sophistication could be built by the IRA. Commander Roy Habershon stated that, "all of our disposal men are highly experienced officers who have great knowledge of dangerous explosive devices. He was very experienced in dealing with such matters." Assistant Commissioner John Wilson was a little blunter in his description of the event, stating "he did not stand a chance."

The surrounding area had to be secured, to ensure no other devices posed a threat to the police and civilians in the vicinity, before Roger Goad's body could be removed from the scene. The ASU had, as intended, killed a member of the Bomb Squad disposal team. They were under orders from GHQ to shift tactics, and their objective was to kill people, and Captain Goad would be the first victim of their cold blooded phase two campaign. Jim Nevill, speaking with Eddie Butler after the IRA man's arrest, asked him about the booby-trapped bombs. Butler described to Nevill that was the intention of the ASU to kill an explosives expert. Nevill said "well, you succeeded didn't you." Butler, allegedly replied, "that's correct; he didn't take his precautions did he." The ASU would complete a hat trick of shop doorway bombs with one more the following day on Saturday, August 30th. The police received the warning, through the Press Association, that there was a bomb in a doorway of the National Westminster Bank in High Holburn, which exploded at approximately 10:15pm, consistent time-wise with the two previous explosions. There were no reported injuries from the blast. The ASU would move on from shop doorway targets, and it would be up to the likes of Jim Nevill and Peter Imbert to work out where they were going to strike next. They had nothing concrete to go on in terms of identifying the members of the ASU or their base, or bases, of operation in and around the London area. However, they did know they wanted to question a possible IRA courier, 21-year-old Margaret McKearnly from County Tyrone. She had been allegedly linked to several possible ASU's across the country and was described by Roy Habershon of the bomb squad has "probably the most dangerous and active female terrorist operative over here." She had been linked to an episode in Manchester of the end of June 1975, where the police had made a significant dent in the IRA's intended activities in the north of England. Brendan Dowd, sent back to England to run a group of less than well-trained IRA volunteers, quickly found himself in trouble. Information gleaned through police informant's led Manchester police to where Dowd was staying, where after a brief exchange of gunfire he was taken into custody, still wearing the watch he had stolen from the briefly abducted PC Lloyd the previous year. The rest of his new ASU were also rolled up in the police net, but McKearnly had escaped. Her arrest was a priority for the Bomb

Squad, as she could be the key link they were looking for regarding the London ASU and a means of cracking the case. The Met still had no real lead on the ASU, hence the urge to find the young Irish woman, but they were determined to be proactive and go looking for the Irishmen, rather than waiting passively for them to make a mistake.

In a combined Met operation between the Bomb Squad, Special Branch and regional crimes squads from around London, a series of dawn raids were carried out on dozens of homes in the capital on the morning of August 31st, 1975. Armed officers scooped up potential suspects in the London bombings, all with Irish connections of some type or another. The four ASU men, sleeping soundly in Crouch Hill and Milton Grove, were not disturbed that morning. The police raids did not produce any more clues to the whereabouts of the IRA cell, leaving the Met still no closer to making a collar in the terror campaign case.

In Northern Ireland, the widely discredited cease-fire was causing significant anger in Unionist politicians and supporters, who accused the Wilson government of taking a soft line against terrorism. What they really meant was that the government was not doing all they, the Unionist, wanted them to do in order to handle the IRA. Their own paramilitary units were, of course, not included in the equation when it came to discussing terrorist organizations. The Loyalists had been rocked back on their heels by an increase in attacks on their paramilitary units by the IRA. The three previous years had seen the bulk of the sectarian violence being directed at the Roman Catholic population and paramilitary groups. The tables had been turned and the Protestants, furious at the Wilson government, were demanding to know what the Northern Ireland Secretary, Merlyn Rees, was going to do about the situation. The Unionists demanded the introduction of a curfew in the Province, but Rees refused to agree to the demand, proposing instead an increase in the level of troops to control the spiraling escalation of sectarian violence.

O'Connell and the ASU were planning another foray on London and made a decision to have the bomb attack, on a prominent Mayfair hotel, coincide with another event taking place the same day. Friday, September 5th was the day of Captain Roger Goad's funeral and the Methodist Church at Basingstoke, in Hampshire, was full to capacity with 250 mourners, relatives, former Army colleagues and fellow police officers, including many of the senior leadership of the Bomb Squad. There was no room for the crowd of 500 outside who lined the approaches to the church.

O'Connell finished making up a ten-pound gelignite bomb and placed it into a nondescript bag, and handed over the device to the two man delivery team, who set off on the drive to the Hilton hotel in London, which at the time was filled to capacity with late-season tourists. The drive was uneventful and the bomb carried into the busy hotel lobby without incident, where it was secretly left under a marble table. At 11:57am, Mr. Albert Pick, a switchboard operator at Associated Newspapers, took a call from a man with a soft Irish accent, who informed Mr. Pick that there was a bomb in the Hilton hotel lobby and that it would explode in twenty minutes. Albert Pick hurriedly placed an emergency call to Scotland Yard about the bomb warning. It would be the eighth warning of a bomb in the Hilton made that week, and the Met were averaging 20 bomb-alert phone calls a day. The call was past to Vine Street police station, who ordered a patrol car to head to the Hilton to assess the situation. The officers at Vine Street also called the Hilton to warning of a possible bomb in the lobby while the patrol car was on route to the hotel.

At the Basingstoke Methodist Church, Captain Goad's widow and her two children, Sharon and Nicola age ten and five, listened to the passionate tribute paid to Roger Goad by the Police Commissioner Sir Robert Mark as he addressed the packed church. "His cruel and wicked murderers are to be pitied for the mindless brutes they are," said Sir Robert, "devoid of reason, devoid of humanity and deserving only of the contempt of their fellow men." Sir Robert continued, "they offer a stark contrast against which the nobility and unselfishness of the gallant man will be judged."

The Hilton hotel security staff carried out a sweep of the lobby, but somehow failed to find the bomb placed there by the ASU. The first police officers arrived at 12:03pm to be told by the Hilton staff they could not find a bomb. The police were understandably reluctant to order an evacuation of the entire hotel, as if a bomb had been placed in the lobby, any evacuating guests could be caught in the blast. A second patrol car arrived at 12:15pm. None of the guests had been asked to evacuate and, at that time, there were about a hundred people milling around the lobby. All the shops and kiosks in the hotel were still staffed, with 33-year-old Molly Bush behind the counter of a jewelry shop, one of many employees in the building, along with her colleague Mr. Edgar Dickinson. At the British Airways desk in the lobby the manager, Anthony Peters, was dealing with customer inquiries. "There was an almighty explosion," said Peters, "the whole place went black. When I looked up, the impression was of pieces of carpet burning." The time was 12:18pm and the ten-pound bomb had detonated under the marble topped table. Molly Bush recalled how the jewelry shop had been destroyed, with the explosion sending very expensive jewelry scattered everywhere. "We were lucky to be standing at the back of the shop, away from the window," she stated. Twenty-two-year-old Philip Power had been passing the Hilton as the bomb went off and immediately rushed into the destroyed lobby to see how he could help with any of the wounded. Mark Colakowski, an assistant in the men's shop in the hotel, tried to comfort an Arab guest who had lost a leg in the blast. Colakowski said "I bent down and tried to do something for him. I tried to stop him from seeing his leg." Mr. Mohammed Ikhlaf, a hall porter, said, "people were running off screaming, lying on the floor. There was glass and dust everywhere." Ikhlaf helped several wounded guests outside, noting that many of the injured were Arab tourists. Two guests, a man and a female Scandinavian journalist, were killed in the blast with 60 injured, many with serious leg and abdomen wounds.

After the funeral service at Basingstoke Methodist Church, the funeral cortege set off to Aldershot for a cremation ceremony, led by a police patrol car. Police officers and men of the Royal Army ordnance Corps, Captain Goad's former unit, lined the approach to the crematorium chapel, saluting Goad's coffin, draped in a dark blue Metropolitan police flag, as it passed by onto his final rest. Back in London, the ASU had killed twice more, with two more families going through the pain and grief of losing loved ones in an instant to the terrorist's bombs. Many more families would have to help the maimed and wounded to pick up the pieces of their shattered lives as they recovered from their wounds and crippling injuries.

Detective Superintendent Peter Imbert, arriving at the Hilton, quickly took control of the situation and established a crime scene, as he would later recall. "I nearly blotted my copy book on that occasion. We had a procedure for collecting evidence at crime scenes like the Hilton. We would section off the area where the bomb had gone off so that we could collect any debris from the explosives, so it would give the scientists an opportunity to determine what sort of explosive had been used, what sort of package it was in and what the detonation mechanism had been. While my lads, the Exhibits Officers, were clearing all this up, suddenly two people appeared in the doorway on the other side of the hall. I called out to them to get back, but they carried on coming. So I said 'Get back! We are clearing up a crime scene!' I was very firm when I called out, only to then realize it was the Home Secretary and the Assistant Commissioner! The Home Secretary was very gracious about it and I heard him say to John Wilson, the Assistant Commissioner, 'you can see who's in charge here!' It didn't matter who it was, we didn't want them treading all over the crime scene and contaminating it. As you can imagine, once we'd caught the gang in a year's time some defense council would have argued that the scene was contaminated and they'd have made a big thing about people walking over it and corrupting the evidence. You have to think well ahead in such circumstances, a year or two ahead for when you have them in court."

Detective Inspector Ron Chapman became assigned to the Bomb Squad two days after the Hilton hotel bombing to run a team of detectives who were, at the time he joined the group, investigating the Hilton incident. Detective Chief Superintendent Jim Nevill informed Chapman that he had considered sending him up to the Hilton to take part in the investigation, but had decided that he would allow Chapman time to familiarize himself with the structure and workings of the Bomb Squad before throwing him into the deep end of an active terrorist investigation. It was a very different setup than he had been used to on Divisional CID work.

Ron Chapman quickly determined the mood in the Bomb Squad, "everybody always thought they [ASU] would eventually get caught," said Chapman, "but there had been such a trail of incidents, with such a frequency that I was surprised how far behind they were in actually finalizing detailed reports about each of the bombing incidents. The basic investigations had been done, but there were things from the early phase of the ASU's campaign that still needed to be topped and tailed. Resources were stretched thin and the number of incidents kept growing." That said, all was not doom and gloom in the Bomb Squad, as Chapman later described, "there was a mood of optimism that, ultimately, we'd catch them. Every dog has his day, as even hardened criminals will get away with a certain amount of crimes before eventually they got caught. The same was true for the bombers, you couldn't guarantee how it would happen–maybe they would blow themselves up by accident, or crash a car in a getaway. Something will always happen, some piece of evidence would come to light, or someone would see something that would result in their capture."

The situation in Northern Ireland was spiraling out of control, with increased violence directed both at Catholic and Protestant targets, while at Westminster, Edward Heath, the former Prime Minister, had been ousted from his position as leader of the Conservative party by something of a coup d'état from the right of the party led by one of his cabinet ministers, Margaret Thatcher, who replaced Heath as party leader. As leader of the opposition party, Thatcher had a keen eye on the political ramifications of the Northern Ireland situation as, after all, if Wilson and his Labour government were to be perceived as failing in their efforts to contain the escalating violence, both in the Province and on the British mainland, then that would work in Thatcher's favor in her bid to become Britain's first elected woman Prime Minister. Wilson's Home Secretary, Roy Jenkins, who had the Metropolitan police commissioner reporting to him, had not demonstrated to the British public a tenacious ability to track down the Irish bombers attacking in the capital. The longer the bombers went undetected, the worse it would look for the governing Labour party. In order to get an inside view on the Northern Ireland situation, Thatcher requested a meeting with Wilson and his Secretary of State for Northern Ireland, Merlyn Rees, at number 10 Downing Street. Thatcher, accompanied by Airey Neave, the shadow Northern Ireland minister, met the two Labour politicians on the evening of September 8th. Wilson and Rees outlined their continued desire to find that a "solution" to the situation in Ulster, but felt they still had a problem with getting Ian Paisley and the Unionists to play ball and consider options other than a return to the old Stormont system of governing the Province. The growing concern for the Labour politicians was Paisley's then leadership of the UWC, which had brought any notion of a power-sharing arrangement to a chaotic end with the national strike of 1974, and they were threatening the same all over again which, with the current state of violence, so Wilson explained, could push the Province into total anarchy. Rees told Thatcher that they had to expect the Irish press to continue to demand a British pullout from Northern Ireland, but this "was nonsense," he stated. Wilson emphasized the point by telling Thatcher that they would "never give in to IRA wishes" as they did not represent the majority voice in Northern Ireland. The two Labour politicians assured Thatcher that no deal had been made, or promised, with the IRA, but Thatcher remained concerned that the violence in London was the direct result of an ultra-violent splinter group from the Provisional IRA with no accountability to the Army Council. Highlighting this concern, Wilson added that the sudden recent arrest of Daithi O'Connell by the Irish government had "removed the one person who was able to exert tight control at the top [of the Provisionals]." The splinter group theory was made all the more feasible given that Sinn Féin had "fervently denied responsibility" for the Hilton Hotel bombing, added Rees. Thatcher stated that politicians on both sides of the House had received numerous letters from their constituents asking why the British government did not pull out of Northern Ireland and added, somewhat condescendingly, that "people unfortunately did not realize that the result of a pullout would be much greater carnage here[in England]." The Conservative party, stated Thatcher, understood the need to protect innocent citizens in all parts of the United Kingdom, "even if this was not widely appreciated elsewhere." Wilson agreed and said that "any impression that the government were taking the line that the Irish could cut their own throats would immediately give the appearance that we [the government] had given in to the IRA." There would be no deals with the IRA, or any pullout from Northern Ireland.

Feeling betrayed by the British government and their continued stance on the refusing to withdraw the troops, despite by veiled hints to the contrary, the IRA stepped-up its campaign of violence in Northern Ireland. On September 22nd, the Provisionals exploded 17 bombs across the Province, including one on a hijacked train. In a statement made by the Republican Press Center, the IRA claimed that the multiple attacks were in direct response to increased security activities aimed at Republican strongholds across the North, including police and army raids in "attempted murder of innocent citizens." The statement continued, "those who think that the Belfast Brigade will allow this harassment to continue should be warned by past events—we consider it alright to take retaliatory action." What had been left of the truce lay in shattered remnants across the Province, with 12 people injured in the blasts. Merlyn Rees was, predictably, furious, stating that the IRA's action in the attack had made a "mockery and a travesty" of the cease-fire. The ASU, already given a dispensation from GHQ to start their mainland campaign, were busy planning the next part of their phase two operations, stepping up the no-warning attacks on the upper echelons of British society, on the assumption that if they attacked and killed people influential with the government, then maybe Wilson and Jenkins would pay attention to what these people had to say. They had two more attacks planned before starting the new tactic, as ordered by GHQ, and struck at one target in Maidstone in Kent on September 25, 1975. The quick actions of the landlord of the Hare and Hounds pub, after spotting a suspicious looking package under the table, prevented a repeat of previous pub bomb attacks. He quickly ordered everyone outside before the bomb exploded, preventing any casualties. The second attack was put on hold by the media conscious ASU, due to events that unfolded on September 28th, that would capture the attention of both the Met and the British media. Rather ironically, given what they would later face themselves, the ASU would let the drama of what would become known as the Spaghetti House siege play out before making another terror strike.

They did not want to share domestic headlines, and they had plans to make, so they would wait.

The Metropolitan police had also been busy making plans. Faced with a slew of hostage situations across the globe in the early 1970's, the Met needed a strategy to deal with a potential terrorist backed hostage standoff, as it had not faced such a situation in modern times. The Met had dealt with an armed siege standoff before, back in January 1911, when a group of Russian and Lithuanian anarchists were disturbed while tunneling through a wall to a neighboring jewelers shop. The gang shot dead PC Choat and Sergeants Bryant and Tucker and fled to their lodgings in Stepney, London. Tipped off to their whereabouts, the Met attempted to get the men out, but they were seriously outgunned. The Scots Guards were brought into the fray, but in the ensuing firefight the building caught fire and the then Home Secretary, Winston Churchill, ordered the fire department to let the building burn, killing the gang in the process. Later dubbed the Battle of Stepney, the techniques employed were evidently not applicable to modern times.

The Met examined siege episodes triggered by the various Middle East and European terrorist groups, and how the law enforcement teams involved handled the situations. The practice of containing the siege situation, and controlling the flow of information in both directions, would emerge as a primary strategy for the Met, reasoning that information was the key element to enable the strategic and tactical control of any siege. C7, the Mets technical support branch, experimented with audio and video surveillance techniques over a period of two years, to allow the police to listen and observe, in secret, what the hostage takers and hostages were doing in a confined space. In such a situation, they would be able to directly observe the reactions of any hostage takers to requests made by the negotiation team, which would help fine-tune the approach being used by the police. It all sounded great in theory, and in training, but how would it work in the real world?

The Spaghetti House Italian restaurants were, and remain, a popular chain of Italian eateries spread across central London. In 1975, it was their practice to gather the day's takings from the restaurants across the city at the Knightsbridge branch and then deposit the cash in the night storage safe of a nearby bank. The Knightsbridge branch was situated in the heart of the capital's foreign embassy district, an area well patrolled by regular Metropolitan police units, and units of the Met's armed Diplomatic Protection Squad. The daily collection of cash from the restaurants would make a tempting target for a holdup, if any villains knew about the practice, which they did thanks to a tip off from a Spaghetti

House employee. Using this information Franklin Davis, originally from Nigeria and recently released from a 10 year prison sentence for armed robbery, aided somewhat reluctantly by two young West Indians, Wesley Dick and Anthony Monroe, attempted to hold up the Knightsbridge branch and relieve them of the collective takings amounting to £13,000. Armed with a sawn-off 12 gauge shotgun and two .22 caliber handguns, the three would-be bandits struck at 1:45am on September 28th, 1975. Brandishing their firearms, the gang forced nine Italian employees down a flight of stairs to the basement, where they were to be confined while the gang made off with the cash. However, the robbers had not figured on the courage of Signor Giovanni Mia, one of the restaurant chain managers, who made a successful dash for freedom down a set of stairs in the rear of the building the robbers had not noticed. Signor Mai ran to the nearby Berkley Hotel to raise the alarm. Being in the heavily patrolled embassy district, it took approximately one minute for four police patrol cars to converge on the restaurant. Davis, brandishing a pistol, called to the officers and told them he had hostages and that he would be making a set of demands.

We have to question the thinking behind the attempted holdup, because the location of the restaurant was, at the time, inside the most security sensitive area in London due to the high concentration of United Kingdom diplomatic offices and homes of the world's governments, all located within a half mile radius of the restaurant. Not a particularly good place for an armed holdup!

With the bungled robbery behind them, Davis and his two accomplices had a hostage situation on their hands, with the three of them holding eight Italian restaurant workers in the basement storage room 13 feet by 15 feet with no windows and only one door. Davis attempted to turn the failed robbery into a political situation. He would tell police officers, on the other side of the basement door, that the gang represented the "Black Liberation Front" but the Met rightly scoffed at the preposterous change in rational. Publicly, they claimed to take the statement seriously, but they were under no illusions they were dealing with a simple robbery that had not gone sour. The robber's demands were for a flight out of the country, but they were unsure of precisely where they wanted to go. Commander Ernest Bond told the press that no deals would be made with the gunman who had "made the usual demands you would expect from a kidnap situation."

The Met had an opportunity to test out their siege strategy. Dr. Peter Scott, a psychiatrist from London's Bethlehem Maudsley Hospital, was brought in to assess the state of mind of three gunmen confined to the basement with the hostages. C7 swung into action and deployed state-of-the-art fiber-optic cameras and audio listening devices through the walls in the basement room, undetected by anyone inside, which provided a clear view and sound of activities in the basement. The press had been informed that the police could hear conversations in the room via a heating vent near the exit, an interesting piece of misinformation deliberately fed to the press to avoid public speculation on the sophisticated surveillance technology they were using. The strategy adopted by the Met was one of containing the hostage takers and making it very clear to them that they were going nowhere and that they were prepared to wait it out, no matter how long it took. A careful employment of the media was a key part of the police strategy; however, the media would be of little use if the hostage takers could not receive any of the coverage, so the Met sent the men a transistor radio on which they could hear the news broadcasts. Sir Roberts Mark, the Metropolitan Police Commissioner, wanted the men to know they had two destinations available to them, "a cell, or by implication a mortuary, if they preferred that."

The Italian consul general in London, Dr. Mario Manca, came to the scene to reissue of the Italian speaking hostages that everything that could be done to secure their release was being done. Dr. Manca, at one point in the six-day siege, offered to take the place of one of the hostages who was feeling ill, but wisely the police declined his courageous offer, as trading one restaurant worker for a senior Italian diplomat would create only more problems for the Metropolitan police, and a potential international incident for the government.

Conditions inside the basement room were hot and rather unsanitary. The police initially sent in a metal bucket for sanitation purposes, but followed up with a chemical toilet. The men had food as the room was a storage area for the restaurant, but the police kept them supplied with water, coffee and cigarettes. The siege finally collapsed through combination of good detective work, video surveillance, and good old-fashioned psychological manipulation. The criminal investigation division (CID) detectives had arrested the Spaghetti House employee suspected of being the inside source of information for Davis. The suspect, in turn, identified a confederate of Davis who had supplied the firearms to the gang. A Daily Mail reporter was present when the firearms supply suspect was taken into custody, and the Met were concerned that it would not take much for the reporter to make a connection back to the restaurant worker and Davis. The Met had managed to contain the radio news about the arrest of the Spaghetti House employee, to avoid having that fact present on the radio to the gunmen. With little else of note in the news, The Daily Mail had a significant scoop on its hands, linking the gun supplier to the Italian employee back to the gunmen. Sir Robert Mark had to go to the editor of the Daily Mail and explain exactly why he didn't want the story to appear, as he would have had an almost impossible task of keeping the story off the BBC airwaves and straight into the basement room via the radio. The news, if heard by the gunman, could trigger a negative reaction towards the hostages, so Sir Robert argued. The Daily Mail editor told Sir Robert, "right, that story's dead!" As part of their strategy to break the will of the three men, the Met supplied a photograph of Davis to the Daily Express newspaper, who happily plastered it over the front page of the subsequent edition. The next day Ernest Bond took a copy of the Daily Express and wrote, in thick black marker, that the arrested confederate had received £500 for supplying the picture of Davis to the press. Ernest Bond slid the newspaper under the door of the basement, while the surveillance team observed the reaction of the gunmen in the room. On the video feed the police could see that Davis, the intended recipient of the message, was sound asleep. Munroe and Dick, puzzled at the message, tore up a newspaper and threw it into a trash bin. The police waited until Davis woke up, and then repeated the exercise. After six days of enduring a hot, smelly, exasperating standoff, the sight and thought of a supposedly trusted accomplice making money out of their predicament, finally proved too much for Davis. The gang capitulated, with Davis making a halfhearted attempt at shooting himself with one of the .22 caliber handguns.

The Met was satisfied with the siege result, based on the tactics they had employed at the Spaghetti House. The Met regarded the six-day standoff as an excellent exercise for any future episode involving diplomatic hostages. One element they needed to improve on was the containment of the siege environment. In most hostage standoff situations, there are two containment areas that law-enforcement groups must secure and maintain. The first is the inner containment zone, which is the immediate area the hostages and hostage takers are confined in. The police have to control every aspect of the inner zone, including the flow of information, supplies and people. The outer containment zone is the area outside the inner zone and may include adjacent buildings, streets and vehicles in the immediate vicinity of the hostage situation. This zone is required to keep the media, and other non-vital services, away from the site to avoid accidentally feeding vital situational intelligence to the hostage takers. The Met failed to effectively control the outer zone during the Spaghetti House siege. Sir Robert Mark felt the police were "besieged" by the media as they "infiltrated the surrounding flats and other premises and every kind of listening and watching device was employed to monitor the drama . . ." The Met would have to do a better job in any future such situation to avoid any uncontrolled flow of media reporting becoming a strategic liability to the negotiation teams and negatively impacting any future hostage situations.

The next establishment target in London for the ASU was the Ritz at 150 Piccadilly, one of the capital's top hotels. From a timing perspective, the previous attack on the Hilton hotel had been a departure from the ASU normal method of operation. Most of their attacks were conducted at night, but they had deviated from that in a gesture of defiance toward the bomb squad as they buried Captain Roger Goad. The Ritz attack would be more in keeping with their demonstrated tactics and was scheduled to take place on the evening of September 9th, 1975. Eddie Butler had helped to build a five-pound gelignite bomb, packed with coach boats as shrapnel placed round the surface of the explosive, timed as per the other placed devices with a modified Westclox timer. Butler and his cover man traveled to the Ritz and Butler entered the lobby, looking for a place to hide the device. The time was approximately 8:30pm. Butler had a problem, as the hotel lobby was far too busy to be able to conceal the device without being noticed or the bomb being seen by a guest or hotel worker. Butler had already "made up" the bomb and set a time delay, so he left the building and defused the device, which would then require being made up again before being placed in the hotel. Butler's plan was to wait a while and try again.

In order to "make up" the device again, Butler would need to find a quiet spot where could work undisturbed. He walked to the nearby Green Park underground station and headed for the men's toilet. Butler found an empty stall, walked in and locked the door, sitting on the toilet as he worked on making up the Ritz bomb one more time. However, Butler must have made some unusual noises as he completed the bomb and set the timer, as a man in the next stall became suspicious, and so he stood on the toilet seat in his stall and peered over into where Butler was placing the bomb into a bag. Fearing the man had seen more than he should, Butler left the toilets at Green Park and headed quickly for the exit. Walking briskly out of the station, Butler passed a nearby bus shelter where he stooped and placed the armed bomb and walked off. Several people were subsequently waiting for a bus when the bomb exploded at 9:00pm, killing one young man in his 20's, and injuring several others including two children, aged three and seven, and 52-year-old Stan Brightwell, a tourist from Chicago. "The bomb went off as I was walking back to my hotel," related Mr. Brightwell, who was treated at St. Georges Hospital for a gash sustained to one of his legs.

The blast seriously concerned the Bomb Squad, being so close to the Green Park underground station. What if the ASU were planning on attacking the underground? A blast of the type at the bus stop, with coach bolts, would be absolutely lethal in the confines of underground platform or, heaven forbid, inside a rush-hour train. They could not know how close they were to the facts. Eddie Butler would later tell Jim Nevill how the ASU had worked out a plan to bomb underground trains as part of their next phase of attacks. The plan involved placing a bomb, with a short time delay fuse, in an empty carriage of an underground train just before it left a station platform. The delay would be short enough so the bomb would explode when the train was between stations, blocking the tunnel in the process. When asked what would happen if someone got into the carriage before the doors closed, Butler just shrugged and told Nevill it would be their "hard luck." But underground trains were not the immediate concern of the ASU, despite the Met being rightfully worried at the prospect of an attack. They had orders from GHQ to target the upper elements of British society and the places they gathered to meet, eat and socialize. Their orders also included the assassination of politicians and prominent business people. They would be keeping the Bomb Squad busy.

The sheer volume of work the ASU had given the Bomb Squad, in terms of crime scene investigations and follow-up reports, was immense and in turn created a backlog of work for the officers involved, scrambling to keep up with the frequency of the ASU's activities. Despite knocking on a lot of doors after getting reports from nervous neighbors saying that the people upstairs, next door, or across the street had been heard playing Irish rebel songs, they still had no real sense of who they were chasing. They were, however, building up a data base of forensic evidence in terms of fingerprints collected from crime scenes that continued to expand, as Detective Inspector Ron Chapman recalled. "Fragments of fingerprints would be recovered, from time to time, from the unexploded devices that were made safe or from safe houses," said Chapman, "such as the one discovered in Fairholme Road after the shooting of PC Stephen Tibble. Unfortunately, you never get four fingers and thumb; you'd get a tip of a finger or maybe a finger and thumb. Every time we came across a new print, it was given a letter of the alphabet code to identify the suspect, such as suspect Q or Z." The growing collection of fingerprints, so it was hoped, would lead the Bomb Squad to find the culprits before they killed anyone else.

The ASU started a new tactic in the campaign against London, switching targets to exclusive restaurants and once again attacking without warning. They were under orders to kill prominent people and hit at the upper elements of the establishment. They had selected several locations to carry out the attacks; the first of this type would be at Lockets restaurant on Marsham Street, just half a mile from the Houses of Parliament. An upscale dining establishment, Lockets was popular with MP's and members of the gentry, making it an ideal target for O'Connell and his ASU. O'Connell, with help from Eddie Butler, constructed a thirty-pound gelignite bomb, making it one of the largest placed timed devices they had built during phase one or phase two. They also packed the bomb with an outer layer of large coach bolts, creating a highly lethal explosive device designed to kill. The bomb was placed in a zip up canvas holdall, required to carry the weight of the completed device, and the holdall was passed to the two-man ASU delivery team for transportation to Marsham Street. The ASU team placed the bomb outside the restaurant, next to a car parked close to the building, and then left the scene.

At Lockets, dinner preparation was in full swing with several members of Parliament anticipating a good meal. Hotel Porter Fred Warren was on his way home from work, walking along Marsham Street as he approached the restaurant. As he got closer, Warren noticed a suspicious looking bag close to a car parked outside the restaurant. He decided to take action, rather than ignore the bag, probably due to the heavy PR campaign from the Met, urging the public to be vigilant about packages or bags left unattended. Fred Warren went into Lockets to seek out the manager, Roberto Caparari, to inform him of the suspect looking bag. Caparai called the police and within minutes 26-year-old police Sergeant Paul Martin arrived on the scene. PS Martin approached the holdall, and carefully unzipped the bag and, to his horror, noticed sticks of gelignite and wires inside the bag. It was a bomb, a large bomb and obviously timed, but with no warning PS Martin could not be sure of how long he had to get everyone out of the restaurant to safety. Going back into Lockets, PS Martin confirmed with the restaurant manager that the bag did appear to contain a bomb and recommended evacuating the building immediately. Paul Martin called in the confirmation of the bomb to the Bomb Squad, who mobilized to get the disposal team in place and cordon off the area. Meanwhile, Roberto Caparai ordered a prompt but orderly evacuation of the dining room. The forty guests complied but many complained bitterly, so Caparai reported, demanding to know what the restaurant was going to do about their meals, as many had not had their dinners. In an inspired move, Caparai ushered the hungry diners to a pub a safe distance down the road to buy them all drinks, and assured them that once the situation was deemed safe, they would all be fed. "I told them the cook would make them all another meal," he said. However, some diners failed to put the inconvenience into its proper perspective. Tory MP Sir Timothy Kitson, emerging from the restaurant as the diners were evacuated noticed, much to his alarm, that the bomb had been placed next to his car! When later asked about the size of the device, one Bomb Squad detective stated that there would have been "appalling" results if the bomb had gone off, but all of this was apparently lost on Sir Timothy who complained bitterly that, his evening ruined, "all I had to eat was a bread roll and butter!"

The bomb disposal team made the device safe, apparently with minutes to spare before the bomb was set to go off. The thirty-pound device would give the Bomb Squad more fingerprint fragments to add to their alphabet collection. They also noted that the device had not been booby-trapped, unlike some earlier setups. The ASU, in order to keep the Bomb Squad guessing, would change targets but with tragic unintended consequences.

On October 22, 1975, Paul Hill, Gerry Conlon, Patrick Armstrong and Carol Richardson were found guilty of carrying out the Guilford and Woolwich pub bombings. They were convicted of murder and sentenced to life in prison. The judge, Justice Sir John Donaldson, stated that he regretted the four had not been charged with treason, which still carried the death penalty.

On the same day, 32-year-old Tessia Oandason, housekeeper to Tory MP Sir Hugh Fraser, answered the telephone at the Fraser's residence. The caller calmly enquired as to what time Mr. Fraser left for his office in the morning. Thinking nothing of the request, Miss Oandason replied that her employer typically left at around 8:00am. O'Connell went to work, constructing a fourteen-pound gelignite bomb with a button switch booby-trap anti-handling device. The bomb was intended to go off in one of two ways: triggered by the timer or the microswitch if the device was tampered with. The intended target, Sir Hugh Fraser, was a staunch proponent of the death penalty for crimes involving terrorism, and was an outspoken member of the Tory party on the topic of Northern Ireland. He had also been a wartime member of the Special Air Service Regiment. As such, he was regarded as a legitimate target by GHQ, and so the ASU planned to assassinate him by placing a bomb under his car.

The ASU delivery team headed out to Fraser's regency house in the elegant Camden Hills Square area in Kensington and arrived at around 6:00am on October 23rd. Eddie Butler covered while one of his fellow ASU members placed the device in position under Fraser's red Jaguar XJ6 car, parked outside his house. At 7:30am Tessia Oandason opened the front door of the house to bring in the daily newspaper; when she noticed something odd placed under one of the front wheels of the Jaguar parked outside on the fairly steep slope of Camden Hill Square.

One of Hugh Fraser's neighbors in the exclusive district was Professor Gordon Hamilton-Farley. At 45-years-old, Professor Farley was regarded as one of the world's foremost experts in the treatment of cancer. He had returned from a research trip to Australia on the previous evening and was, according to Dr. Michael Whitehouse, one of his deputies at St. Bartholomew's Hospital, full of fresh ideas for his work in the treatment of adult leukemia. Reunited with his two poodle dogs Emmylou and Bimmy, who had been cared for in his absence by his sister, Professor Farley decided to go for an early morning walk. His wife, Daphne, was due back from a trip to China and he was looking forward to being reunited with her and their four children. Professor Farley had brought back a lot of work from Australia and planed to tackle it over a long weekend before going back to the hospital on Monday. After a long journey the previous day, the walk would be a welcome change.

Hugh Fraser had a houseguest that Thursday morning as 17-year-old Caroline Kennedy, daughter of the late John F. Kennedy, was staying at his home on a trip to London. At approximately 7:50am, Fraser was about to go to his car with the young Kennedy as he had promised to give her a lift into town on his way into his office at the House of Commons. However, he stopped, turned around and returned inside with the young American following him. It was Fraser's habit to converse on the phone with his friend and fellow MP Jonathan Aitkin and he had realized he had not called Aitkin as previously planned. On this occasion, so his housekeeper recalled, Fraser and Aitkin talked for about ten minutes on the subject of Saudi Arabia. Phone call completed, Fraser prepared to once again leave his house accompanied by Caroline Kennedy.

Outside, 13-year-old Derek Britnell and his friend were on their way to Holland Park comprehensive school. They noticed Professor Farley, walking his two dogs, as he came parallel to Hugh Fraser's Jaguar. They watched as he stopped, and stooped down to examine something under the front of the car. The fourteen pounds of gelignite detonated, killing Professor Farley instantly, with the blast flinging his lifeless body into the Fraser's front garden, blowing the Jaguar ten feet into the air. The two schoolboys witnessed the horror, and Derek Britnell stated that "the car flipped over in the air and came down with a bang." The two boys were blown off their feet. "We heard windows splattered all around," said Britnell, "there were bits of everything all over the place, a lot of blood too. It was horrible."

Police officers were quickly on the scene, as two officers on traffic duty were in a patrol car at the end of the street when the bomb went off. A call was made to the Bomb Squad incident room and the duty officer, Inspector Ron Chapman, was called to the scene. "I was duty officer and had been on reserve since midnight," recalled Chapman, "I was actually making my way in to The Yard when I got a call directing me to attend the scene, because if you are the duty officer you take over and deal with the investigation. This was effectively the first incident I had attended since being posted to the Bomb Squad in September. I found my way there, and when I arrived I found there were a lot of senior officers already on the scene, in fact the place was swarming with police, because it was a main thoroughfare into London and a lot of senior officers used it as part of their route on their way to The Yard."

Detective Inspector Chapman arrived on the scene at around 9:30am and described what he was faced with. "The thing that struck me the most was that being October, there were still a lot of leaves on the trees, but the explosion had not only lifted a Mark 10 Jaguar into the air, which had landed across the street on its roof, but had blown all the leaves off the trees in the Square, leaving a carpet of them on the ground."

Ron Chapman's job was to secure the crime scene, begin the search of evidence and collect statements from the people on the scene who had witnessed the explosion. One other eyewitness was the Fraser family nanny, who was on her way to the house to collect mail for his estranged wife as Ron Chapman later recalled, "It would seem that Professor Farley noticed something underneath the front wheel of Fraser's Jaguar and bent down to inspect it. Hugh Fraser's nanny was driving down the road at the time and saw the Professor bend down, and she was a couple of car lengths away when the bomb blew up. She let go of the steering wheel and her car crashed into a tree. It must have been a great shock to have that happen right in front of her."

There were many people for Chapman and his incident team to interview, and a lot of debris that would require collection for examination by the forensic team, as Ron Chapman described, "we had a team of officers that would come out and sweep areas and everything would go into bins and be taken away to look for the smallest parts of the device.

So, at the scene it was a question of dealing with the witnesses and gathering evidence, once the site was secure."

Chapman also described the task of dealing with the body of Professor Farley that had been blown into the front garden of Hugh Fraser's house. "The deceased was certified dead by a divisional surgeon,"said Chapman, "and Detective Superintendent Peter Imbert and I subsequently went to the postmortem which was held later that afternoon. I'd been to many before, but this was particularly sad, given the circumstances. It's one of those things where you have to switch off."

Chapman interviewed the housekeeper who revealed to the officer that she had seen a strange object under the car as she collected the newspapers earlier in the morning, but had not mentioned the event to anyone. Ron Chapman explained, "she thought it was a stone or something that might have been put there as a sort of wedge, as the road had quite a slope, to stop the car from rolling down the hill. Things could have been different if she had drawn Fraser's attention to the object. He may have been wary enough to call the police."

Fraser had escaped death by minutes and the IRA had killed a highly regarded cancer specialist by mistake. The nation was outraged. There was brief concern and speculation that Caroline Kennedy may have been the target, but that was quickly squashed as the Met issued warnings to all MP's to check under their cars every day. Fraser stoically commented that the attempt on his life had made him all the more determined to "stamp out terrorism." He noticed how close he had come to being killed, "I would have been in that car had I decided to leave at my normal time." He was saved by the almost forgotten phone call he had promised to make that morning.

On arriving at the House of Commons, Fraser was cheered by many MP's as he made a stern warning to members of the House that "every politician in the house is at risk." Roy Jenkins, the home Secretary, urged the entire nation to be on the lookout for suspicious packages and . to report any unusual behavior to the authorities. Jenkins demanded of the House the "wholehearted cooperation of each of us to combat and certainly not to be intimidated by the viciousness of terrorism." There had been no warning by the ASU.

The public outcry at the senseless death of Professor Farley was again causing some members of Parliament to lift the lid off the capital punishment debate one more time. The call for this debate would increase over the following weeks as the ASU continued to execute their deadly plot of terror. The Bomb Squad detectives were no closer to rounding up the bombers, despite two dawn raids on addresses in

Wimbledon and Morden that resulted in nine people being taken into custody for questioning, held under the Prevention of Terrorism Act, all of whom were released within days. The ASU, unperturbed by the death of a prominent scientist mistakenly killed instead of their intended target, moved on with their plans to attack the places where the elite of British society gathered to relax and enjoy a meal.

Wednesday, October 29 was a slow night for the upscale Italian restaurant the Trattoria Fiore situated at the junction of Mount Street and South Audley Street. At 9:00pm that evening there were ten diners in the restaurant and eight members of staff preparing meals and waiting on tables. Half a mile away in the Hilton hotel, Deputy Assistant Commissioner Ernest Bond was attending a police dinner at the previously attacked establishment. Mount Street is not a particularly busy road and at 9:00pm that night it would have been quite dark, dark enough for the two man ASU delivery team to pause outside the restaurant and leave another timed gelignite bomb containing fourteen-pounds of explosive along with the now familiar shrapnel components. The bomb, placed outside one of the restaurant windows, would remain undetected. Inside the Trattoria Fiore, Mr. Edwin Daly, a lawyer visiting London with his family from Philadelphia, was having dinner with his ten-year-old daughter Ruth. Daly, an Irish-American Catholic, would later recall how a year before his trip to London he had been approached on the telephone by lady in her 70's, who had managed a children's hospital for many years. She asked Daly if he had any connections that could "render aid" in Ireland. Daly suggested the Catholic Bishops relief fund, but immediately realized that was not what she was looking for. What she wanted was money to buy guns for the IRA. Daly was immensely frustrated at what appeared to be a fairly common theme amongst Irish-American Catholics, namely a romantic attachment to a cause most did not fully understand in a land many had never visited, a notion that the guns were for a historical cause being fought against the Protestant Unionists backed by the British government. Such American supporters of the IRA would drape themselves in the flag of Irish Nationalism, wash down their St. Patrick's Day corned beef and cabbage with green beer and pass the hat for the lads back in the old country. As Daly would later comment, "these people want the right to have a riot with Ian Paisley, and his supporters, with no outside interference."

The ASU's bomb exploded outside the restaurant at 9:24pm, with the blast shattering windows up and down Mount Street and South Audley Street. Patrons drinking in the nearby Audley pub were knocked off their feet by the force of the blast. Inside the restaurant, Daley and his daughter received cuts and lacerations from flying glass and were among the seventeen people wounded in the blast, six of them seriously. A waiter was knocked unconscious by part of the ceiling as it collapsed back into the building. Corin Moore, who lived opposite the restaurant, ran immediately to aid the injured and stated that he "grabbed all the sheets and blankets I could and tried to bandage people with them. It was pretty awful." Customers of the upscale seafood restaurant Scott's, just yards away in Mount Street, also felt the blast in what would be a chilling portent of the future role the establishment would have in the soon-to-be rapidly converging fortunes of the Bomb Squad and the four elusive members of the ASU.

Arriving at the restaurant, Detective Superintendent Peter Imbert took control of the crime scene. Imbert made an appeal, through the media, for people to come forward if they had seen anything suspicious in the area during evening before the blast. Detective Sergeant David Waghorn, also with the Bomb Squad, would note the street address and time of the bomb detonation as part of his crime scene duties. Waghorn, posted to the Bomb Squad in February 1974 from the CID, worked in the Bomb Squad operations room to help control and coordinate the activities of the police teams investigating the bombings and shootings committed by the ASU. David Waghorn would also note that again, like many other bomb episodes in the capital over the past year or so, it was another dry evening. The investigating crime scene officers had rarely experienced rainy evenings on arriving at a bomb site. This struck David Waghorn as strange as this was London, after all, and it did tend to rain a lot. Waghorn started to wonder if the absence of bad weather on the evenings of the ASU's attacks could be a factor to consider as they strove to find a way to catch the men. He also wondered if other factors could be part of some type of pattern in the ASU's actions, noting that the bomb attack on the Trattoria Fiore restaurant occurred only half a mile from the Hilton hotel site and close to other locations also attacked by the ASU. Was that pure coincidence, Waghorn wondered?

Later, back in his office in the Bomb Squad incident room, Waghorn decided to take a map of central London and began flagging all the incidents that had occurred since late 1974. As he would later explain, "eventually it occurred to me that there was in fact a pattern to their activity, not a precise pattern, but it was still a pattern." Waghorn drew a circle around the bulk of the bombing and shooting incidents in central London and was amazed to find that the ASU were, in fact, confining themselves to a very definite area of activity in the city. Fascinated, Waghorn looked more closely at the circle, "within the area, you could take out whole chunks as they consisted of residential districts and we knew the ASU were attacking establishment type addresses. It turned out they were working in a very limited area." It was a startling revelation to the young policeman who continued to cross-reference other factors in the ASU's apparent modus operandi. Waghorn's discovered that there also appeared to be a pattern regarding the days of the week they made their attacks. They also had a penchant for stealing Ford Cortina's to use on their jobs, and they disliked rain as Waghorn had noted at the Trattoria Fiore. That may have been the due, Waghorn reasoned, to the fact that the rain could have caused a short circuit in the timed devices they planted or make lighting a fuse difficult, making them wary about choosing rainy nights, which pointed to another element in the pattern. Most of their bombs were set to explode, or were thrown, during certain hours of the evening, Waghorn noted, calculated to catch the maximum number of available targets in the area at the time of detonation. This in turn led David Waghorn to deduce that the ASU team would be at a minimum of three people, given the need to have a driver, a lookout and one person to place or throw the device. He also concluded that they would be nervous or careful in their initial approach to a target, possibly approaching with caution and maybe taking a reconnaissance swing by their target before finally attacking. David Waghorn's analysis also showed that the ASU had a tendency, within the area they were focusing on, to go back to the same streets or locations more than once to carry out an attack. So, in total, Waghorn had a theory that, if correct, predicted the area they were operating in, potential days of the week the attacks might come on, the approximate time of day they would strike, the type of vehicle they may use, how many people may be involved, their method of approaching a target and what type weather they would prefer to operate under. Waghorn continued, "I argued that if you put enough police officers in the areas that contained the establishment type targets, and they sat there and watched and waited long enough, the ASU would be identifiable. I always had a theory that they would be more vulnerable on the job than when they were not, as by nature they were a secretive bunch and could not go down the pub and boast about the things they had done."

The concept was fine in theory, but Waghorn had to sell the idea up the chain of command, as the Met, like any hierarchical organization, had a political sensitivity to such a proposal, and coming from a junior officer it would potentially make some of the senior ranks less than enthusiastic about adopting the scheme. Waghorn took his map, and his theories, into the office of Chief Inspector Graham Ison of the Bomb

Squad. Ison was very supportive of the ideas that Waghorn put forward and encouraged the young officer to put the concept into writing in the form of a report that would, in time, be sent to the senior leadership of the Bomb Squad for evaluation. David Ison realized that Detective Sergeant Waghorn may have come up with the one plan that could bring the ASU down and get them off the streets of London, and also realized that internal politics may make the proposal a tough uphill sell for the young policeman.

However, the ASU were pressing ahead with their agenda. In an almost carbon copy of the attempted assassination of Tory MP Hugh Fraser that went tragically wrong, resulting in the death of Professor Farley, the ASU struck again with a car bomb. Their intended target was a prominent London businessman who lived in the exclusive Connaught Square area of London. The ASU carried out the reconnaissance and established their target, but missed the mark. Instead of placing a booby-trapped device under the target's car, it was mistakenly left under the metallic gray Mercedes of London lawyer Richard Charnley. Leaving his house in Connaught Square, Charnley got into his Mercedes at 9:10am, just as Korean War veteran Ian MacPherson was taking his morning run and was approximately 30 yards from Charnley's car. Out of habit, Charnley buckled his seatbelt before starting the car, and as he started the engine the bomb exploded, sending the vehicle somersaulting through the air, where it landed in the street on its roof. One of the front wheels, blown off in the explosion, crashed through the living room window of a house opposite, where it proceeded to ricochet off the interior walls for several seconds, leaving behind a bizarre series of skid marks. Ian MacPherson ran to the upturned Mercedes to find the injured, but conscious, Richard Charnley held upside down in the driver's seat by the seatbelt fastened seconds before the blast. MacPherson recalled that Charnley worried the petrol tank would explode, but MacPherson reassured him the tank was intact and not leaking. He would also not release Charnley from the seatbelt as he was concerned that the driver's spine could have been damaged in the blast and subsequent impact with the road.

Police and emergency services reach the scene and Charnley was carefully freed and rushed to St. Mary's Hospital in Paddington. As Charnley was wheeled into the operating theater, he managed to tell people nearby, "I don't feel too bad, thanks." He sustained a broken left leg in the explosion which required surgery to pin it together. That Charnley's injuries were relatively light, considering the bomb blast, had the bomb squad officers shaking their heads in disbelief when they examined the mangled wreck that, earlier that morning, had been an expensive motor car. Commander Roy Habershon said, "I cannot explain why his injuries were so minor, except that it was an act of God. He is a very fortunate man indeed." Detective Sergeant David Waghorn would add another flag to his map that day, as he continued to build his data in the hope that his concept for trapping the ASU would be adopted by the Bomb Squad leadership.

The next day, November 4th, from his hospital bed Richard Charnley made an appeal to the ASU to stop their campaign of "senseless" attacks on people in London and the surrounding areas. Charnley stated that the killings "cannot help in any way in resolving the problems in Ireland." At a press conference held the same day, a different philosophy toward the ASU bombers and their fellow countrymen unfolded before the British media. Mr. Ross McWhirter, who with his brother Norris was one half of the editing team of the best-selling Guinness Book of Records, had a message for the people of Britain. For several months, the right-wing leaning McWhirter had been toying with the idea of a direct appeal to the public on the issue of Northern Ireland. He told the press, "people are beginning to see there is no end in sight, and they are very, very angry." Working with a few like-minded individuals, Ross McWhirter formed the organization called Self-Help, which proclaimed it was against "socialism, extremism of either left or right, nationalization and bureaucracy and for free enterprise." At the November 4th press conference, Ross McWhirter presented a Self-Help pamphlet entitled "How to stop the bombers," as the British Government had not been able to stop them as they were too concerned with the civil liberties of the few that impacted the relative safety of the many, so the document argued. Self-Help's position advocated that all citizens of the Irish Republic, living in Britain, would be required to register with their local police and be issued with a pass required to either leave or enter Britain. Should any Irish citizen check into a hotel, boarding house or apartment, they would have to leave a signed photograph matching the picture in their passport, with the proprietor or landlord, for purposes of future identification of terror suspects. McWhirter further added that the British government would be pressed to have any suspected bombers charged with treason instead of murder to ensure they would be put to death, if found guilty. Self-Help's final element would make the ASU sit up and pay attention. Ross McWhirter announced that a fund had been set up to provide £50,000 to anyone who supplied information that resulted in the arrest and conviction of the people responsible for the London bombings. Somewhat akin to a new sheriff in town, McWhirter had nailed a wanted poster on the hitching post outside the town saloon. The ASU now literally had a price on their heads, thanks to the actions of someone who usually pursued a cause through the courts, behind closed doors, and not in the public forum, which naturally would include the very people he had taunted with a hefty reward. The fact that he had put a contract on his own head with the announcement of the reward must have occurred to McWhirter, but it appeared to not have deterred him in his resolve to bring the ASU to justice, and stamp out the Irish factor, in his view of the British way of life. By his own actions, McWhirter has added his name to the ASU hit list. However, there were several names ahead of McWhirter's that the ASU had plans to visit before attending to the newest addition.

Edward Heath was still on top of the ASU hit list, as the Prime Minister responsible for Internment. They had missed him by 10 minutes the previous December, with a thrown bomb, but a change in tactics would be employed for the second attempt on the life of the former Prime Minister.

The ASU tried a different approach to planting a bomb under a parked car. They had been unsuccessful in their first two attempts to actually get their intended target, and so made a decision to physically attach the bomb to the underside of Heath's large Rover V8 motorcar, a powerful vehicle in its day, which they carried out in the early hours of the morning on Saturday, November 8th, 1975. Edward Heath had made plans to have dinner that evening at the Royal yacht club in Lymington, on the Hampshire coast, as a guest of honor of the club's Commodore. It would take Heath approximately two hours to cover the 100 miles to Lymington from his home at 17 Wilton Street in Belgravia, but his day did not go as planned. After lunchtime meeting with President Sadat of Egypt, whose was in the country politicking for the ability to purchase British Jaguar fighter bombers, Heath had an unexpected meeting with his legal advisers regarding a potential scandal in the press involving the investment firm of Slater Walker, the company that managed his investment portfolio. The meeting lasted until past 6:00pm, and made Heath late for his dinner engagement. After informing the Royal yacht club of his delay, Heath changed into a dinner jacket and hurried to his car parked outside his house. As Heath would later describe the scene, "I slammed the door, started the engine, put my foot down hard on the accelerator, shot out to the end of the road . . . and made my way as speedily as to possible to Lymington."

Heath's haste to get to his dinner engagement on the south coast probably saved his life. As the powerful Rover leapt from the street outside Heath's house, the bomb, attached to the underside, was torn away by the acceleration and landed, without detonating, in the street where Heath's car had been parked. Blissfully unaware of what had happened back in Wilton Street, Heath arrived at the Royal yacht club as a guest of honor late for dinner, rather than ending up as a late former Prime Minister. It was his second lucky escape from the IRA bombers, who had inadvertently deposited a live bomb in Wilton Street. After Heath's speedy departure toward his dinner engagement, a young couple, out for a Saturday night on the town cruised around Belgravia looking for a parking space. They found one, much to their delight, outside 17 Wilton Street where they parked their Mini in the spot and headed out for the evening.

Returning several hours later, the young couple decided it would be a good idea to follow the police instructions about looking for suspicious parcels before driving off. The young woman got down on her hands and knees and looked under the Mini. What she spotted made her jump up screaming, as she had noticed the package that had fallen off Heath's car and landed in the road. The couple had evidently not noticed the package in the dark as they parked their car over it several hours earlier. Running off for help, they found a police officer at the nearby Victoria Station who called the event into the bomb squad. Realizing it was Edward Heath's address, Bomb Squad officers raced to the scene along with two bomb disposal officers led by Major Geoff Biddle. Wilton Street was again cordoned off and the residents moved to a safe spot while Major Biddle and his assistant tackled the device. Biddle had to lay prone in the gutter to work by flashlight on the ten-pound bomb. It was a cold night, and the stoic Biddle's only complaint was that it had been an uncomfortable experience as, "the wind was blowing up my trousers." Apparently, with only minutes to go, Major Biddle managed to disarm the bomb and render the area safe again.

Heath arrived back from his dinner in Lymington at around 2:00am only to find his street cordoned off with police tape once again. The Bomb Squad officers present at the scene related the story of the evening to Heath, who naturally wanted to meet the bomb disposal officers involved. Major Biddle explained to Heath that the device was unlike any they had experienced before, but that they managed to defuse it in the nick of time. The enthusiastic Biddle was keen to show the bomb to a somewhat nervous Edward Heath, who reluctantly followed the Bomb Squad officers to the back of a van, where Biddle produced "a large block for me to examine," recalled Heath. Turning the block over, Major Biddle proceeded to explain to Heath the subtle differences he had found in this bomb as compared with others he had examined. Heath, looking increasingly anxious in the close proximity to the disarmed IRA bomb, was spared anymore of the Major's enthusiastic debriefing by the other bomb disposal officer, who kindly suggested that perhaps Mr. Heath would like to go to his home as it was getting late. As he walked back towards his door, one of Heath's young neighbors, ten-year-old William Meriwether, admonished the former Prime Minister in a worried tone, concerned that the bomb could been placed under his father's car by mistake adding, "that would have meant my daddy's Mercedes going up in smoke!"

Heath and the residents of Wilton Street had avoided the IRA bombers, who had killed one unintended victim and wounded another with two of their bombs-under-cars tactic and had thankfully failed to kill Edward Heath with a third. While Detective Sergeant David Waghorn added the incident to his growing list noting time, place and weather, the ASU were evidently becoming frustrated at the lack of success in their recent activities and needed a result keep GHQ off their backs. The stalemate in Northern Ireland required the ASU to keep up the pressure on the Wilson government, and that pressure would not be applied if they were missing their targets. They were angering the British public with their attacks, which would occur regardless of who they targeted, but politically they were wasting opportunities to strike at their designated targets: the upper elements of British society. Two high profile eateries, popular with establishment figures, had not been visited by the ASU. The establishments were two miles apart and firmly inside Detective Sergeant Waghorn's theoretical zone of ASU operations. The first of the two to be attacked would be the world-renowned Scott's seafood restaurant and oyster bar at 20 Mount Street, just yards from the previously attacked Trattoria Fiore. Founded in 1851 by fishmonger John Scott, the restaurant became popular in its original Haymarket location, where the writer Ian Fleming is said to have discovered the dry martini, shaken not stirred. The restaurant relocated to Mount Street in 1968 and established itself as a place popular with film stars, royalty and politicians. Clientele in 1975 included Prince Charles and Edward Heath, to mention just a few.

Wednesday, November 12th, 1975 was yet another dry evening in London. Two, possibly three, members of the ASU had stolen a Ford Cortina and were heading for Mount Street. They had with them a five pound gelignite "thrower" packed with ball bearings and bolts as shrapnel and fitted with a short fuse. At 9:28pm, with Eddie Butler acting as cover man, the bomb was thrown at one of the two large round windows in the front of Scott's that fronted the oyster bar, where approximately 30 customers sat enjoying their drinks and food, with a further 100 customers eating in the dinning room behind. As the bomb crashed through the plate glass window, it exploded sending a shower of lethal shrapnel through the bar. The sound of breaking glass, as the bomb crashed through the window, alerted several people in the bar that a bomb could have been thrown at the restaurant. One customer, Silvio Varviso, music director of the Stuttgart Opera House, recalled "I knew it was a bomb and my wife and I threw ourselves to the floor. There was a big bang and a lot of smoke." Waiters helped uninjured customers out of the restaurant through a cellar exit as police and ambulances arrived at the restaurant. The Bomb Squad officers on the scene quickly cordoned off the area and began to search for clues. One eyewitness stated they had seen three men drive off in a Ford as the explosion occurred. Commander Roy Habershon was certain as to the perpetrators of the crime, as he stated that, "there is no doubt we are dealing with an intensive IRA bomb campaign aimed at Mayfair eating houses." One person had been killed in the bomb attack and 15 others injured. In the aftermath of the deadly attack, Habershon speculated on the possible need for all restaurants to have metal grills installed over their windows to protect them against the thrown bombs of the IRA. David Waghorn had more data to back up his assertions that the ASU was sticking to a pattern, as the location matched, the time of day fitted, it appeared the gang had used a Ford, and the eyewitness claimed to have seen three people in the car. The Met had a plan on the table that could catch the ASU in the act, but it would require somebody in authority to approve the proposal and set the wheels in motion. The situation, for the young officer, had become frustrating, but he was not alone. Commander Roy Habershon allowed his obvious frustration, at the inability of the police to identify and arrest the ASU, to leak through in a comment to the press. "I want to make it clear to everyone," he said, "all members of the public, that this is their fight. It is up to them to put the finger on these people."

Nerves were becoming frayed and tension increased as the hunt for the elusive terrorist team of the ASU continued. However, Detective Superintendent Peter Imbert had an uninteresting and highly perceptive insight that would add considerable weight behind David Waghorn's proposal to trap the ASU. Imbert was at home watching the late news coverage of the bomb at Scott's, as he later recalled, "on the news there was a man who you might call a typical upper crust Englishman, speaking with a cut glass accent, saying that there would be no way the IRA was going to drive him from his favorite eating place, and that he would be back again. I thought to myself if the IRA had seen that TV coverage, I dare say they would be back there again as well. "

Scott's would be a key element in the future fate of Peter Imbert, many of his colleagues, and the ASU. The destinies of the two sides would converge, at some point, someone in the zone of activity, identified and drawn up on David Waghorn's map. Neither side would know the significance of Imbert's observation from the news broadcast, where the very embodiment of the British establishment, on the TV news, had thumbed its nose at the ASU terror campaign. What the IRA had failed to factor into its calculus of mayhem was the very fact that the British establishment would never yield to terror tactics. They would return time and again to "their" places in a deliberate, almost bloody-minded, resistance to the terrorists. The IRA would have to continue to bomb and kill, for the people they had targeted would never yield. They could not, for to do so would be tantamount to an admission of weakness and failure in the face of adversity. The cold showers and tough discipline of England's top private schools, topped off by Oxford and Cambridge, turned out the civil servants, captains of industry and government mandarins, all steeped in the belief of the stiff upper lip of the English gentleman. They would not yield to a bully, they would rather roll up their sleeves and fight back and give the bully a bloody nose. The IRA, to some extent, were missing the point, and in fact their tactics concealed a paradox, for while they attacked the gathering places of the upper crust, they were, by virtue of the means of attack, targeting the people who worked in the clubs and restaurants of the West End, who were not the people of privilege that came to their places of employment for entertainment. It would be the working classes who would share the wounds and fatalities handed out by the ASU, and their bombs were fanning the flames of outrage in the British population across the social spectrum. The tide of pro-capital punishment support was again rising in direct response to the IRA campaign both in England and Northern Ireland. Pressure was mounting on the Wilson government, politically and financially, at home and internationally, and the pressure was growing daily to find a solution to the Irish question. Some of that pressure would be redirected toward the Metropolitan police to find the IRA men responsible and stop the bombings in London. The Met, through the initiative and ingenuity of David Waghorn, had a potential answer to the problem right at their fingertips, if they chose to recognize the plan as a solution in their fruitless hunt for the IRA killers abroad in London.

Six days after the attack on Scots, O'Connell, Butler and one other ASU member set out again on a bomb throwing attack. Their target on the night of November 18th was Walton's restaurant in Chelsea, at the Junction of Walton Street and Draycott Avenue. The restaurant had the reputation of being one of the most expensive in London at the time, with actors Elizabeth Taylor and Peter Sellers among the glittering and titled customers who visited the establishment on a regular basis.

In a flat above the restaurant, 34-year-old Peter van der Vlugh was spending the Tuesday evening at home with friends while O'Connell and Eddie Butler drove toward their selected target in a "borrowed" car, carrying an almost exact copy of the five-pound bomb used against Scott's, complete with ball bearings and bolts. At 9:52pm, van der Vlugh heard a screech of brakes from the street below as the stolen Cortina came to a sudden stop outside the restaurant. Butler acted as cover man while the bomb was lobbed through the front window of the restaurant, behind which sat approximately 80 customers all innocently enjoying their evening out. The bombs smashed through the plate glass window and landed on a table where two couples were dining. Mrs. Ivy Brenton, dining at Walton's with her husband and friends, recalled seeing the bomb, "I remember looking across at the table where the bomb had landed and saw red sparks like sparklers. Then I heard a glass breaking and the next thing I knew there was a big explosion." The four customers sitting at the table where the bomb landed did not stand a chance. Two were killed in the blast, with the others sustaining "terrible injuries," according to one of the restaurant waiters, 38-year-old Donato Chezzi. "After the terrific explosion," Chezzi recalled, "came a silence. Then I heard women and grown men screaming. It was terrible."

Mr. George Robertshaw was drinking in the Queens Arms pub across the road from the restaurant when the bomb exploded. "We heard a loud crump," he said, "at about ten of us ran outside. The front of the restaurant had been blasted out and there was glass and debris all over the street." Robertshaw and other customers of the Queens Arms clambered through the shattered windows of the restaurant to help move tables and chairs from wounded victims. On hearing the explosion, van der Vlugh ran downstairs and into the restaurant. "It was a shambles," he recalled.

Detective Inspector Ron Chapman was duty officer again that night and was at Scotland Yard when the call came about the bomb at Walton's restaurant. "Because we were getting these late-night incidents, when you were a duty officer you worked a rotor and you would be on duty for 24 hours," said Chapman, "but you've virtually worked 4:00pm to midnight on reserved, just being available late at night. We traveled to Walton's from The Yard in the incident van, and when we got there it was like a war scene, it was horrendous. The ambulances were still there and smoke was everywhere, it was a real horror scene, with a fire burning in the restaurant."

While Mr. Robertshaw was in the process of helping a victim into the street, the police ordered everyone to get out, as they were concerned about a second bomb in the area. Many of the wounded suffered horrific injuries inflicted by the ball bearings and coach bolts the ASU has used as shrapnel.

Chapman needed to coordinate the police effort at the scene and make sure that as much evidence as possible could be collected. This added a somewhat grisly element to the work the police had to carry out in connection with the wounded being taken to hospital, as Ron Chapman later explained, "there was an ambulance just leaving the scene and I recall grabbing a Constable and telling him to get in the ambulance and get back to us with where it was going. You needed to know to get a situation report about injured people and where they were being taken for treatment. We needed to get officers to the hospitals, as if any of the victims had something removed by one of the doctors, a piece of shrapnel or something, that is a potential exhibit and you needed to take possession of any bits recovered. Recovery of that type of evidence would not be foremost in the minds of the doctors and nurses treating the wounded, but it could be the vital piece that would tell you it was from a bomb. It could be a piece of table, but equally it could be a piece of the bomb."

There was also the task of collecting as much in the way of eyewitness testimony as possible, as every clue the police could obtain would be of vital use to them in piecing together the event and linking it to the bigger picture in their hunt for the elusive ASU. The challenge for the incident team would be collecting statements from people at the scene, as Ron Chapman explained, "not everybody comes forward after an event like that, and so it occurred to me to have an officer take note of all the car registration numbers in the area around the restaurant because if people drove away, you would then have some way of tracking down potential witnesses."

Many of the wounded were taken to St. Stephen's Hospital, where Dr. Lawrence Martin commented "I had been involved with the victims of nine bombings, but these are the worst injuries I've seen." Ron Chapman echoed Dr. Martin's words, "there were a lot of ball bearings used in the bomb, and when we went to the postmortem of the two people killed there were many ball bearings removed from the bodies of the deceased."

The time and location of the attack matched the pattern established by David Waghorn's analysis. Another flag on the map, the right time, dry conditions, just about everything matched. Finally acknowledging that the detection of the ASU, through conventional police work, may not net them a result fast enough, the Met decided to adopt the plan put forward by Detective Sergeant Waghorn to flood the suspected area of operation with police officers in plainclothes in an effort to catch the ASU in the act. Walton's restaurant proved to be the final piece of the puzzle for the Met, aided by Peter Imbert's hunch that the ASU would be tempted to have another go at Scott's, once the restaurant had recovered from the bombing of November 12th. Plans for the flood operation were approved by the police senor leadership team, and they would waste no time in putting the plans into action. As David Waghorn would later put it, "eventually it was realized that it was as good an idea as any. There was a pattern, a loose pattern, but it was there."

Based on the premise that the ASU were likely to revisit some of the same locations, or operate in limited area in London, the Bomb Squad leadership team, including Jim Nevill and Peter Imbert devised a scheme based on Waghorn's analysis and concept of basically just watching and waiting for the ASU to show themselves. In order to do this, they came up with a plan to flood the streets of London, inside Waghorn's deduced area of operations, with pairs of plainclothes officers to watch for the appearance of the ASU if they made another attack. If Waghorn's theory was correct, the flood plan would see pairs of unarmed plainclothes officers watching and waiting for O'Connell and his team to show up, and then call in the armed uniformed officers of the SPG to apprehend the IRA men. The flood plan was to be put into place on Friday November 21st with police officers, out of uniform, on duty outside potential targets and the selected leaders of the observation teams were called into Scotland Yard for a briefing at 1:30pm that day. Following the meeting, an unidentified source from inside the Met called the offices of the London *Evening Standard* newspaper and leaked the story, which was subsequently bannered across the front page of that day's edition– and by doing so alerted the ASU to the presence of a dragnet operation in London to trap them during their next attack. The exposure of the secret operation rendered it useless, wasted a lot of time and police money, and distressed a lot of the police involved. Many of them were furious at the breech of confidence. One officer commented, "there is always someone who can't keep their mouth shut. They should have been bloody hanged."

The then commissioner, Sir Robert Mark, had been on a campaign to improve the relationship between the Police and the media during the preceding two years. He took this slip on the *Evening Standard's* part hard, and wrote to the owner of the paper to complain at what he saw as a breach of trust and the destruction of a secret operation. He received no reply, but did get a telephoned apology from the very embarrassed newspaper editor.

The front page article in the *Evening Standard* gave the ASU a glimpse into what the police could have in store for them if they dared to venture out onto the streets of London again with murder on their minds. It demonstrated to the IRA men that they could not rely on their past ability to strike and escape before the police arrived on the scene. In fact, their next attack could very well be directly observed by the police, if the information in the *Evening Standard* front page article was in fact accurate. The ASU had several options in front of them. They could change tactics and avoid the area in London they had targeted or simply stop operations altogether. The latter was not really an option, as they had not been compromised and so would not be able to justify their "retirement" to GHQ. Alternatively, they could continue with their campaign but limit their attacks to drive-by shootings which would carry less risk of being apprehended than stopping the car to place or throw a bomb. With the threat of discovery in their usual area of operations, as a team they decided to send a message to the government, the British people and the media who reported every bloody deed they conducted in their terror campaign. They would strike a soft target of opportunity in Enfield, north London.

During the early evening of Thursday, November 27th, Harry Duggan and Hugh Dougherty set off on the eight-mile journey from Milton Grove to Village Road in Enfield in another "borrowed" car. They parked away from the target's address and walked the remainder of the distance, then waited in the dark and secluded garden of the large of . north London house. There were lights on in the house, so one of the two people who lived there was already home. They would wait, hidden in the dark, for the second to arrive.

At 6:45pm the headlamps of Rosemary McWhirter's blue Ford Granada illuminated the driveway of the home she shared in Village Road with her husband Ross, as she swung the car into the drive. Her two sons were away at boarding school in Marlborough, leaving the large house occupied by just herself and her husband. As she turned off the ignition, Rosemary McWhirter was confronted by Duggan and Dougherty who were both pointing hand guns at her. They demanded that she hand over her keys, which she did, and then ran from the two armed men straight to the front door of her house. Unable to get in, as the two ASU men had her keys, she frantically rang the doorbell. Her husband Ross, aged 50, opened the door to have his wife run screaming past him toward the kitchen. Harry Duggan had followed Rosemary to the door, where he was faced by Ross McWhirter. Duggan fired one round from his .357 Astra Magnum at the surprised McWhirter, the bullet hitting the publisher in the abdomen, and at such close range, probably knocked him off his feet. Duggan fired a second shot which struck McWhirter in the head. Leaving him for dead, the two IRA men took Rosemary McWhirter's car and drove off, heading back to their base. As they drove away, Mrs. McWhirter ran to a neighbor's house to raise the alarm. Police and ambulance teams arrived at the scene and rushed Ross McWhirter to Chase Farm hospital in Enfield, where he was pronounced dead.

As the two ASU men drove away, Harry Duggan opened the cylinder of his revolver and extracted the two spent cartridge cases, and replaced them with live ammunition, putting the two spent rounds in his jacket pocket. The police would later find the stolen Granada in Devonshire Hill Lane in Tottenham, halfway between Crouch Hill, Dougherty's address, and the house in Village Road, Enfield. Back at Milton Grove, Duggan took the two spent .357 rounds and placed them in a drawer for safekeeping.

The Met were under no illusion that the assassination Ross McWhirter was the deadly handiwork of the Provisional IRA. A Sinn Fein spokesman in London said of McWhirter, "by his actions he was encouraging people to inform on the Irish. He was the target for any Irishman, politically motivated or not." The forensic teams from the Met had a field day with the stolen Ford Granada. They found fingerprints that positively linked the suspect Michael Wilson with the murder of Ross McWhirter, which gave the bomb squad good cause to be excited. They had uncovered a link to the Provisional IRA cell that had previously operated out of the bomb factory found at 39 Fairholme Road after the murder of PC Stephan Tibble. The link connected that event with the activities of the current bombers, so it was not too much of a stretch to imagine that Michael Wilson was a common thread and could possibly be the key IRA operative on the British mainland. The Bomb Squad would add the recovered fingerprint fragments to those already collected in their database for bomb suspect code named Z, Michael Wilson. They had a name, but no history or criminal background to go with it, and although they did not know who this man was, or where they could find him, he had become the most wanted man in Britain.

In the House of Commons the following day, Home Secretary Roy Jenkins found himself under considerable pressure to explain to the House the "additional measures" he planned to introduce to combat the IRA terrorism in England, and what precisely the police were going to do about the situation. Jenkins wisely avoided giving any details, stating that, "there is, at this stage, no further information I can add and I believe it would be preferable, from the point of the Metropolitan police, for me to not speculate about the enquiries which they are pursuing with the utmost vigor." Pressed for further information by Jeremy Thorpe, leader of the Liberal party, on the threat risk to other prominent people in public life, Jenkins again refused to move, citing the debacle of the *Evening Standard* one week prior. "It would not be right for me to announce the operational plans which the police may have in hand. The House may recall," Jenkins said, "that an important plan last Friday was nullified by publicity in a newspaper during the afternoon." Jenkins closed by saying "I hope the House will not expect me to say more."

As Sir Robert Mark would later comment, the mood in the Met was optimistic, "tales were well up, however, and there was an unmistakable feeling of the hunt closing in for the kill." After the disastrous newspaper publicity of November 21st, the Met were going to try David Waghorn's flood plan again, but without the press publicity. It was a gamble, but a gamble they had to take. As Detective Sergeant David Waghorn would later put it, "when you're clutching at straws, it seemed like a good one to clutch onto."

doi:10.1300/J173v08n01_04

Chapter 4

December 6th, 1975

The assassination of Ross McWhirter on November 27th, after his much publicized reward offer and list of nationalistic approaches to dealing with the IRA problem, was the catalyst for the Met to throw the dragnet out over central London again, but this time in total secrecy from the media. They realized that the leak of the previously planned operation may have heightened the ASU's vigilance to police operations to apprehend them, possibly making the plan less effective, but that was a risk deemed worth taking. The Met want to catch the ASU in the act of carry out a bombing, which would require them to get out of any car they were using. The biggest risk the plan faced, after being compromised in the press, revolved around the fact that the officers looking out for the men were on foot and would be relying on the response time of the armed SPG officers who would have to respond to any call for help from the plainclothes officers. Their worst nightmare was that the ASU would not get out of their car, but just use the vehicle for a drive-by shooting. That would make their capture and arrest a very difficult prospect.

The revised effort was again dubbed "Operation Combo," nicknamed "The ring of steel" by some officers, as described to the author by Peter Imbert. "We had a few hundred officers out on a number of nights setting a trap for them. The plainclothes officers taking part in the operation were not armed. There was a concern about the two man groups' mistakenly opening fire on other policemen, so it was the uni-

[Haworth co-indexing entry note]: "December 6th, 1975." Moysey, Steven P. Co-published simultaneously in *Journal of Police Crisis Negotiations* (The Haworth Press, Inc.) Vol. 8, No. 1, 2008, pp. 129-160; and: *The Road to Balcombe Street: The IRA Reign of Terror in London* (Steven P. Moysey) The Haworth Press, Inc., 2008, pp. 129-160. Single .or multiple copies of this article are available for a fee from The Haworth Document Delivery Service [1-800-HAWORTH, 9:00 a.m. - 5:00 p.m. (EST). E-mail address: docdelivery@haworthpress.com].

Available online at http://jpcn.haworthpress.com
doi:10.1300/J173v08n01_05

form boys who were armed. They were in what we called personnel carriers [the ubiquitous Ford Transit van of the era] dotted around the
periphery of the search areas, waiting to be called. We had thought of
the likely places, such as Downing Street, Houses of Parliament, resi-
dencies of royalty and cabinet ministers, so that we could put officers on
observation near to them."

The chance that the ASU would, in fact, attack some of their previous
targets again, in light of the leaked *Evening Standard* piece, was still
considered to be a worthwhile opportunity to catch them in the act and
arrest them. It was thought that some locations would hold more of a
draw for the ASU than others, but the Met team decided to cover all
eventualities, even some that were considered less likely than others. As
Peter Imbert explained, "they'd been three times to the vicinity of Bak-
ers Street underground station, so they had a habit of going back to
places. So it was thought, with the little team of us trying to work out
where the officers on Combo should go, it was thought that Scott's was
low percentage likelihood." While considered a long shot, Scott's restaurant, in Mount Street, would be covered by a pair of Combo officers
during the operation, on the off chance that the ASU would take another
look at the establishment.

Imbert was also convinced that the next attack would not be on a Saturday. The statistics gathered by Detective Sergeant David Waghorn
tended to back up Imbert's assumption, as only seven of the thirty-two
ASU assaults to that point had occurred on a weekend day, with the remainder happening during the week, with Thursday as the most active
day. The ASU's changed tactics, during their phase two operations, had
targeted establishment figures and the upper elements of British society
and the places they frequented, so weekdays would be more likely to
find this demographic still in London, rather than away from town for
the weekend. This would also support the low count of episodes on a
Friday, as the target population may have been heading out of town. The
obvious divergence from this logic would be establishment figures,
such as former Prime Minister Edward Heath, that lived in London on a
week round basis.

After the false start of November 21st, Operation Comb commenced
the first week of December, under orders of strict secrecy, with five
hundred officers in pairs, on the streets of London. Inspector John
Purnell, from Paddington Green police station, and Sergeant Phil
McVeigh of Harrow Road police station, had already spent several
rather dull, cold nights in plain clothes on surveillance in Portman
Street. They were covering the location as it had been the site of two

previous gun attacks by the ASU, one on the Portman Hotel and the other on the Churchill Hotel. The two unarmed officers were watching and waiting for any sign of terrorist activity, listening in on the radio carried by McVeigh for any activity observed by fellow officers in the Operation Combo area. Nothing had happened.

The bitterly cold London weather of December 1975 was making the surveillance operation an uncomfortable exercise for all involved. John Purnell later described the night of December 6th, "it was, as I remember, bloody cold that night. We were taking hot soup and standing in shop doorways to try and stay warm. We were getting bored out of our boxes really and just waiting around, because we couldn't get involved in anything else. We weren't allowed to get involved in anything even if we'd seen something. We were under orders to pass it along to a uniformed unit to deal with. Basically it [6th of December] was a night of boredom."

At 6:00pm on the evening of the 6th, one of several armed teams of the uniformed Special Patrol Group [SPG] division of the Met were preparing for their night as part of the Combo operation. There were six officers in the team; two armed with .38 Smith and Wesson six round revolvers, one assigned to driver duty, one to radio operator and another as map reader, in case they received a call to move into position to confront the ASU. Their roles were interchangeable, as each of the specially trained officers could carry out any of the roles assigned to their teammates. They left their base in South London and headed for the West End area of London to watch and wait, like all the other Combo participants, in their assigned observation sector.

At around 7:30pm on that Saturday evening, two members of the ASU stole a Ford Cortina from outside a house in Porten Road, Hammersmith using one of the many Ford keys they had in the ASU for "borrowing" cars. They drove to 61 Crouch Hill to pick up the rest of the team. Butler, a keen soccer fan, had spent the afternoon watching Arsenal play Leeds United at home, and had later prepared the equipment for the night's activity, wrapping the Sten gun and M1 carbine in an old shirt and placing them into the canvas holdall bag he had purchased from a store on Hornsey Rise several weeks before. The M1 carbine had a modified stock, so that it could be folded up and concealed inside a bag or under a coat. The modification was relatively crude, using a door hinge and a simple gate hook-and-eye fixture, but was adequate for the job. Spare gun parts and extra magazines were also stored in the bag. Each of the four men carried a personal hand gun and extra ammunition, including the Astra Magnum, carried by Duggan that had been used to shoot Ross McWhirter. Butler and Dougherty were carrying .38 Specials and O'Connell had the second .357 magnum. They also had a .45 caliber Star semi automatic pistol as a back up. The equipment was loaded into the stolen car and all the members of the ASU, for the first time since becoming fully operational in 1974, got into the car to head off for the selected target for that night: Scott's Restaurant on Mount Street in Mayfair, leaving Crouch Hill at approximately 8:40pm to cover the six miles to Scott's. The establishment had been targeted again as it was an "exclusive restaurant," as Butler would explain to Jim Nevill. The significance of the four men going on the raid was critical. Butler was later asked why, on that occasion, did all four of the ASU go on the shooting mission, when in previous operations only two or three of them would have gone. Butler allegedly replied that it was to "see to anyone who got in our way." The leaked police operation, published in the *Evening Standard,* had contributed to a change in tactics for the ASU, who were taking the additional precaution of bringing along with them extra firepower in case they had to "see to" any police operations they may run into that night. The leak, which was viewed as being so detrimental at the time, may actually have helped to trap the four men into launching an all out effort that night. They did not know it at the time, but they were to drive into a web of police officers just waiting and watching for the ASU to show up, looking for any sign of suspicious activity.

The SPG team assigned to the West End had parked in Cambridge Circus, in the Soho district of London, famed for its theaters and nightlife. The officers had been taking a snack break, eating potato crisps and drinking cans of Pepsi Cola while they watched the Saturday night crowds of people bustling around the West End. They were also amused by one street entertainer who was keeping people in the street enthralled with a troop of performing parrots. As Officer A[1] would later recall, "we were watching him rather than anything else."

The ASU headed out from Crouch Hill, driving to Mount Street. On the way, they stopped so that Butler could purchase an evening newspaper to check the classified football results. They arrived at Mount Street at around 9:00pm, driving slowly toward Scott's from the east. Two plainclothes officers, stationed in Mount Street as part of Operation Combo, watched the approaching car slow to a halt and noticed a rifle barrel protruding from the front driver's window. O'Connell, aiming the M1 at the restaurant window, fired two rounds. Butler, in the rear right hand passenger seat, pulled the trigger on the Sten, only to have the unreliable submachine gun jam on him once again. The stoppage was a difficult one to clear and so the ASU moved away from Scott's without firing any further shots at the restaurant. As they drove away, Butler stowed the Sten and the M1 carbine back into the canvas holdall, removing the magazine from the jammed submachine gun in the process. The quick-thinking plain clothes officers in Mount Street broadcast the make, number of occupants and license plate number of the car to the rest of the Combo team, together with the direction the vehicle was traveling in the one way traffic system in the Mount Street area. The ASU made a right hand turn into Park Street and continued straight ahead toward Oxford Street, heading to where John Purnell and Phil McVeigh were on watch, feeling cold and bored as the night dragged on.

Four other officers taking part in Operation Combo were patrolling the Knightsbridge area that evening in a bright Canary yellow Ford Granada. Detective Constable Bob Fenton had recently joined the Flying Squad, the elite plainclothes detective branch of the Met, and was in the "Yellow Peril" that night with Detective Inspector Henry Dowswell, Detective Sergeant Phil Mansfield and the highly experienced police driver PC Peter Wilson. The hand-held radio they had with them was proving to be a problem, as Bob Fenton would later recall, "we had bad radio signals, so Henry decided to return to the Yard, which was not far away, and change the radio." The four unarmed officers set off on the short drive to Scotland Yard to swap out the faulty radio set.

The Cambridge Circus parrots were still entertaining the SPG officers, but the radio call from the Combo team in Mount Street immediately caught their attention. As a team, they decided to head off in the general direction of the reported event, "as it sounded like it was a genuine call, "said Officer A, "rather than one of the many false calls that had come over the radio." Officer A also added that although the location was out of their assigned Combo sector, the team responded to the call as, "being armed, we thought we should head over there."

John Purnell later recalled how events unfolded after he and McVeigh received the broadcast from the officers in Mount Street: "It was a bit of a one way traffic system and so I said to Phil, 'Christ that means they are coming toward us!'" The ASU would have the option to take a left turn at the junction with Oxford Street, where Park Street changed to Portman Street, so Purnell and McVeigh hurriedly walked back down Portman Street toward the intersection in case the car made the turn. Before they reached the junction, the car with the ASU on board came into view, as John Purnell described, "and sure enough, the next thing we know the suspect's car was coming up [Portman Street] toward us! We could see there were four guys in the car, so we flagged down a taxi cab and I got Phil to circulate on the radio that we had sight of them. We got into the cab and after identifying ourselves as police officers, I literally said to the cabbie, 'follow that Cortina!' He made a joke, 'blimey, I've always wanted this to happen!' Of course, we didn't tell him it was full of armed terrorists! He was pretty good, a good cabbie and kept his cool and just followed the Cortina."

Portman Street changes to Gloucester Place just north of the intersection with Wigmore Street, with several sets of traffic lights along the way. Purnell and McVeigh had a lucky break in that the traffic lights stayed in their favor, so they could avoid having to run a red light to stay with the stolen Cortina, as that would have confirmed the ASU's increasing suspicion they were being followed. To drive back to either Crouch Hill or Milton Grove, the ASU would have needed to turn right onto the Marylebone Road and then take a left turn onto Albany Street, the A4201. Becoming increasingly suspicious of the taxi cab tailing them, and probably not wanting to have a police tail back to their base of operations only four miles away, they continued over the Marylebone road and stayed on Gloucester Place, which flows into Park Road.

Driving north along Tottenham Court road and then onto Oxford Street, the SPG team were tracking the broken messages coming over the radio. "We knew the suspect car was being followed, but we didn't know who it was in pursuit at that time or what vehicle they were in," Officer A related.

McVeigh radioed to Scotland Yard that they were following the suspects into Park Road, but there was an apparent transcription error, made by the radio operator at The Yard, that would cause a delay in the vital armed backup teams from entering into the chase. Peter Imbert would later describe the confusion: "The officers were leaning out of the cab window trying to talk on their personal radio to let Scotland Yard know which way the fugitive car was going, so that the personnel carriers with the armed officers could close in and head them off. But as usual, there was a little bit of a cock-up on that occasion, because the fellow at The Yard misheard the officers when they said they were on Park Road–I think he took it down as Park Place or Park Street."

It may also have been an error on the part of the police officers in the cab. McVeigh was giving the running commentary to The Yard dispatch officer, but being based at Harrow Road, which was slightly further west, he would have been less familiar with the area than Purnell who was a local. Regardless of how the communications error occurred, the mistake would subsequently put both Purnell and McVeigh in considerable peril.

The ASU had become suspicious of the taxi cab tailing them, despite Purnell's instruction the cabbie to keep a good distance from the stolen Cortina. The cab driver would later tell the BBC's Radio 4 news that the driver of the stolen Cortina had not been driving erratically as he tailed the vehicle, "he wasn't going mad, this car. There was no way, you know, he wasn't causing any attraction to himself."

John Purnell described the scene as they continued to tail the Cortina, "the whole time they [ASU] were pretty jumpy and they were turning round and looking at us. Just past Rossmore Road, opposite the [Regents] park, they pulled into a little close [Alpha Close, a cul-de-sac] and we drove a little bit further beyond them [along Park Road], about thirty yards, and told the cabbie to pull over." The cabbie also said he pulled up past the stolen car so as to "not give the game away."

The ASU had pulled into Alpha Close, which was just a small pull in, to determine if the cab was indeed following them. If the cab kept going, they were clear, if it pulled to a stop then they would have confirmed their suspicions and they were being tailed. The cab pulled to a stop. McVeigh radioed the location of the parked stolen Cortina, which then highlighted the mistaken location transmitted to the armed SPG groups, as Alpha Close was off Park *Road*, not Park Street.

Back at Scotland Yard, Henry Dowswell had changed the defective radio set, as Bob Fenton would recall, "as Henry returned to the vehicle, we started to hear over the radio about shots being fired into a restaurant and that a chase was ongoing and so we headed in the direction of the chase, rather than going back to Knightsbridge." He added "it was pure fate that we were closer to the chase as the result of a bad radio." The Flying Squad car, driven by PC Peter Wilson, sped through the Saturday night traffic, siren screaming, to cover the three miles between The Yard and the location called out by McVeigh. PC Wilson's knowledge of the streets of London and his experience as a first class police driver aided their fast response towards the then ongoing chase. Former Flying Squad Detective Alec Edwards had the following comment about the requirements for drivers such as Peter Wilson, "to be a Flying Squad driver, you had to be Class One certified by the Metropolitan police, which was the highest level of training conducted at that time. The officers who applied to be Flying Squad drivers would have to prove their skills and demonstrate they could get on with the Flying Squad team they would be assigned to. It was very much a team environment, and so the drivers would come up, and some would make it and some wouldn't and then if they got on well with the team, we would take them. But they had to be very good drivers in any case."

The two officers in the cab following the IRA men were not aware of the error in communication and were naturally expecting to see the armed units turn up at any minute and take over the pursuit. It is worth pointing out, again, at this juncture that Purnell and McVeigh were unarmed, had no body armor to protect them and they were also aware that the ASU were armed, given the report of the shooting in Mount Street. But, no back up was in sight despite the sounds of sirens in the distance. Purnell did not know which units the sounds of the police sirens were coming from, or if they were in fact armed units responding to McVeigh's radio call. This put Purnell and McVeigh in a difficult position. They could not afford to let the ASU escape, but at the same time they had no way of defending themselves if the ASU started shooting. John Purnell described the scene that he and McVeigh faced as they left the relative safety of the cab: "We got out of the cab and started to walk towards the Cortina, because by that time the four of them were out of the car. They looked at us and I thought at that point they were going to separate but they didn't, they stayed together."

For a few seconds the two groups stood apart looking at each other, formulating their next moves. The jammed Sten and the M1 carbine were stowed in the canvas bag. Not having these weapons available would prove to be a serious mistake on the part of the ASU and a probable life saver for the two policemen who were faced with a decision to make in terms of whether they should wait for backup or give chase. The ASU made up their minds and took off as a group, walking away back south down Park Road. Butler would later state to Jim Nevill that they thought the two men in the taxi were plain clothes police officers. "He was right!" stated Purnell, and he and McVeigh followed the four men down Park Road at a walking pace, about thirty yards behind, as their intent was to keep sight of the group and not apprehend them. The two unarmed officers would have been overpowered, or shot, if they had attempted to stop the group.

"They then started to run south down Park Road toward Rossmore Road," said Purnell, "and we were running after them. It was at that time they turned round and started firing shots at us! We just carried on chasing them. I shouted out, rather foolishly, 'police stop!' or something stupid like that, but they kept on and turned right into Rossmore Road, which is a bridge going over the Marylebone Station train tracks."

The ASU themselves would later admit that not having the Sten working and available was a mistake. Peter Imbert would later taunt Harry Duggan during his subsequent interrogation about the quality of their guns, reminding him of the jammed Sten. Duggan shrugged and commented that it was just one of those things. He chillingly added that the subsequent chase on foot would have had a different outcome if the Sten had not jammed earlier and had been available. Quizzed further by Imbert, Duggan added, from a cell in Paddington Green police station, "well, it wouldn't have ended like this."

Undaunted by the small-arms fire being directed at them, Purnell and McVeigh continued to pursue the ASU up Rossmore Road, and it was at that point they could hear the sirens of the approaching armed backup. John Purnell recalled later, "by this time there was the sound of sirens going off all over the place. You could hear the bloody sirens everywhere, the world had gone mad! They were firing shots at us and we were leaning flat against walls when they turned around to fire at us. We were just clinging to walls and running!"

As the SPG van came to the junction of Park Road and Rossmore Road, the officers on board saw Purnell and McVeigh heading up Rossmore Road, pointing ahead of them. "Our driver took us into the road," said Officer A, "and so we drove along the left hand side of the road and, looking further up on the right hand side, we could see four men jogging along the pavement."

The burden of hauling the bag of weapons and spare parts was too much under the chase circumstances for the ASU, and so the canvas holdall was ditched in Rossmore Road. O'Connell would later tell Jim Nevill that, "we couldn't have carried it much further, it was heavy and awkward when you are running." The bag and its contents would later reveal vital forensic evidence. The group of IRA men, still pursued by Purnell and McVeigh, now faced the SPG officers, as John Purnell described the scene: "The SPG carrier came into Rossmore Road and came up past us, drove up level with the suspects and then pulled in front of them."

The SPG van pulled to a stop 30 feet ahead of the running ASU members. Officer A: "My partner was seated in the back of the vehicle and I was in the left hand side, by the side door. I told my partner I was going to get out through the side door, and that was the last thing I remember saying, as then there was gunfire being directed at us." Officer A's partner got out through the rear doors of the Transit van and exchanged fire with the ASU. "I was by this point prone in the road," said Officer A, "using the double rear wheels of the vehicle as cover." He also remembered that, "I could not have got any flatter, spread out in the road, and I realized that this was not a training exercise. Looking up from my position behind the rear wheels of the vehicle, I saw the four men and the flashes of gunfire. I fired two rounds at the man nearest to me who was firing a pistol at our vehicle." Both rounds missed their target. "One of them was later found about half a mile away in dairy," recalled Officer A, "the scientific people were very thorough in recovering all the rounds. The other was found a little closer, in the side of the bridge."[2] The ASU and the SPG exchanged further shots, as Officer A related to the author, "during this brief period of the firefight, the driver of the SPG vehicle, realizing he had unarmed colleagues in the back who were in some danger, drove off at speed a fair few yards down the road, thereby removing my cover! One minute I was feeling fairly safe, and then I was sprawled out in the middle of the road feeling quite exposed! At that point, the four men turned around and ran away from us, back down the direction they had come from."

John Purnell recalled the moment, "that was okay, but of course what happened then was that the ASU were cut off, so they turned around because those SPG guys were armed. They were firing at the SPG and the SPG were firing back at them. Then the terrorists started running back towards us! We were in danger of not only being hit by the terrorist bullets, but also the SPG! We could have easily been hit by friendly fire."

Bob Fenton, in the Flying squad car, recalled arriving on the scene. "As we approached the Rossmore road area," he said, "we could hear shots being fired. We actually overshot Rossmore Road going north on Park Road. We noticed the vehicle that had been reported parked in Alpha Close and did a U-turn back towards Rossmore Road."

With the armed ASU team now running back toward them, Purnell and McVeigh frantically tried to find a means of defending themselves. Being level with the bag dropped by the ASU, Purnell crouched to the floor, unzipped the bag and pulled out what he thought was the butt of a gun, but it later turned out to be just a gun barrel, probably one of the spares for the Sten. With no means of defending themselves in the face of the advancing ASU team rapidly bearing down on them, Purnell later confessed to being genuinely afraid: "When we were just chasing them up Rossmore Road, I don't remember being scared out of my wits. But I was I was in fear of my life when they were running back towards us. I was still with Phil then and you do take comfort in being with other people. I was clearly frightened, but at that stage I wasn't thinking 'God, this is it!'"

Purnell and McVeigh ran back the way they had come on Rossmore Road, now pursued by the ASU with no place to take cover. The arrival of Bob Fenton and the other officers, in their bright yellow Flying Squad car, saved Purnell and McVeigh as the Flying Squad officers pulled to a screeching halt between the ASU and the two unarmed policemen, shielding Purnell and McVeigh from the ASU's line of fire. Bob Fenton: "We turned right onto Rossmore Road to be confronted by four men who started to fire shots at us, at the car, as we pulled to a stop. I could hear the shots and see the little flames [from the muzzle flashes], but nothing appeared to be happening, no whizzing bullets or the sound of metal hitting metal. I saw John Purnell who was holding what appeared to be a submachine gun, kicking a holdall."

Bob Fenton also recalled how the bullets punctured the car radiator and hit the engine block, which protected the officers, "It was quite a large vehicle, with Henry and Peter in the front and me and Phil Mansfield in the back. The only way we could look forward was by moving our heads to the left and right, so we were peering between Henry and Peter, so our heads were all in a line through the windscreen. If one of those rounds had gone through the windscreen, it would have taken one of us out."

The ASU continued to fire on the car of Flying Squad officers while the SPG fired at the ASU. Bob Fenton later recalled, "As they came towards us they were in a group of four as they shot at us. Then they split into two groups with two going round on one side of the car and two round the other side. Just after we got out of the vehicle and headed towards them, one of them turned back and let rip with his gun." Aiming at Henry Dowswell, Harry Duggan fired his .357 magnum from approximately fifteen feet at the Detective who instinctively flinched away from the shot, which miraculously missed him, passed between Fenton and Mansfield, through the rear of the Canary yellow Granada and lodged in the soft furnishing of the rear seat where they had been sitting seconds earlier. PC Wilson, still sitting behind the wheel of the Yellow Peril was unharmed, although his car had been wounded, as Alec Edwards explained, "he would have been most upset if his car had been damaged, he would have created hell! The Flying Squad drivers looked after their cars like babies; it was 'their' car!"

Still in danger of being fired on by the ASU, Purnell and McVeigh took cover behind a bus that had turned onto Rossmore Road, as part of its usual route, directly behind the Flying Squad officers. The unmarked police car had blocked the road and the bus could not get through. The situation was one of absolute chaos with officers taking cover behind vehicles as the ASU continued to fire at all of the police groups in Rossmore Road as they diagonally crossed the street and made for a set of steps that run into the street below. John Purnell later described to the author the scene he and McVeigh faced:

"Just behind the [Flying Squad] car was a bus, and Phil and I ran behind the bus to take cover. The terrorists crossed the road and ran down steps which led from Rossmore Road down to Taunton Place which runs parallel to Rossmore. Three of them ran into Balcombe Street from there and one went down Taunton toward Boston Place. I told Phil McVeigh to give the details of where they were going over the radio, because at that point it was just Phil and I as everyone else was still further back and taking cover. We were by the bus which was right next to the steps [to Taunton Place] and Phil radioed the details of where they were heading."

Watching the four ASU men making an attempt at escaping caused Purnell and McVeigh to rapidly weigh up the options facing them. The group had split up, with three heading south down Balcombe Street and one making his way down Taunton Place toward the very dark and narrow confines of Boston Place, a street lined with numerous doorways and parked cars, affording the fleeing ASU member plenty of opportunity for a well covered firing position. There was a very real risk that all, or some, of the ASU may get away from the police, and so Purnell made a decision: chasing the three would be a higher risk option than just going after the lone ASU member, but neither option was particularly attractive to the unarmed officer and the longer he deliberated, the greater chance the officers had of losing the opportunity to catch the ASU. Purnell reacted to the situation unfolding in front of him, "as I ran down the steps on my own, I thought I'd have a go at going after the single guy."

Officer A had his attention on the scene briefly interrupted, "what distracted me for a short time was a man running back toward me from where the terrorists had gone down the steps, as I didn't know if he was one of the terrorists. I called on him to stop, lay prone on the ground and show me his hands, all at gun point." The man was handcuffed and later taken into custody, but as Officer A later recalled, "It turned out he was just an innocent civilian running to get out of the way of all the shooting!"

The enormity of what he was doing hit Purnell as he ran down the steps and into Boston Place. He was chasing an armed and dangerous member of the ASU on his own, with no radio or back up, in a dark and narrow street. The single ASU member had gone down the steps and turned right on Taunton Place which leads to Boston Place, a street that runs parallels to Balcombe Street. Purnell, despite being very frightened for his personal safety, was determined to not let his target escape. "It was pretty dark and the road [Boston Place] was narrow and I was really quite worried that he was going to take cover in a doorway, and that would have been it for me. I've got to say that I wasn't really afraid until I was on my own. I was okay when I was with Phil and I wasn't really thinking about the danger. When I did feel it was when I went down those steps [to Taunton Place] and I was on my own. I felt very vulnerable then and I thought, 'what have I done!' I worried I would never see my wife Margaret and the kids again!" For a split second Purnell thought about turning back, but just as quickly resolved to continue the pursuit.

With three of the ASU running down Balcombe Street, the lone ASU member was pursued down Boston Place by Purnell, who watched the IRA man as he then turned left into Ivor Place. By sheer luck, as Peter Imbert later put it, "the luck of the Irish," the four men met up again at the junction of Balcombe Street and Ivor Place. Henry Dowswell, leaving his fellow Flying Squad officers at the railings in Rossmore road with McVeigh, also followed down the steps into Taunton Place, followed by Officer A and his partner.

As Purnell turned into Ivor Place, he noticed a lone man standing outside the door of number 21. Still carrying the gun part taken from the ASU's bag, that Purnell intended to use as a club if needed, he charged at the unsuspecting bystander, believing him to be the ASU member he was pursuing. Purnell grabbed the man by the lapels and slammed him into the front door, where the man collapsed at Purnell's feet. "He probably thought he was being attacked," said Purnell, "well, he was really, wasn't he?" Purnell immediately realized this was not the person he was chasing, so he made a very hasty apology to the prostrate bystander and continued the short distance down Ivor Place to Balcombe Street. A group of bystanders pointed down the street, indicating the direction the four men had taken, so Purnell continued to give chase, and he was worried that the man he was chasing had in fact escaped, but the bystanders indicated that four men had run off down the road, and Sergeant McVeigh had seen the group join up again in Balcombe Street.

The sounds of a rapidly approaching and growing police presence in the area convinced the ASU they needed to get out of the street and quickly, so they attempted to escape through an apartment block and out the back onto Boston Place. The ASU had entered the front door of the apartment block, number 22, as Purnell ran from Ivor Place into Balcombe Street: "They all then continued down Balcombe Street and then into the block of flats, which was opposite the Portman Arms pub,[3]" stated Purnell, "I didn't see them run into the building, but as I arrived there I saw a woman frantically pointing at the flat block yelling, 'they're in there, they're in there!' That was it; I ran into the pub and asked them to call the police, to make sure they knew where they had gone. I was there about a minute before anyone else got there. Henry Dowswell was the next one on the scene then we took cover behind cars that were parked opposite the flat." Dowswell was closely followed to the scene by the two SPG officers, who took up covering positions outside the apartment building.

Sergeant McVeigh had stayed behind the railings on Rossmore to report the movements of the four men to the police headquarters, as his position gave him a clear view down Balcombe Street. Purnell and Dowswell then waited for additional armed backup to arrive and were keeping an eye on the building in case the ASU came back out the front. They did not, and finding there was no unlocked rear exit out to Boston Place, the ASU ran up the stairs of the apartment building to the flat with a light on, to number 22b.

Inside 22b, John (54) and Sheila Mathews (53) had previously settled down for the evening to watch television. They had been enjoying an episode of the Telly Savalas New York detective series "Kojak," and were unsure if the gunfire they could hear was coming from the TV set or outside. John Mathews went out onto the balcony off the living room of the two bedroom flat that overlooked Balcombe Street, to see what the commotion was about outside. He described it as "a lot of shouting from the street." Stepping out on the balcony, he noticed Purnell and Dowswell crouching behind a car in the street opposite the flat. He was noticed by Purnell: "I didn't know who he was at the time, but someone came out on the balcony and we told him to get back inside and stay there!" John Mathews was told that there were armed men around and, heeding Purnell's advice, returned to the living room. At that point the doorbell rang and, believing it was the police, John Mathews opened the door only to be faced with the four armed members of the ASU. Jim Nevill would later ask Butler how they got into the flat. Butler replied, "I rang the doorbell. Himself [Mathews] answered the door." Butler pushed past Mathews and entered the living room. The other three then dragged Mr. Mathews into the living room and the ASU looked for material to tie up the couple. They found panty hose and used this to bind their hands and later their feet as well. Within a short space of time, Balcombe Street was flooded with police vehicles with sirens blaring and armed police personnel, "the cavalry had arrived," as Purnell put it. Butler moved into the bedroom, next to the living room, to take a look outside at the scene developing in the street below. Movement of the bedroom window curtain was observed by officers in the street.

By this stage in the events, the armed units arriving on the scene were directed by Purnell and Dowswell into the apartment building, where they went door-to-door looking for the ASU. They reached 22b and hammered on the door and rang the door bell, announcing that they were police officers. Duggan forced a distraught Mrs. Mathews, at gunpoint, to the front door of the flat where she was told to tell the police to go away. Duggan also told the police, in very graphic and invective laden language, to clear off. As Butler would later put it, "we wanted to make sure they [the police] knew we had hostages." The police would also be told by members of the ASU, during subsequent interrogation that the hostages would have been shot if there had been any attempt by the police to break in. They wanted to deny the police any satisfaction of getting them out alive.

O'Connell called the police from the Mathew's living room at approximately 10:00pm, identified himself as a member of the IRA, and stated that they were holding a couple as hostages in Balcombe Street. The initial call was handled by the main Met incident center and the officer taking the call asked if there were any other hostages. Given an opening for deception, O'Connell replied that there was a child in the apartment, a deliberate ploy to throw off the Met in their tactical assessment of the situation. The call was routed through to Deputy Assistant Commissioner Ernest Bond of the Metropolitan police. O'Connell again confirmed that they were members of the Provisional IRA and made a set of demands that, he assured Bond, would secure the safe release of the hostages: A car to take them to London airport and a plane to fly them safely to Dublin. Mr. Bond refused to give in to the IRA demands and insisted on the release of the hostages–despite the ASU's threats to execute Mr. and Mrs. Mathews. O'Connell warned Bond by saying, "Do not attempt to break in."

To avoid compromising aliases, and the weapon and ammunition storage safe houses they had been using, should they be captured, the four ASU men burned all their forged identity documentation in a metal waste bin. The stand off between the IRA ASU and the Metropolitan police had started.

The events of the night had made the TV news and inside the apartment the ASU watched the coverage with some reported amusement. The BBC news footage showed the bullet-riddled Flying Squad car and Mr. Mathews later said that the ASU members had laughed at the scene on TV as the police, so they stated, had shot some of the holes in the vehicle themselves.

In Oxfordshire, the news was also being watched by the wife and sister-in-law of a sleeping Peter Imbert. Convinced that Operation Combo would not result in any action on a weekend, Imbert and his wife had made a visit to his brother and sister-in-law for the weekend. Imbert was taking a nap on the couch while the TV news reported the events of the evening. This was causing a heated debate between the two women watching both the news and the slumbering Imbert. Peter Imbert later described the scene: "I was having a sleep at my brother and sister-in-law's house in the north Oxfordshire countryside as we'd gone there for a weekend off. The news came on and it said there had been another terrorist incident in London. Apparently, my wife and my sister-in-law debated whether or not to wake me up. My wife said, 'no, he needs the sleep,' but my sister-in-law said 'he'll murder you if you don't wake him up!' But, before they could make a decision, my immediate boss [Chief Superintendent] Jim Nevill had telephoned–he knew where I was staying–and asked me if I could come back to London. He said they had done a shooting, had been chased and were holed up in flat in Balcombe Street and had hostages."

Nevill and Imbert discussed the logistics of getting the ASU out of the flat, and into custody, and freeing the hostages. The two experienced officers felt it should be a straightforward exercise that would not take too long. Imbert suggested to Nevill that as he was on the scene, he should talk them out of the flat that night, and then Imbert would come down to Paddington Green police station first thing Sunday morning to start the interrogations. Imbert and Nevill were very pleased and relieved that Combo had paid off as hoped. The Met had been desperate to capture the ASU and now it appeared they had them trapped in 22b Balcombe Street and would soon be pressing charges on the group. The siege was just what they could have hoped for and Imbert would later say, "that was our good luck! We'd had almost two years of bad luck, like a bad dream reaching out to get them and they'd already gone." This sentiment was also echoed the night of December 6th by Deputy Assistant Commissioner Peter Walton who stated, "we have got them surrounded in the way we want."

With logistics agreed for the following day between the two senior bomb squad officers, Imbert retired for the night with the comforting knowledge that the almost year-and-a-half hunt for one of the IRA's most prolific ASU's was drawing to a close. There remained the issue of extracting both the IRA men and the civilian hostages alive, if possible, but confidence was high that this could be achieved. It was important to the men of the Bomb Squad to have all the occupants of the flat out safely and in one piece. Imbert's personal motivation to secure the release of the hostages, together with that of Jim Nevill, was high and for a good set of reasons, "the immediate thing was to get them out, keep them all alive and I mean the terrorists as well as the hostages," said Imbert, "we wanted the hostages out alive as they were innocent people. We wanted the terrorists out alive so that we could interrogate them about the offences which had been committed–the murders, the attempted murders and all the damage they'd caused–and get them before a court. I was also very much aware that if we got them out and into custody, that was the end of the IRA campaign at that particular time. It had probably been the most vicious terrorist campaign that we had had in this country during the 20th century. They had been calculated killers."

Not everyone in the Met shared Imbert's opinion regarding getting the hostages out alive. Sir Robert Mark considered Mr. and Mrs. Mathews as "expendable." The view among the senior leadership of the Met, heading into the siege, was that the sacrifice of the hostages, and the terrorists, would be preferable to violating the prevailing government principle against allowing the use of violence, by terror groups, to extort a desired outcome, while at the same time compromising the law enforcement position. They had carried this logic through to the point where there was an unwritten rule that, if any senior Metropolitan police officers were captured by the IRA, they were to be "written off."[4] However, Sir Robert and the other senior Met officers were going to have to play a careful balancing act over the course of the following days to avoid handing the IRA a televised martyrdom of the ASU.

Following the practiced hostage protocol that had worked well enough for the Met at the Spaghetti House Siege, the police team went into action. A careful, but "noisy" evacuation of the occupants of the apartments above, below and around 22b was carried out that evening, including people from the flats on the opposite side of the street: Their apartments would be used to house the sharpshooters from the Met's Blue Beret's–the armed response and firearms training team of SO19. Over thirty people were evacuated and moved to temporary accommodation in order to free up space for the tactical operation teams, the hostage negotiators, and to protect the public. This act would also prevent the press from using one or more of the apartments to observe the unfolding drama, thereby securing the outer containment zone, unlike the September siege at the Spaghetti House where the Met had failed to adequately control the press access to the scene.

Police dog handlers took "hard nosed dogs" into the apartment beneath 22b to make a lot of "unfriendly" noises. The dogs were encouraged to bark and growl so that the ASU could clearly hear their presence. The combined commotion coming from all around 22b served to convince the ASU they were at risk of being overrun. They gathered bare essentials from the rest of the flat and blockaded themselves, and their two hostages, in the living room of the apartment. The Met would not know this for several hours and continued at act as though the ASU had full run of the apartment.

Outside, the area was contained by setting up barriers at each end of the street. Motorists in the area were required to abandon their vehicles to the care of the police, for the duration of the siege or until given the all-clear to collect them again. A mobile command post was positioned near the junction with Ivor place, acting as a barrier at one end of the street. The other end of the street, just south of the cross road junction with Dorset Square, was blocked off by a barrier manned by uniformed officers. The press would be required to remain behind this barrier, some distance from number 22b. Many TV cameras and telephoto lenses were trained down the street to monitor the events outside the building, but the press had been denied the chance to get closer to the hostage scene. The police became concerned about the flow of uncontrolled information, potentially being relayed to the ASU via the media coverage, until they could gain and maintain tactical command of the situation, which would take a several hours to establish, and so in order to centralize the press interest and act as a focal point for all information flow from the Met to the press, Jim Nevill commandeered space at the British Rail headquarters building, opposite the nearby Marylebone Rail Station, to act as the overall tactical command post. Press conferences and briefings to the media would take place from this building, leaving the mobile command post, situated in Balcombe Street, to operate unencumbered without the necessary, but tactically risky task, of liaising with the press. Space was also commandeered in the Portman Arms Pub as a rest area for the officers near the occupied flat, a move that would prove popular with the police and the publican, as his pub had been cut off from trade with the outside world until the siege was over.

The Met started the process of communications with the various outside agencies needed to support their efforts, should the siege become a protracted event. Messages were sent to the Home Office to have a liaison officer in attendance, as the members of the ASU were assumed to be Irish origin and therefore the Home Office would be required to deal with any international ramification of the siege, especially if the Met decided on a "tactical" resolution to the standoff. In that regard, contact was made with the Ministry of Defense, and arrangements made to deploy the Special Air Service [SAS], the army's elite Special Forces regiment. At this point in time, the British public had little previous exposure to this very secretive clandestine operations group, but the IRA knew them well through numerous clashes north and south of the Irish border. Their reputation was one of ruthless efficiency. Following the request for deployment the SAS would build a mock up of the balcony and living room of the flat at their London barracks in Chelsea after obtaining floor plan layouts for the apartment. This would be used to practice storming the building, should they be required to do so at the behest of the police, or the government.

The psychiatric team, headed by Dr. Peter Scott from Bethlehem Maudsley Hospital, deployed with much success during the Spaghetti House Siege, was put on standby for duty on the following day. The relationship between Dr. Scott and the eventual team of negotiators would be an important factor in the eventual outcome of the siege. Dr. Scott, described by Sir Robert Mark as a "gentle, though firm and determined man," would provide a much needed check and balance for the police team as the days unfolded.

The Spaghetti House experience gained by The Yard's C7 Technical Support Branch would also play an important part in the unfolding Balcombe Street episode. The team was preparing to install video and audio surveillance equipment into the flat in order to provide covert tactical intelligence to the negotiation team. However, to do this undetected, they would need to know the overall layout of the apartment, such as the placement of furniture in relation to adjoining apartment walls, and an overall footprint of the floor plan layout. To gain this information, they interviewed neighbors, family friends, and members of the family for recollections of the layout or better still, any photographs taken recently inside the flat. The C7 team could not proceed without this vital information, as any discovery by the ASU of the surveillance equipment would undermine the negotiators position. They were a confident team, as their efforts had basically resulted in the collapse of the Spaghetti House Siege earlier in the year. During the night, the C7 team would also tap the phone line to the flat to monitor, and if required block, calls into and out of 22b. The press, family members and well wishers had all tried to call the Mathews, and tactically, the Met could not afford to have the ASU making any calls out of the flat to the press, or GHQ for other cells to initiate a rescue, diversionary tactics, or a parallel hostage situation.

With the inside and outside areas contained as best they could for the evening, the Met's last act that night was to place high intensity spotlights in the street outside the apartment building, with the beams trained on the outward facing windows of 22b. With the serenading of the barking dogs below and the illumination of bright lights, the occupants of 22b settled down for what was to be a long first night confined to the living room of the small flat. Mrs. Mathews later said that she "prayed like hell. I never thought we'd get out of there alive." Mr. Mathews described how they "smoked and smoked" through the night, drinking small bottles of mixer drinks, but the ASU members did not touch any of the available alcohol in the drinks cabinet. The ASU also did not put down their guns the first night, according to the Mathews', and kept them trained on the couple the whole time. While not physically abused, Mr. Mathews said that they did speak "roughly" to the couple. John Mathews was forced to stretch out on the couch, bound hand and foot, while his wife, likewise bound, was forced to curl up in an armchair. The ASU men sat on the floor and would later take turns napping in pairs, while the others kept guard.

John Mathews, a Chief Inspector in the Royal Mail postal service, based at Paddington in London, was regarded by some of his colleges as "unflappable" and was accustomed to dealing with "emergencies and major problems." He had also been called as "cool as a cucumber" when faced with tension. This coolness nearly cost the hostages their lives, according to John Mathews' later accounts of that night. He attempted to engage the ASU members in conversation to try and discover why they [the hostages] were being treated as they were, and what the ASU were trying to achieve. He stated that this was almost a "fatal mistake" as the ASU members became very angry and started blaming the British for everything "that had gone wrong" in the world. The couple did not dare to try to reason with the ASU again, but resorted to "speaking only when spoken to," a behavior that would work well for the couple as events unfolded.

The Met forensic team had also been busy, collecting evidence from the stolen car and the holdall of guns and magazines. The stolen Cortina had been removed for fingerprint and ballistic evidence and the holdall would be examined extensively for prints in the hope of identifying someone on record, as that would give the police a chance to formulate a profile of who may be in the flat with the hostages.

Later that evening, Officer A and his partner were asked to meet Sir Robert Mark, the Met Commissioner, in Rossmore Road to show him the shot-up SPG van. "He had a look at it, had a look at the bullet holes in it and the broken glass," recalled Officer A, "he had a look inside and was 'impressed' by all the abandoned Pepsi Cola cans and crisp packets, said something to the effect of 'well done' and that was that."

The chief architect of Operation Combo, Detective Sergeant David Waghorn, was at home on the evening of December 6th as the events of the chase and the siege broke on the news. He called into the Bomb Squad's operation room, where Chief Inspector Graham Ison was directing and coordinating Operation Combo that evening. Waghorn simply asked Graham Ison, who had been a big supporter of the young Detective and his theory about the movements of the ASU, if Combo had been operational that night. He was told that yes, it had been. "That was very satisfying to know," said David Waghorn.

There had been a few casualties from the events of the evening, but no one had been seriously hurt. The only people requiring medial treatment were three women, from the Balcombe Street apartment building, that had to be taken to the nearby hospital suffering from shock as a result of hearing the gunfire in Rossmore Road.

Back at Paddington Green police station, the evening was over for John Purnell and Phil McVeigh. The significance of what they had helped to achieve had started to sink in with the two officers after returning to the police station to fill out their paperwork. They had, unarmed and without backup, given chase to one of the IRA's most valuable operational assets and, through their sheer determination, had ensured their eventual capture and removal from active status. The shock at how close they had come to being killed had also began to set in, but not to the extent they had expected, as John Purnell would later describe, "interestingly enough, we were okay after it was all over that night. We weren't too bad; in fact we went back to the station, had a cup of tea and wrote out our statements."

Purnell and McVeigh talked about the events of the night as they pulled their statements together. They made a commitment to tell the story exactly as it unfolded, and while not motivated by recognition from their peers, they did discuss the events of that night in terms of whether they would get some from of official commendation. "I said to Phil McVeigh afterwards that if this comes off," said Purnell, "we've captured four terrorists who have killed a lot of people, so I suspect we would likely get some sort of Commissioner's Commendation. If you capture four terrorists it's almost inevitable. What I also said to Phil was that we had to tell the events as they had happened. We didn't want to flower it at all, we just put down exactly what we did and what happened, just simply that."

Statements completed, Purnell recalled calling his wife on the phone. "I remember ringing my wife and asking her if she'd seen the TV news. She asked me why I wanted to know. I said to her 'some terrorists are holed up in Balcombe Street.' She said, 'yes, I saw that!' I told her I had been involved." John Purnell paused in his retelling of the story to the author, and then finished his commentary, "she just asked when I was coming home."

NOTES

1. The member of the SPG team interviewed for the book has requested anonymity for himself and his team members. Out of respect for this request, I will refer to him as Officer A.

2. This should not be construed as a commentary on Officer A's marksmanship. As part of the research for this book, the author took a one day training course on handguns under the expert guidance of Jon Green, director of training for the Massachusetts based Gun Owners Action League. Even with the absence of time pressure and incoming shots, the author can attest to how difficult it is to hit a target consistently with a .38 revolver.

3. The pub is now called the Hobgoblin.

4. In his autobiography, Sir Robert recalled he was asked what would happen if politicians or cabinet ministers were taken captive. His response was "Ask them if they would like a few more."

doi:10.1300/J173v08n01_05

FIGURE 1. The shattered Horse and Groom pub, Guilford, after the October 5, 1974 attack by the IRA. Four people were killed and 50 injured.

Source: Empics–Press Association. Used with permission.

FIGURE 2. Aftermath of the explosion at a telephone exchange at New Compton Street on the night of December 17, 1974. The ASU attacked a total of three exchanges that night.

Source: Empics–Press Association. Used with permission.

FIGURE 3. December 19, 1974. Selfridges, in Oxford Street, after the explosion of a 100-pound car bomb the ASU parked next to the store.

Source: Empics–Press Association. Used with permission.

FIGURE 4. Scott's Restaurant, in Mount Street, site of one bomb attack and the shooting incident on the night of December 6th, 1975, that resulted in the pursuit of the ASU and the start of the siege.

Source: Monica Hatch. Used with permission.

FIGURE 5. The steps leading down from Rossmore Road to Taunton Place. The ASU ran down the steps to escape the police.

Source: Monica Hatch. Used with permission.

FIGURE 6. John Purnell, GM QPM, in February 2007, on the steps to Taunton Place looking down Boston Place, where he chased a lone member of the ASU on the night of December 6th, 1975.

Source: Monica Hatch. Used with permission.

FIGURE 7. John and Sheila Mathews, photographed at a dance in 1974.

Source: Empics–Press Association. Used with permission.

FIGURE 8. Outside view of the siege flat in Balcombe Street. Number 22b is on the left on the second floor, shown with the shared balcony.

Source: Monica Hatch. Used with permission.

FIGURE 9. Floor plan layout of 22b Balcombe Street.

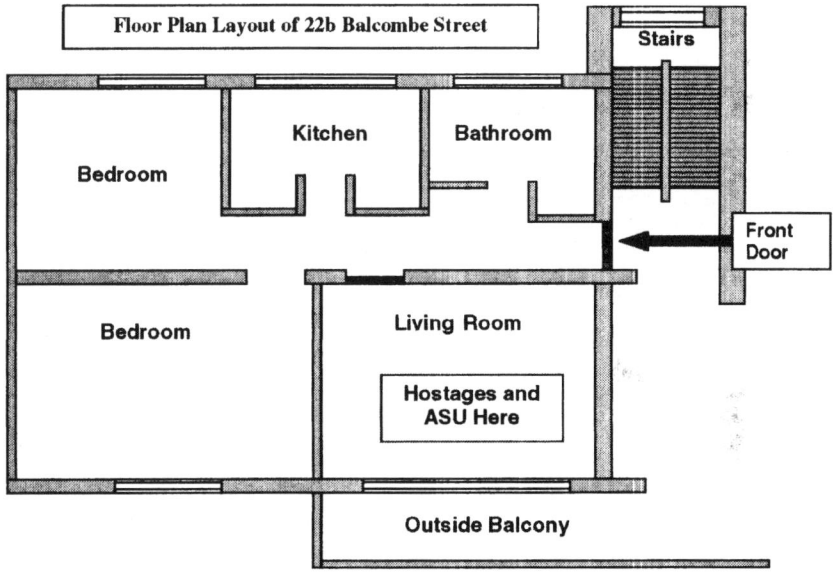

Source: Steven P. Moysey

FIGURE 10. The Met kept the media confined outside the siege area. View looking north up Balcombe Street from the barrier south of Dorset Square.

Source: Empics–Press Association. Used with permission.

FIGURE 11. Police Commissioner, Sir Robert Mark, discussing the siege with uniform officers at Balcombe Street.

Source: Empics–Press Association. Used with permission.

FIGURE 12. Detective Superintendent Peter Imbert on the field telephone with "Tom" during the siege.

Source: Peter Imbert. Used with permission.

FIGURE 13. View looking North up Balcombe Street, showing the sight screen. The officer in the doorway is holding one of the flags used to signal to other officers leaving or entering the building.

Source: Empics–Press Association. Used with permission.

FIGURE 14. Wide angle view of the siege flat, circled on the left, and the flat used by Imbert and Nevill, on the right, at 20 Dorset Square.

Source: Monica Hatch. Used with permission.

Chapter 5

The Siege, December 7th-12th, 1975

SUNDAY DECEMBER 7TH

Balcombe Street is a relatively quiet residential area of central London. It runs North-South and is approximately one mile long, bordering Marylebone rail station to its west and quaint mews lined streets to its east. The street itself is largely made up of town houses, many of which have been converted into apartment buildings. The street is also linked to several fashionable areas of London, such as Dorset Square. One block west of the Dorset Square crossroad junction with the street is an imposing building, number 222 Marylebone Road. Originally built as a 19th century railroad hotel at the height of the steam era, the building in 1975 was the headquarters for the nationalized rail service, British Rail. Being conveniently located close to the barricade erected by the Metropolitan police to cordon off the south end of Balcombe Street, the building was to be used by the Met to hold press briefings and as a base for the senior leadership team. The cordon at the north end of the street was formed by the mobile command post placed there by the Met as their forward command base. In addition to the command post, one other vehicle was positioned in the street outside the apartment building. A private collector had an WWI four-wheeled armored vehicle, minus the engine, on display as a monument outside his home in nearby Huntsworth Mews. This was wheeled into Balcombe Street by the proud

[Haworth co-indexing entry note]: "The Siege, December 7th-12th, 1975." Moysey, Steven P. Co-published simultaneously in *Journal of Police Crisis Negotiations* (The Haworth Press, Inc.) Vol. 8, No. 2, 2008, pp. 161-233; and: *The Road to Balcombe Street: The IRA Reign of Terror in London* (Steven P. Moysey) The Haworth Press, Inc., 2008, pp. 161-233. Single or multiple copies of this article are available for a fee from The Haworth Document Delivery Service [1-800-HAWORTH, 9:00 a.m. - 5:00 p.m. (EST). E-mail address: docdelivery@haworthpress.com].

Available online at http://jpcn.haworthpress.com
doi:10.1300/J173v08n02_01

owner to act as an armored shelter for the forward officers, should the ASU decide to start shooting into the street. The armored car was to be reminiscent of the Siege of Sydney Street, back in 1911; later called the battle of Stepney. The presence of the vehicle, despite its obvious vintage, led some observers to speculate that the SAS were already on the scene, which in fact was the case, but they were in plainclothes to scope out the siege site and not inside armored vehicles.

As of the Sunday morning, the Met were still unsure as to the exact number of IRA members in the flat. They believed there were at least three gunmen in the apartment, with some eyewitnesses stating that they had seen four men run into the apartment building. The Met could not discount that fact that one of the ASU may have slipped away during the foot chase, but Purnell and McVeigh had stated they had tracked four men–once they met up again at the junction of Ivor Place–who had fled down Balcombe Street toward number 22. However, as Purnell had stated on the Saturday night, he had not seen the men enter the apartment building, so there would remain a level of uncertainty regarding the exact strength in numbers of the ASU. The Met also knew they were armed with handguns, but did not know if they had any explosives or hand grenades in their possession. They also had no positive identification on the hostage takers; however, Chief Superintendent Jim Nevill would tell the press later morning that some of the officers involved in the chase did get "a good look" at the fleeing ASU team.[1] Detective Chief Superintendent Nigel Reid, head of Enfield CID and Commander Roy Habershon, head of The Yard's Bomb Squad, had spent several hours with the police involved in the Saturday night chase, in an effort to build up a picture of who they had trapped in the apartment.

Sunday would start early for the police and the press. The Met, from the outset of the siege, knew how important it would be to establish a co-operative relationship with the press. The media would have an important role in bringing the armed standoff, so the Met believed, to a satisfactory conclusion, so as part of the effort to control everything the hostage takers would receive in the way of information, regarding police activity, securing the cooperation of the media would be critical, even if this meant the Met had take advantage, at times, of the interest the media would have in the case. At 3:00am Sunday morning, the Met held the first press conference of the day at 222 Marylebone Road British Rail HQ. Sir Robert Mark, the Met Commissioner, led the police team addressing the media. Sir Robert would adopt a hard policy toward the ASU in his public communications with the press, a position he would maintain throughout the siege, in the full knowledge that, at that point, the ASU still had TV and radio access. At the early morning press conference, Sir Robert left no one present in any doubt of his position toward the IRA men. He referred to the ASU as "ordinary, vulgar criminals" whose only destination would to be to a "cell in Brixton prison" and not a plane to Dublin. Sir Robert would also later say that the ASU had ended up in number 22b by "their own stupidity."

It was clear that the police were prepared for a lengthy standoff. Despite his private views that the hostages were expendable, his public statements that morning focused on the primary concern of avoiding bloodshed and being patient to ensure the safe recovery of the two hostages. Sir Robert stated that they were prepared to surround the flat until "these people see reason." When asked about supplying food to the hostages, and the ASU, Sir Robert emphatically stated that no food whatsoever would be sent into the flat. Sir Robert elaborated, in that a human being could survive on water alone for some considerable time and presumably the ASU had access to water.

The press conference ended with an interesting request from the police to the media. Sir Robert urged the press to be careful what they wrote and broadcast, as it was to be assumed that the ASU had access to the TV and radio. He was also mindful of what the IRA could do with certain information and this would mark the beginning of the Met's concerns about a counter action by the Provisionals in an effort to rescue their top assets trapped in number 22b. He asked the media to review what the police communicated to them, and that if they felt the police had given any information that was inappropriate for sharing with the general public, he implored the media to not report the information and to point out the error to the police.

The statement made by Sir Robert, regarding the water supply situation in the flat, was based on an assumption by the Met that the ASU did, in fact, have free access to the kitchen and bathroom, and therefore, a supply of drinking water and available bathroom facilities. The Met did not realize, at that stage in the day, that the four ASU gunmen had confined themselves, and their two hostages, to the small living room in the flat, which had only two access points–through the doorway into the interior hallway of the flat, or through the doors onto the balcony. The lack of access to toilet facilities would quickly become an issue inside the apartment. The men had been urinating into empty soft drink bottles, while Mrs. Mathews was in a very distressing situation, sharing the room with her husband and four hostile men. Her discomfort and embarrassment would grow by the hour. The six adults had also been deprived of water, other than the short supply they had in terms of mixer drinks and so they had a worsening spiral of a lack of toilet facilities and a shortage of water.

The belief that the ASU had the full run of the flat would also cause the Technical Support Team of C7 a series of dilemmas. They had several options regarding the placement of the fiber optic TV and audio probes they planned to insert through the walls from adjacent apartments. The probes would have to be placed so that they could see and hear the activity in the flat, but at the same time they needed to remain undetected by the ASU. Positioning the probes would be a critical factor in gaining intelligence from inside the flat that would be both usable and actionable by the negotiation team, once this was established and operational.

As part of the C7 assessment of the flat's layout, neighbors and friends were questioned on the location and placement of furniture inside the apartment. During these interviews, it became clear to the team that the ASU had been bluffing regarding the fact that a child was in the apartment. Neighbors confirmed the Mathews, who had two adult daughters that lived away from home, lived alone in the flat, which they had moved into about one year earlier. The child story had been a deliberate ploy, told to the Met officer on the phone with the ASU Saturday night, to fog the tactical focus of any armed response unit that may have deployed against the hostage takers.

Detective Inspector Ron Chapman had been out at a social function the night of December 6th, and had gone to bed without hearing the news of the chase and the beginning of the siege. He received a phone call early Sunday morning and was requested to make his way to the British Rail headquarters building commandeered as an operations center. Ron Chapman's role was to take over from Detective Chief Inspector Dave Monday, who had been manning the incident room all night. Chapman's was to run the incident room from 10:00am to 10:00pm when he would then hand over control of the room to Dave Monday for the night shift. The primary function of the incident room was to lead the investigation into the events that led up to the chase and siege, and to coordinate on-site support for the negotiation team. The officers involved would interview witnesses to obtain statements, collate the evidence and ensure the preservation of the integrity of the evidence as it was collected. They were also responsible for collecting statements from the officers who took part in the events of Saturday night.

At approximately 7:30am, Deputy Assistant Commissioner Ernest Bond called the Mathews' telephone in the flat. O'Connell, the ASU's commanding officer and, by default, the group spokesman, answered the phone. O'Connell repeated the group's demands for a car to London airport and a flight to Dublin. Mr. Bond again reiterated the Met's position, demanding the safe release of the hostages before any considerations could be made to the hostage takers demands. The call lasted ninety seconds and ended with O'Connell telling Bond, when asked again about the safe release of the hostages, "we'll see about that." Fifteen minutes later at 7:45am, a brief press conference was again held at 222 Marylebone Road. Mr. Bond related the details of the conversation with the ASU and informed the press that the police would be contacting the ASU again in about one hour's time. Bond urged the press not to call the Mathews' flat as this was creating difficulties for the police, as C7 were swamped with calls attempting to get through to the Mathews' phone number. The Met were also mindful that the ASU had been attempting to call the press from the flat.

Superintendent Peter Imbert arrived on the scene of the siege after driving back in the early hours from his weekend away in Oxfordshire. During the drive, he had heard the news broadcast where the commissioner had made his "vulgar criminals" commentary on the IRA men in the flat. That commentary would later prove to be a challenge to Imbert. Peter Imbert later stated that on the Sunday morning he was "surprised to find they [ASU] were still in the apartment!" and not in custody in prison ready for interrogation. As one of the Met's Bomb Squad officers that had been tracking the ASU since 1974, Imbert was rightly expecting to be a part of the team involved in the delicate task of talking with the ASU in an effort to end the standoff without bloodshed. However, the invitation to participate in the negotiations did not come in quite the way Imbert had expected, as he later related to the author: "When I arrived on the scene, I was met by the Commissioner [Sir Robert Mark] and the Assistant Commissioner. Sir Robert said to me words to the effect of 'now, you're not a bad bloke, Imbert, you talk to them and get them out!' But, he'd already gone public saying that they were nothing but common criminals and they were going nowhere except to prison, so I'd got nothing left to bargain with! Well, I had to think of something else–I had to think about getting on a level with them so that they trusted me."

The primary negotiation team, comprising of Jim Nevill and Peter Imbert, would need a base of operations to work from away from the forward command post in Balcombe Street and the press briefing area of 222 Marylebone Road. Deputy Assistant Commissioner Wilford Gibson had secured an apartment in a building directly across the street from number 22, on the corner of Balcombe Street and Taunton Mews–number

20 Dorset Square. The room was on the ground floor and afforded a reasonable view of the balcony and bedroom window of the siege flat on the second floor across the street. Peter Imbert, getting into the mindset of the negotiator and thinking tactually, did not favor the selection when shown the room by Gibson. Imbert later recalled, "Mr. Gibson said, 'we've got you a room from which you can work.' It was the ground floor room on the corner. I said, 'well look, I think it would be better if I can look down on them, if we could get one of the upper floor rooms.' One then had the psychological advantage of looking down on one's prey."

Gibson, who had studied the psychology of hostage negotiation, agreed with Imbert's assessment. Arrangements were made to secure a second room, on the third floor, which afforded Imbert the professed desire to look down, like a circling hawk, on his IRA prey. All the frustrations of the past months, searching for the ASU, would have to be held back. All the recollections of the dead and maimed at the bombing sites they had visited, the postmortems they had had to attend for identification continuity evidence purposes, the broken and destroyed property, and the shattered lives of those who had lost loved ones, could not leak through into their voices. The images of a dead PC Stephen Tibble, the funeral of Captain Goad, and the grieving Rosemary McWhirter–all of these painful and emotional memories had to be suppressed if Imbert and Nevill were to be successful in their roles of the primary negotiators. Whatever personal feelings they may have had toward their long-term adversaries, now surrounded and holding two people hostage across the road would have to be put on hold. Their primary task was to establish a rapport with O'Connell on the phone and build whatever trust they could between the two sides. "Creating trust with the ASU for me meant talking to them with no trace of panic in my voice," recalled Imbert, "keeping things cool and calm. One needed to do that not only for the terrorists, but also for the hostages and for all of the police officers on duty around the area."

However, the Mathews' phone had become an increasing tactical liability to the Met. The press and news media had repeatedly called the number, as had numerous members of the Mathews' friends and family, watching or hearing the hostage drama unfold on the radio and TV news. The phone also offered the opportunity for the ASU to call the outside world, if C7 didn't intercept the call in time. Based on the tactical needs of the situation, the Met decided to disconnect the main phone line after they had told the ASU of the decision and gained their agreement. It would serve no use to the Met's cause to have the ASU upset at the disconnection of their only lifeline to the outside world. Arbitrary disconnection of the phone would not have helped in the building of trust with the ASU, which would be essential in any subsequent negotiations, and driven a wedge between the two groups looking to establish at the very least a basic working relationship.

Base of negotiations established, Imbert and Nevill's next task was to find a replacement for the phone line as a means of secure communication between the ASU and number 20 Dorset Square. Radios were ruled out, as the Met had found out at the Spaghetti House siege that amateurs, and some of the press, had found it relatively easy to intercept transmissions on the unscrambled police frequency. Such an interception, at Balcombe Street, which unlike the Spaghetti House incident involved highly trained IRA operatives, could have been a definite tactical advantage to any other IRA cells in the area planning a counterstrike operation. The Met were genuinely concerned at such a prospect and were therefore being ultra-careful when it came to securing communications. They needed to control the flow of information into and out of the flat, in the same way they needed the covert electronic surveillance intelligence that they could not, under any circumstance, allow the hostage takers to know that they were being monitored. That said, the Met, despite Sir Robert's "vulgar criminal" comment, were well aware they were dealing with a group of highly trained IRA field operatives who would have been well briefed about revealing as little as possible in the close confines of the flat, in anticipation of being bugged by police surveillance teams. The only means available to the police in terms of a secure, scan proof communications tool was a direct hard wired field telephone. This would have a base unit in each location, powered by a set of internal batteries and would be directly connected via a transmission wire. The Met had two pairs of field telephone systems available and arrangements were made to bring one pair of the sets to Balcombe Street.

At around 11:30am, Jim Nevill addressed the ASU using a hand held megaphone from the street below the balcony of number 22b. Nevill informed them that, in the best interests of confidentially, the police wanted to disconnect the regular phone line and supply the ASU with a field telephone hand set. After a short deliberation, the men signaled their approval to Nevill. Officers in the apartment above 22b lowered the handset, connected to the transmission wire, to the flat below. The ASU opened the balcony window and a man in a maroon sweater [O'Connell] was observed as he pulled the handset into the flat, closing the doors behind him. The C7 team disconnected the regular phone line, leaving the field unit as the only means of direct two-way communication, which closed a tactical gap in the Met's strategy.

The police initiated contact with the ASU over the new field telephone. Imbert called and O'Connell answered at the other end. They agreed on what to call each other–Imbert and Nevill would use their first names, Peter and Jim. O'Connell was asked his name and gave the reply, "Tom." Probed by Imbert for the names of the other members of the group, Tom, rather tongue-in-cheek told Imbert they were called "Mick" and "Paddy."[2] So it was Tom, Mick, and Paddy in the flat with the Mathews. The negotiating team laughed–at least the ASU appeared to have a sense of humor. Imbert asked if he could speak with Mrs. Mathews and she was placed on the phone. Imbert asked her how she and Mr. Mathews were being treated. "Well," she responded and Imbert noted that she spoke with "calmness and self possession." Mrs. Mathews told Imbert she was in some pain, due to the uncomfortable position she was being kept, and the fact that she had received some dental work some days before that was troubling her. Imbert agreed to send her some painkillers, which were lowered to Tom later from the balcony above 22b. However, as the minutes ticked by on her conversation with Imbert, Tom became increasingly irritated and eventually took the phone away from her. Neither of the hostages would be allowed to speak on the field telephone again.

Imbert and Tom continued to converse during the course of the afternoon, circling each other like a pair of professional boxers, sizing each other up, probing, testing. At one point, Imbert told Tom, "either come out or stick it out, but you've got to come out at some point." Imbert reminded Tom that they were "both involved in the situation." He was right, as both Imbert and Nevill, in consultation with Dr. Peter Scott, would bear the psychological burden of the Mathews' safety. What if their strategy and tactics were wrong? What if they misinterpreted or misread a statement or, worse, used an inappropriate expression that triggered the ASU to take a violent course of action in the flat? Both sides had entered into a high stake battle of wits, and both sides had a lot to lose. The lives of the Mathews, and to a lesser extent the lives of the ASU, were literally in the hands of Nevill and Imbert and they desperately wanted to get them out alive. Imbert continued to press Tom, "when you come out, I don't want you to do so with more on your conscience." Tom replied, "if anything does happen [to the hostages], it's your fault . . ."

The conversations that Sunday tended to gravitate toward the ASU requesting food and cigarettes. Imbert, in a softly-softly approach initially refused to entertain any such requests. The key thing both Nevill and Imbert needed to focus on was building trust and developing a relationship, as best as they could, with Tom as the principle contact with the ASU. Butler would later tell Nevill and Imbert that he had been the voices of both Mick and Paddy. Dougherty and Duggan would keep relatively quiet–they had both been seen, and heard, by a credible witness at a crime scene: The assassination of Ross McWhirter. Rosemary McWhirter had seen their faces and heard them speak. But, at that stage the police still did not know who was in the flat. Forensic evidence would change that situation later that day.

At the police training college at Peel House in Hendon, Superintendent George Howlett had a strange request presented to him in his office by the supplies storekeeper.[3] The storekeeper, a man who would obsessively care for the flow of material into and out of his stores, said he had received a requisition from the "Balcombe Street team" that had him scratching his head. The request was for the training school to send the siege scene six pairs of plimsolls in a number of different sizes. The storekeeper was concerned at this unusual request for gym shoes to be sent to a crime scene, and so asked Howlett who was going to sign the requisition to allow the plimsolls out of his stores and, most irregularly, off the school premises! Howlett, suspecting what the shoes would be used for, signed the requisition and told the storekeeper to issue the requested footwear on the double! The bemused storekeeper issued the shoes, and would spend the following six months trying to reconcile his stock books, as he would never see the shoes again, something he would not forgive Howlett for in all the years he remained with the school. The rubber soled gym shoes were to be used by the team of officers from C7 that would later install the sensitive surveillance equipment, feeling that the gym shoes would make less sound than their regular street shoes.

With the negotiation team in place and operational, Imbert would take the day shift, while Nevill would keep up the pressure at night, the need for obtaining real time covert intelligence from inside the flat was now critical. The Technical Support teams of C7 officers were working out the best location for the TV and audio probes, based on the assumption that the ASU had free access to the entire flat. This assumption would be shattered in dramatic fashion.

Imbert was talking with Tom on the field telephone when an almost innocent, off-the-cuff comment from the ASU man made Imbert freeze in his tracks. Peter Imbert later describe that moment: "We'd heard accounts that somebody had been seen in the bedroom window and round the back we had officers observing, and one or two had said they had seen curtains move. So, when I was negotiating on Sunday morning I was under the impression that they [ASU] were covering the whole of the flat. And that's why our lads didn't storm in because they might have come into contact with them if they had gone through the front door. So, we thought they were in the whole of the flat. Then Tom said to me that Mrs. Mathews wanted a drink of water. I said 'well get her one then.' He said something like 'not bloody likely, your guys are all over the place!' "

Peter Imbert had to catch himself to prevent his surprise, at Tom's innocent statement, leaking through into his response. Without missing a beat, Imbert continued his conversation with Tom, momentarily letting the water request go unanswered, "one could have been so easily caught off balance and said in reply 'no they are not, you can get to the kitchen and we'll let you go back.' But it just immediately came to me if he is saying that they haven't got access to the kitchen, so the passageway is empty as well. That was a very important discovery, to know that they had confined themselves to that one room [The living room]. It was important to find that out. But, that was part of my job, to find out where they were, how many there were, what weapons they had got, and how determined they were in terms of their state of mind."

The importance of this discovery cannot be underestimated. The Met's evolving strategy of wait-and-see had received an enormous boost in terms of tactical control. Their whole thinking, tactically, would have to be revisited, as they now had a situation where the hostage takers had no access to bathroom facilities, and with a female hostage in the close confines of the living room, this was going to create a complicated dynamic. They also had no access to the kitchen, where water and food would have been available. The ASU's requests for food now fell into place–they had nothing available to them. There was also no place, except the floor, for them to sleep. All of these factors added up to one huge tactical advantage to the police, as the hostage takers would be totally dependant on the negotiation team for everything. The sanitation and water problem would rapidly deteriorate into an unacceptable situation to put the hostages through, so Imbert and Nevill made arrangements for the delivery of a chemical toilet and bottled drinking water to be brought to the scene. They would make the ASU wait until Imbert was ready, before delivering the supplies, as Imbert was not going to let the tactical superiority he had gained go unused from a psychological perspective. He would use that against the ASU once the armed units, being called into place to occupy the areas inside the apartment to totally contain the ASU, were firmly in place.

With Imbert's discovery regarding the location of the ASU inside the flat, the police could make plans to enter 22b to complete the containment of the ASU. However, in order to gain entry to the apartment, the police would have to avoid going directly in through the front door. They did not know if this had been barricaded, which in fact it had been by the ASU placing a chair behind the door. Breaking in through the front door would then alert the ASU that they were attempting to enter the flat and potentially create a confrontation. The ASU believed the police were already in the apartment, so they would need a more stealth-like approach to gaining ingress to the flat to maintain that belief. The answer was for the police to gain entry to the flat from a rear window accessed by a ladder from Boston Place. As well as being highly trained law enforcement officers, some of the Met had also picked up a few tricks from their adversaries in the housebreaking business, enabling a quick and relatively soundless entry through the rear window. Once inside, the police team would remove the chair from the front door and open it for the rest of the team to quietly enter the flat.

This vital piece of tactical intelligence, regarding the location of the ASU in the apartment, was rapidly disseminated to the C7 team, who went into action, stealthy equipped with their training school plimsolls, to deploy the surveillance equipment through the living room outside walls and from adjacent apartments. To do so they used a low speed, low vibration drilling system that had a penetration rate of less than one inch per hour–a slow and painstaking task of drilling slowly and carefully through the walls in areas, they hoped, the ASU would not notice. The flat still had electricity and the ASU were monitoring news reports on the TV, so that C7 could use the sound from the set as a cover for their drilling operations. Once in position, the TV probes and microphones would provide a source of real-time and recorded information for the use of the negotiation team and for analysis by the psychological team headed by Dr. Peter Scott. Over the following few days, Imbert and Nevill would need to be incredibly disciplined so as to not use, refer to or comment on anything gathered via the surveillance tools rather than directly communicated to them by the ASU over the field telephone. They were eavesdropping on the team of people they wanted to build up trust with, and revealing they were snooping on them would not help the trust process.

The forensic investigations conducted on the ASU's stolen Ford Cortina and the canvas holdall of weapons and gun parts, recovered after the chase on the Saturday night, revealed valuable information. Ballistic tests carried out on the Sten gun and the M1 carbine showed a match with rounds recovered from the scenes of the gun attacks on the Portman and Churchill Hotels, plus a match with rounds recovered from the attack on the Cavalry and Guards club. From these positive forensic matches, the Met could be sure they had indeed cornered the crew they had been chasing across London for over a year. Ballistic evidence, recovered from the Flying Squad car and SPG van in Rossmore Road, revealed a similar ballistic fingerprint to the caliber used in the assassination of Ross McWhirter the previous month–a .357 magnum. The question still remained as to the identity of the three or four men in the siege apartment. The only common theme in the investigation to date had been the forensic evidence linking the suspect Michael Wilson, suspect Z in the Met's crime scene finger print collection, to the Ross McWhirter shooting and the ASU bomb factory at Fairholme Road, discovered after the murder of PC Stephen Tibble. Forensic data gathered from the stolen Ford Cortina from December 6th, and the contents of the bag dropped in Rossmore Road, presented another link: Michael Wilson's prints were found on parts in the canvas bag and in the stolen car. The Met were excited at the findings, as this meant they now had a firm link between Wilson and the ASU's activities over the past fifteen months. Wilson was a key prize in the Met's search for the identities of the ASU team members, but to that point no matches had been made with any fingerprints in the Irish Garda databases. The key question for the Met was, at that point, where was Wilson? Was he trapped inside number 22b with the other ASU members, or had he escaped the net that past Saturday night and slipped away? If the Met did have Wilson contained in 22b, he had already proved how dangerous and ruthless he could be in the gunning down of Ross McWhirter in front of his wife, and the Met leadership speculated if he was in fact the leader of the London ASU. What would Wilson do regarding the hostages if things did not go the way the ASU wanted? Would he be prepared to use the hostages as a human shield and attempt a break out? He was a demonstrated cold-blooded killer, so if Wilson was in number 22b, the stakes were raised in terms of the potential for the standoff to spiral into violence. There was an equal concern regarding his possible escape. Would he be free to marshal other IRA resources for a reprisal raid on a soft target, stage another hostage standoff to free the ASU, or drive a bombing event to force the hand of the police? The issues of some kind of counterstrike by the IRA, either on the British mainland or in Northern Ireland, was a real concern to the Met, as Peter Imbert would later describe, "we were very worried about that happening. We thought there would be some attempt at distracting our attention elsewhere, like another siege or hostage situation, or a bombing. In fact we fully expected that to happen."

If Wilson was inside 22b, the Met wanted him out alive. He would be a big prize and his capture would be a blow to the ambitions of the IRA. But, the big questions still remained unanswered–who was he, where had he come from, and who was working with him?

With the Met's armed officers in position inside the apartment and controlling the space around the living room, Imbert would use this as a first psychological jab at the ASU, who had believed they had been cut off from the rest of the flat since the Saturday night. This information was delivered to the press in a briefing held at 222 Marylebone Road at 6:30pm. Commander Bill Fleming explained to the assembled media how the police had the living room under confinement, which had isolated the hostages and the IRA men to the one room. Commander Fleming added that the siege "could be over quicker than we thought." Sir Robert Mark also spoke with the media that Sunday evening. He stated that it was "sadly inevitable" that Mr. and Mrs. Mathews would suffer hardship under the Met's policy of "no surrender." He again emphasized that no food would be sent into the flat for either the hostages or the hostage takers, but assured the press that the police would be seeking medical advice, from time to time, to ensure the health of the hostages. The objective of the police, he explained, was to "sustain human life." Sir Robert closed his remarks with a carefully measured statement deliberately aimed at the hostage takers. "The best thing they can do," he stated, "is to give themselves up and come out." He was confident that they could avoid bloodshed, "we are in no hurry," he stated, adding that the IRA men were going nowhere and that they should realize their situation was hopeless.

Each of these direct and calculated comments would have been heard by the ASU on the radio or on the TV. The words being used by Sir Robert and other senior officers had a far harsher tone than the carefully paced words that Peter Imbert and Jim Nevill were attempting to use to engage with Tom, who was proving to be a difficult customer. One officer noted that Tom "had a gift for invective," as many of the exchanges with the Irishman were laden with four-letter expletives and were prone to being terminated abruptly.

The commentary to the press from the Met leadership was also being closely monitored by the psychological team. They were becoming concerned that the hard tones from Sir Robert may be working against a successfully negotiated outcome of the siege by making the ASU feel there really was no hope of any concessions, no matter how small. In Dr.

Scott's opinion, this could stall the development of a relationship with the negotiation team if they had to constantly reposition themselves against the statements made by the senior police leadership. The situation would require close monitoring as events unfolded.

Later that evening, Post Office executive Don Phillips offered his services to act as a go-between with the hostages, should the gunmen allow them to use the phone. Wisely, under the circumstances, Imbert and Nevill politely declined the offer and continued to act as the primary negotiation team, in consultation with Dr. Scott.

In another effort to establish psychological dependency in the ASU, Imbert had deliberately kept them in the dark about plans to provide a supply of bottled water and a means of solving the lack of sanitation facilities in the flat, having now firmly cut off any opportunity for the ASU to access the bathroom. Imbert called Tom on the field telephone and informed him that, out of concern for the comfort of the hostages, water and a portable chemical toilet was to be lowered to the balcony of 22b by officers in the apartment above. Tom asked Imbert to send in cigarettes with the supplies, but Imbert made a counter demand. He would send in cigarettes if Tom agreed to release Mrs. Mathews. The deal was refused. At approximately 10:00pm, under sniper cover, the supplies were lowered to the ASU from the flat above 22b and taken into the living room. It had been twenty four hours since anyone in the living room had access to proper toilet facilities. The chemical toilet was not ideal, as it would quickly become smelly in the close confines of the small room with six people depending on it, but given the situation it was a reasonable solution. There still remained the issue of a measure of privacy for Mrs. Mathews, a person with a nervous disposition at the best of times. Mrs. Mathews, in order to maintain some level of dignity, created a makeshift screen from a collapsible wooden clothes drying frame with a blanket draped over it. This was placed in front of the chemical toilet after it was positioned in one corner of the small room. Toilet in place, the occupants of 22b settled down for a second uncomfortable night, with John Mathews still confined to the couch, and Sheila Mathews curled up in an armchair. ASU and hostages alike were all beginning to feel hungry and in need of food.

There would be one final news broadcast from the briefing center on the Sunday evening. Deputy Assistant Commissioner Peter Walton, speaking with the BBC's Geoffrey Wareham, had messages that night for the hostages and the ASU. To the Mathews, he urged that they remain calm and trust that the IRA would eventually "see sense" and release them unharmed. To the ASU, he added that there was "no way out" for them, other than to surrender. Once again, the senior officers in the Met were using a term "surrender," that Nevill and Imbert were determined not to use with the ASU. Peter Imbert later stated that he and Jim Nevill avoided using the terms because it sounded like a taunt, "almost like crowing over a victory," as Imbert put it. The negotiation team would have their work cut out on message control with Tom, and a lack of food and increasing stress would start to exact a growing toll on the ASU in the close confines of the small living room of number 22b.

MONDAY DECEMBER 8TH

By Monday morning, there was a considerable uniformed and plain clothes police presence in and around the Balcombe Street area. Such a large police contingent in the location would demand careful logistical management if the Met were to maintain operational efficiency. One element of on-site logistics the Met have always taken very seriously is the welfare of the officers involved in any operation, and this would translate into keeping them all well fed and watered at Balcombe Street. Mobile police canteen vehicles were brought into the area to supply the officers with endless cups of tea and coffee during the cold December weather, and a good supply of bacon sandwiches and other staples of the 1970's British diet, to keep the police team from being hungry. The police also used the Chevron Club, in Dorset Square, as a place for the officers to get a hot meal, such as a traditional English breakfast of eggs, bacon, sausages and toast, again all washed down with steaming mugs of tea or coffee. A police force in a mid-winter siege situation, rather like an army, would rely on being fed and provided with hot beverages to keep effective.

There would be no bacon sandwiches, fried eggs, and hot cups of tea for the four men of the ASU and their two hostages inside number 22b. Monday morning arrived and all they had to look forward to was cold water, supplied courtesy of the Metropolitan Police, and an increasingly uncomfortable environment which was, with six adults in close confinement, becoming somewhat unpleasant, a situation not helped by the odor of the chemical toilet. The small living room still had electricity for the lights and TV and mains gas for the gas fire that heated the room, but the lack of food was becoming a problem. No one inside the flat had eaten since the Saturday evening, so for at least thirty six hours they had all gone without food, and while food was becoming an increasingly desirous commodity, the ASU, under considerable psychological and physical stress, were craving cigarettes. The lack of available cigarettes to the group–Mr. Mathews had said that the first night they "smoked and smoked"–would be an additional factor in the increasing stress level the ASU were exposed to, and for Imbert and Nevill to deal with. The police negotiation team wanted Tom, and the others, to be as calm and rational as possible, but with increasing hunger levels and nicotine cravings, maintaining a calm and rational discourse over the field telephone would be an increasing challenge to the Met team.

Dr. Peter Scott and his team reviewed the recorded surveillance material and the tapes of the field telephone conversations with the ASU, which primarily featured either Imbert or Nevill talking with Tom. There were occasions where one or two other voices were noted on the ASU end of the line, but these voices would defer to an off-line decision maker in any conversations with the Met team. Dr. Scott was acutely aware of the knife-edge balancing act the negotiation team was performing and, from a tactical standpoint, he needed to feed the negotiators a psychological assessment of the ASU's state of mind and likely reaction to pressure levels, no matter how subtle, in order to leverage the knowledge of the negotiation team. From his time on the Special Branch Irish Squad, Imbert was something of an expert on the Irish political landscape and history of the IRA, from the eighteenth-century Protestant founder of modern Irish Republicanism, Wolfe Tone, to the then current leadership of Daithi O'Connell. As one of the two principle negotiators at Balcombe Street, it was essential for him to have a working understanding of the Republican movement and to use this knowledge in the negotiations with the ASU. This knowledge, in conjunction with the advice from Dr. Scott, would enable the negotiation team to develop a strategy for dealing with the IRA men in the flat opposite their base in 20 Dorset Square, but truly effective tactics would prove difficult to develop on the Monday, given the continuation of the publicly espoused hard line adopted by Sir Robert Mark.

Early Monday morning Imbert called the ASU on the field telephone. Tom repeated the ASU's demand for a car to Heathrow and a plane and safe passage to Dublin in exchange for the safe release of the hostages. The police Commissioner's position on the negotiations was tying one arm behind Imbert and Nevill's collective backs. The policy of "no surrender," and absolutely no concessions on allowing food of any sort being sent into the apartment, was becoming a problem. From a negotiation standpoint, Imbert needed to obtain from Tom, and give in return, some form of concession, no matter how small or seemingly insignificant to the outside observer. He could not gain their trust any other way.

The Met were not going to give the ASU safe passage under any circumstances, but to avoid tipping the IRA men over a point of no return, where they became so frustrated and desperate that they resorted to violence, they needed a means to have the ASU feel their situation was not entirely hopeless in terms of gaining something from the Met. The psychological team had concerns that without some form of relaxation on the current strategy, the ASU could either kill one of the hostages in the flat in retaliation to refused demands, or resolve to attempt a break out with John and Sheila Mathews as human shields, an act that would surely result in a bloodbath. Dr. Scott, having listened to the tapes of the negotiations to date, urged Sir Robert Mark to move away from his position of standing firm against any demands made by the ASU. From a negotiation standpoint, the ASU were being painted into a corner by the all-or-nothing stance that Sir Robert was publicly advocating the police should continue to adopt. Dr. Scott, along with Imbert and Nevill, pushed the senior leadership to soften, privately if need be, the "no deal" tactic to enable the negotiation team a chance to gain some concessions from the ASU. The result of this urging would be noticed during the remainder of the day.

The Met were still desperately concerned about a counterstrike by the Provisionals, in some shape or form, in an effort to force the British government's hand to release the cornered ASU. These concerns were well founded, given the IRA's past efforts to free trapped or imprisoned operational personnel. On October 3, 1975, Dutch industrialist Dr. Tiedde Herrema, chief executive of the Dutch-owned Ferenka factory in Ballyvarra, County Limerick, was abducted at gun point on his way to work by Provisional IRA operatives Eddie Gallagher and Marion Coyle. He was held as a hostage in an effort to secure the release of three IRA prisoners being held in Lymerick jail, including Bridget Rose Dugdale, who was serving nine years for her part in the 1974 IRA art robbery. Dr. Herrema was finally released, after lengthy negotiations with the Garda, on November 7th, 1975. The IRA prisoners Gallagher and Coyle had demanded to be released stayed firmly in their prison cells. After his release, Dr. Herrema showed the press the souvenir given to him by Gallagher–a bullet from the gun Gallagher had held to his head during his kidnap. There had also been a successful rescue of three IRA prisoners from the Mountjoy prison in Northern Ireland. On October 31, 1974, the IRA hijacked a helicopter and forced the pilot to land in the exercise yard of D Wing, where at 3:40pm, J.B. O'Hagan, Seamus Twomey and Kevin Mallon were flown to freedom to resume their IRA activities. One of the prison guards claimed he thought it was the new Minster of Defense arriving by helicopter. One IRA wag, also in the prison, cheekily told the guard it was the IRA's new Minister of Defense leaving! The escape would be immortalized in the Republican ballad "The helicopter song," which includes the line "it's up like a bird and over the prison. There's three men missing I hear the warder say."

The IRA had demonstrated that they were perfectly capable of going after assets that were of value to them, or staging hostage situations to secure, or attempt to secure, the release of IRA prisoners. The Met had every right to be concerned that some form of counterstrike could take place at any point in the standoff.

The counterstrike options would have included a car bomb, so all vehicles attempting to enter or exit outer containment zone around the Balcombe Street-Dorset Square area were stopped and searched for explosive devises. Office workers, who had to report to their place of work inside the containment zone, were issued passes and could not enter or leave their employers' premises without first having their passes checked by a uniformed officer. There was also a concern about the security of the Balcombe Street apartment building. Despite the ASU's failure on the Saturday to exit via the rear of the building into the parallel street of Boston Place, there was in fact a means of entry and exit into the street out back. To ensure this road was covered from either an attempt to enter or an escape effort by the ASU, three sandbag emplacements were set up in Boston Place. These were manned by armed officers, day and night, to cover and secure the rear of the building. Officer A, from the Special Patrol Group, took part in the manning of one sandbag emplacement on the night shift during the siege. The weather remained as cold as it had been on the night of the fateful chase and shoot out on Rossmore Road that had led to the siege, in fact it was so cold one entrepreneurial Londoner set up shop, just outside the barrier off Dorset Square, selling warm blankets to the officers on the night shift. Officer A recalled buying two blankets, at £2 each, in an effort to keep warm against the bitter winter chill.

The Met were ready and waiting for any attempt to break out the trapped men of the ASU. But would the IRA attempt a rescue, or would the ASU try and break out? They would have to wait and be patient, as the nation watched and waited with them.

Publicly, the Met were still admitting to being unsure as to the precise number of IRA men inside the flat. At a press conference that morning, Deputy Assistant Commissioner Earnest Bond indicated to the media that there may only be three hostage takers inside 22b, despite the eye witness accounts from Saturday that stated four men were seen running into the apartment building. He stated that they had spoken to "three different voice, all with Irish accents." He, like the rest of the Met, was unaware that Eddie Butler was playing the parts of Mick and Paddy, as he would later own up to Imbert and Nevill, and Duggan and Dougherty were keeping relatively quiet. The police were publicly stating that Michael Wilson was involved in the Saturday chase and may well be inside the flat. Mr. Bond also relayed to the gathered members of the media that Mrs. Rosemary McWhirter would be assisting the police by listening to the recording of the field telephone conversations between the police and the IRA men in the hope that she would be able to recognize the voice of the man who murdered her husband. This news would be a strong motivator for the ASU to say as little as possible. It would also be a motivator for Duggan and Dougherty to say even less.

A communications breakthrough occurred that Monday morning. Up to that point, all communications with the ASU had been initiated by either Imbert or Nevill calling the men on the field telephone. For the first time since the units had been in place, the handset rang in the negotiators flat. Imbert answered the call, to find Tom on the other end with a fresh set of demands. Rather than reiterating the ASU's demand for safe passage, Tom was requesting hot food and cigarettes be sent into the apartment. The negotiation team had been presented with a golden opportunity, in terms of the psychological to-and-fro of the telephone exchanges to that point. Tom had opened up an opportunity for Imbert, and Dr. Scott, to increase the growing sense of dependency the ASU were experiencing. This also presented Imbert with the chance to soften the police hard-line tactics, as urged by Dr. Scott, without having to be the party that initiated the conversation, a clear psychological advantage. Tom had made the opening gambit and the negotiation team would leverage this for all it was worth.

In a classic rejection and retreat tactic, Imbert made a counter offer while at the same time not squashing the original request from the IRA man: If they released Mrs. Mathews, the police would send in hot soup and cigarettes for the ASU and the remaining hostage. The counter-proposal apparently surprised Tom, who initially stalled when presented with the option by Imbert. The police sensed a degree of indecision in Tom, who appeared to need time to discuss the proposal with the other ASU members. Telling Imbert that they would "think it over," the negotiations paused to allow a decision to be reached by the IRA men.

In order to further leverage the situation, the Met called a press conference to share the details of the soup-for-hostage deal with the media. Once again, they knew the ASU had access to the news media inside the flat and the public discussion of the decision they were facing would add to the pressure they were facing to come back with an answer to the negotiation team. At the press conference, held at 222 Marylebone Road, Deputy Assistant Commissioner Peter Walton laid out the deal offered to the hostage takers. The ASU had not told the police how long they required to reach a decision, stated Walton, and the police were not pressuring them to make up their mind. Mr. Earnest Bond added that, "the ball is in their court," and the police were quite content to wait for their answer to the proposal. Mr. Bond also added that the police were prepared to accept the word of the ASU that they would indeed release Mrs. Mathews, even an hour or two after the hot soup and cigarettes had been sent in. He said he was prepared to take their "promise or guarantee," as, after all, "all we have to lose is the food."

However, the Met secretly had grave concerns that Mrs. Mathews would not be prepared to be separated from her husband, even if the ASU agreed to the deal. They were a devoted couple, and so the thought of forcibly separating the two would be a tough decision to make and actually carry out. The image of the ASU handing over a kicking and screaming Mrs. Mathews to the police would provide the media with an unfortunate spectacle. In fact the notion of providing the press with *any* visual scoop of a number of potential scenarios would be highly undesirable for political reasons. The Met's main worry would be press images of an attempted break out by the ASU, which would almost inevitably result in a bloody shoot out, as the Met would not let the ASU escape–Sir Robert had made that very clear since the beginning of the siege. The Met did have the media contained at one end of Balcombe Street, but they could still observe the street area in front of the apartment block. The British Government could not allow, or afford, to hand the Republican cause any images of bloodshed on the streets of London involving the IRA being gunned down by the police. The Met would have to work out a means of denying the media any opportunity to film events outside the apartment block, should things deteriorate to the point of shooting.

The ASU called Imbert again, but there was a problem with the field telephone that became increasing increasingly faint as the conversation went on. The negotiation team told Tom they were sending him a new battery pack for the base unit, which was installed and the conversations resumed. Tom informed Imbert of the results of the discussions among the ASU regarding his offer of soup for Mrs. Mathews. They refused to release the hostage under any circumstances, but they still wanted the food and cigarettes to be sent in. Imbert, calmly but firmly, restated the terms he was prepared to move forward with, namely the release of the hostage, even if it was several hours after they had eaten the soup. The police would later comment that they felt Tom was more concerned about getting the cigarettes than the food, which again fed into the overall tactics being employed by the negotiation team, focusing on the elements they believed the ASU would find the most important in obtaining a concession from the police. Tom, with his "talent for invective," made sure the negotiation team understood his refusal of the deal and the frustration that was building in the ASU team. Again, he was pushed to release Mrs. Mathews, replying "not on your life," and angrily disconnected the field telephone, cutting off communications with the negotiators in 20 Dorset Square.

The police called another press conference to inform the media how the ASU had refused the offer of soup and cigarettes in exchange for the release of Mrs. Mathews. DAC Wilford Gibson told the press the offer of soup was an act of "good faith on our part," and that the soup would be kept hot in a mobile police canteen near number 22 "in case they changed their mind." Mr. Gibson informed the press that negotiations had stopped for the afternoon as the police were having difficulty in getting in touch with the ASU. He did not mention anything to the press about the disconnection of the field telephone, as this would have been fed back to the ASU via the broadcast media and the concern would be that it would give them a sense of gaining a psychological advantage over the negotiation team. Mr. Gibson did add that the state of mind of the ASU was becoming a puzzle to the police and that conversations with Tom were "unpredictable" in that sometimes he could be "reasonable," and at other time "extremely rude." The psychological team was becoming concerned at the behavior of the ASU and the way they were communicating with the police, especially as the ASU had disconnected the field telephone and were limiting the options for communications. However, Tom's apparent erratic behavior may have just been his way of keeping the negotiating team on edge as they tried to guess what his next move would be

Imbert and the negotiation team had to resort to moving back to the hand-held megaphone, hailing the ASU from the street below the balcony of 22b for three hours until they persuaded Tom to reconnect the field telephone. The refusal of the exchange deal, and the subsequent disconnection of the field telephone, became a major concern to the negotiation team. In the formation of a strategy for negotiation, Imbert and Nevill needed to get some level of understanding regarding the motivation behind the ASU's actions. The immediate answer–avoiding incarceration–was obvious, but what else was driving them to stay in the flat, surrounded by the police and the national media? GHQ in Dublin would be following events through the news coverage, but what would they do in response? Were the ASU holding out in the hope of rescue or some other tactic to secure their release? Imbert and Nevill could not know any of these details, but how were they to proceed? Should the negotiations move toward a more aggressive, psychologically taunting nature, to attempt to dent the egos of the ASU and demoralize them into submission? The Met still had the option to disconnect the electrical and gas supply to the flat, creating a cold and dark environment for the Irishmen, but this would also negatively impact the hostages. The police knew the Mathews had a battery-powered transistor radio in the room, so even with the power off they could still use the broadcast media as a means of influencing the actions of the ASU. A decision on disconnection of services to the flat would need to be made on a tactical basis, depending on how future negotiations unfolded. But, what was the ASU's driving motivation to hold out? Could Imbert and Nevill, with the support of Dr. Scott, push the group to the point of breaking, or would this be too dangerous for the hostages? The police in the flat and the surveillance team had reported some conversations between the ASU team about making a break for it with the hostages, but they did not know how seriously the IRA men were treating the notion, or if it was misinformation for the digestion of the police. Despite Sir Robert's "vulgar criminals" comment, the Met had a healthy regard for the crew they had been unable to apprehend for the previous fifteen months. They knew they were not dealing with armed robbers holding restaurant workers hostage after a botched holdup. These were the elite of the IRA, well trained and highly experienced urban guerilla warfare operatives. How far could they push them before they resorted to violence? It would be a calculated risk, but the growing opinion was that the negotiation team should look for ways to dent the self esteem of the ASU men however they could. It would be a strategy that would not be without some degree of hazard to the hostages, but had the potential benefit that it could shorten the siege. It was a risk deemed worth taking, but it would be for Imbert and Nevill to find the right balance to get the ASU out of the flat and keep the hostages alive as they did so. The ASU and the hostages would be getting physically weaker the longer they went without food, and this would be a key element in the strategy as the negotiation team set out to wear the men down. Outside the apartment, the police canteen trucks and the Chevron Club were doing a brisk trade as evening closed in on Balcombe Street, with officers warming their hands around steaming mugs of tea and coffee in the cold December night air. There would be no supper again for John and Sheila Mathews, confined in their own living room by men Mrs. Mathews described as treating them "as if we weren't there."

In the incident room at 222 Marylebone Road, one statement taken from a civilian eyewitness had Detective Inspector Chapman puzzled. The witness stated that on the Saturday night of the chase, they had seen a man in a light-colored overcoat brandishing a gun running down Balcombe Street, and then crouching behind a car opposite the flat where the IRA men were holed up, still brandishing the gun. Ron Chapman had to go back to the officers involved that night and determine what each of them had been wearing. Going over the information from the officers on the scene, it turned out that the armed mystery man in the light overcoat was, in fact, Inspector John Purnell who had totally forgotten he was still holding the gun part he had taken from the bag on Rossmore Road as he reached number 22 Balcombe Street. Inspector Purnell had later handed the gun barrel to an exhibits officer at the scene on the Saturday night, who tagged the gun part as evidence.

Sir Robert Mark held the final press conference of the day that Monday evening. He made a direct and passionate appeal to the population of Greater London to help the police identify the men holding the two hostages in the small room in Balcombe Street. He appealed to the landlords and landladies of London to look for tenants who had been absent since Saturday night. He said that someone may notice that a flat or studio apartment usually occupied by a "young Irishman" had been empty since the weekend. If anyone had suspicions, he urged, they were to call the Bomb Squad at Scotland Yard. "We should be very grateful," he stated, to find where the men had been living prior to the siege. He also restated the public message that the police objective was to "save the life" of everyone inside number 22b.

Jim Nevill would keep the pressure on the ASU during the night, but the men were in no mood for conversation. The spotlights again illuminated the living room with their flood of electric light. The dogs, now on the other side of the living room door, sounded even more menacing as the six adults settled down for another cramped night, with Mrs. Mathews becoming increasingly uncomfortable curled up in the armchair, despite the use of the painkillers sent into the flat for her on Sunday. Mr. Mathews was still confined to the couch. He would later report a growing sense of nonverbal communication with his wife while they endured their confinement with the four gun toting IRA men.

Peter Imbert was feeling the pressure of his role in the negotiations. As he left the confines of 20 Dorset Square, friends in the force would ask him when he was going to "get them out?" Even his sixteen-year-old son would ask him, "are you going to get them out tomorrow dad?" He would later report that he would wake up during the night, searching for the right words to use in the conversations with Tom, fearing he had made some unnoticed error that would put the lives of the hostages in jeopardy. The pressure was building on both sides.

TUESDAY DECEMBER 9TH

The beginning of the third day of the siege had both the police and the ASU on edge. Increasing concerns regarding the state of mind of the IRA men inside number 22b was growing by the hour. Deprived of food for almost three days, the medical advisors were becoming increasingly vocal about giving the ASU, and the hostages, some form of nourishment. The police, mindful of the need to use the supply of food as bargaining collateral, were reluctant to send in food with the prospect of receiving no tangible benefit in return. The media, always looking for a dramatic viewpoint on the siege, were printing the opinion of medical professionals not involved with the negotiations. In one such example, Dr. William Sargent, a consulting physician at St. Thomas's Hospital, when asked by the media about the effects of hunger on the ASU stated that he was "extremely alarmed" that the IRA men and hostages had been deprived of food for such a length of time. His expressed viewpoint was that a deterioration in the standoff could, if it occurred, be directly attributable to a lack of nourishment and that a shootout was more likely if the police deliberately kept them hungry as the ASU would most likely become "bloody minded."

Inside the apartment, the ASU were becoming increasingly resistant to the developing control tactics employed against them by Imbert and Nevill from the flat across the street. This did not go unnoticed by Commander Roy Habershon, who told the assembled media that morning that the ASU may fear they were being "talked into something." He was right, for that was exactly what Imbert was attempting to do in the sometimes brief conversations with Tom that were always terminated by the Irishman, sometimes abruptly and often with Imbert in mid speech. It was becoming obvious to the ASU that the tactics being employed against them were in an effort to control every element of the negotiations, and this was becoming irritating to the group. They were a highly trained, tight knit unit that been very "successful" in their campaign of terror, against the elements of British society in and around the streets of London. Apart from the need to split up and then regroup after the murder of PC Stephen Tibble, and one brave taxi driver they shot at to warn him off after he gave chase to two of the team after one attack, they had not come anywhere near discovery or capture. Everything changed for them in one night, due to an error in their adopted tactics of revisiting attack scenes and the heroic tenacity of Inspector John Purnell and Sergeant Phil McVeigh. They had been chased, as a group, for the first time and were confined to the small living room of a middle aged London couple with little hope of evading eventual capture, and a long incarceration courtesy of Her Majesty's Prison Service. They had been accustomed to planning and executing their missions on an almost autonomous basis, taking the occasional tactical or strategic direction from GHQ in Dublin. They now had to depend on the smooth talking Peter Imbert and his immediate boss Jim Nevill for everything, and they were not getting much in the way of satisfying their increasing need for food and cigarettes.

Imbert called the flat on the Tuesday morning only to find the field telephone connection was dead. Tom, in an effort to play Imbert at his own game, had taken to disconnecting the phone in an attempt to establish an element of control over the negotiators. This tactic forced Imbert into the street to use a loudhailer to reach the ASU, an act that was not hard for the IRA men to ignore if they chose to do so. It would require extensive patience on Imbert's part to communicate with the men in that fashion, as unlike the field telephone where his words were for Tom, the surveillance team, and Dr. Scott when required, the loudhailer could be heard by the press behind the barriers south of Dorset Square. This would cause Imbert to be careful with his choice of words, concerned that the open communications could feed directly to any Provisional IRA unit monitoring the siege. At a second press conference that morning, Commander Habershon insisted that the disconnection of the field telephone by the ASU was not going to impact the Met's overall strategy of patience and wait-and-see. However, the strategy would be modified as the day unfolded. Pressure from Imbert and Nevill, supported by Dr. Scott, had persuaded the Met senior leadership team to relax their "no deal" policy. At the same press conference, DAC Peter Wilton told the Media that if it was felt necessary, based on medical advice, they would send in food and cigarettes to the ASU and the hostages. This would only happen, he continued, in the event that the doctors on the scene made the recommendation with regards to the medical wellbeing of Mr. and Mrs. Mathews, both still confined to the couch and armchair in the apartment. Sir Robert Mark gave his assurance to the ASU that, should supplies be sent into the apartment, there would be no attempt to put drugs in the food to incapacitate the men inside the flat.

A further change in strategy would involve Imbert becoming deliberately more assertive with Tom over the field telephone, when the ASU agreed to connect it again. After a three hour break in communications Tom reconnected the phone, and communications between the ASU and Imbert resumed. Tom's position was unchanged in demanding food and cigarettes be sent into the flat. Imbert's position was also unchanged, requiring the release of Mrs. Mathews in exchange for hot soup, coffee and cigarettes. Tom, from a counter-positional standpoint, wanted to hold out for a full hot meal for all of the people in the flat, without the condition of releasing a key collateral bargaining chip in Mrs. Mathews. Imbert countered again with an offer of hot soup and cigarettes. Roy Habershon described the details of the communications with the ASU at the next press conference. He described how Detective Superintendent Imbert had been dealing with the ASU in a "quiet, calm and even charmingly cajoling'" manner, in trying to convince the ASU to take the offer of hot soup and coffee in exchange for Sheila Mathews.

While the negotiations proved to be difficult, Peter Imbert regarded himself as someone who could "talk himself in or out of any situation," as he would later tell the author. He was regarded as "Mr. Smoothie" by some of his fellow officers, having honed his negotiation skills on the streets of London by persuading recalcitrant members of the general public to be reasonable and do things his way, using his street smarts and common sense, rather than resorting to slapping on the handcuffs. His negotiation skills were legendary even within his family. Peter Imbert related a brief anecdote to the author on this subject. His daughter, aged fourteen during the time of the siege, announced her intentions to attend a local disco club and this did not go over well with either of her parents. In an effort to be reasonable, Imbert invited his daughter to sit down with him and discuss the matter. On overhearing this, his sixteen-year-old son blurted out to his sister, "don't talk to him; he'll talk you out of anything!" Now all he had to do was talk the ASU out of apartment 22b, and do so with the hostages alive.

In terms of getting out of the apartment and achieving safe passage, one avenue had been closed to the ASU by the Irish government. The public demands made by the ASU for safe passage via airplane to Dublin had caused the Irish coalition cabinet considerable embarrassment, as at the time they were highly sensitive to outside criticism of their internal security policy. The ASU's demand for safe passage to Ireland, and the subsequent debate it had generated, had again opened up the highly sensitive issue of extradition of identified IRA terrorists. Some ministers in the Irish cabinet speculated that the demands made by the ASU were a deliberate attempt by the Provisional IRA to discredit the Irish government's policy on law and order. The Irish made it very clear to the Wilson government that under no circumstances would the Irish cabinet grant landing rights to any aircraft carrying the IRA men, or any other terrorists, seeking sanctuary in the Republic. The British government also had concerns that the IRA may step up the terror campaign if the political peace process did not make better progress. The pressure was building on the Wilson government, and a peaceful, or at least bloodless, resolution to the standoff in Balcombe Street was becoming increasing important. They could not afford to have the situation deteriorate into a shootout and give a propaganda coup to the Provisionals. All political pressure rolls down hill, so the Met were under no illusion that the government wanted a peaceful end to the situation, but still they had the SAS building a mockup of the flat, and training to break in and either disable or kill the hostage takers, should things deteriorate into shooting inside number 22b.

At a midday press conference, held again at 222 Marylebone Road, the Met announced that they knew for certain the man known to them as Michael Wilson was a key IRA operative, and had been involved over the past fifteen months in a series of bombings and shootings in and around London, and he could well be inside number 22b. The Met reported a very good response to Sir Robert Mark's appeal for landlords to be vigilant for missing tenants or flat mates. Sir Robert told the media they had established his identity without any doubt, including his address, adding, "we know everything about him." That was not entirely true, as at that point the police had no history on Wilson other than the evidence they had gathered, but it made for good media coverage. An artist's impression of Wilson had been constructed and circulated to the media and other police forces. DAC John Wilson, at the press conference described Michael Wilson, code named Z, as a "good class man, in criminal terms," a comment that must have surely irked the Commissioner who had repeatedly called the ASU "vulgar criminals." Outwardly calm, Sir Robert added that Michael Wilson was someone they were "most anxious to get our hands on." If and when the police apprehended Wilson, Sir Robert continued, he would be charged with almost "every variety of serious crimes" in relation to "guns, bombs and terrorism generally."

The Met had originally thought the identity of Z could have been Kieran McMorrow; a British Army deserter who had joined the IRA and was wanted in connection with terrorist activities in Ireland and the UK. The final break that linked Wilson back to the IRA came through cooperation between the Irish Garda and the Metropolitan police at Scotland Yard. During the first days of the Balcombe Street siege, Garda fingerprint experts found that the Met had collected forensic evidence from the Ross McWhirter murder, the Fairholme Road flat, and the stolen Cortina getaway car. This material matched prints they had for a wanted IRA operative, obtained from an abandoned house near Charlestown, County Mayo, after a shootout between Garda forces and two IRA men at the scene resulting in the eventual escape of the IRA. The prints found in the abandoned house had proven a match with the prints obtained by the Met. This man was wanted by the Garda in connection with the April 1974 £8 million art robbery from Sir Alfred Beit's collection, taken from his home in County Wicklow. The Garda now had a name to the unidentified prints, and the Met apparently had an address to go with it.

The ASU and Imbert conversed over the field telephone further that afternoon. The focus was again on food. Switching topics, Imbert offered to replace the chemical toilet, in use by six adults since the previous Sunday, but in an act of counter control, Tom refused. The offer of a replacement was viewed by the IRA as another control tactic on Imbert's part to exert his authority and dominant position in the negotiations. Imbert again refused to make an offer of food to the men without an exchange of a hostage in return. The tension was increasing on both sides. Not only did the IRA men have to put up with yet another refusal of food, but Tom also had to endure Imbert's extensive knowledge of Republican history that the police officer was only too happy to share with the Irishman. Imbert later related to the author how he had "lectured" Tom on Republican lore, obviously irritating the Irishman to the point where he would slam the phone down, cutting Imbert off in mid sentence. This was a deliberate tactic being used by Imbert in an attempt to belittle Tom, to see how far he could push him and what his reaction would be. It was a highly risky tactic, but one the negotiation team felt it worth taking. It was appearing to work, as from the ASU's perspective they were refused food for a third day, Tom was being subject to increasingly demeaning tactics by Imbert, and they were trapped with an increasingly nervous Mrs. Mathews. The chemical toilet would, by this point, be a rather unpleasant object to have in the room, but by the virtue of the tactics the ASU were using back against Imbert, they had taken a stand against its replacement. The situation inside the flat was bad and getting worse for both the ASU and the hostages.

John Mathews again later described how he felt an increasing ability to communicate nonverbally with his wife. Caught in the middle between the ASU and the negotiation team, he said that they were able to pass messages to each other with a "merest flick of an eyelid," or a slight body movement or jerk of the head, which Mr. Mathews said meant nothing to the "others in the room." Watching his wife suffer increasing discomfort from the "chronic back trouble" she was developing from being forced to curl up in an armchair was becoming too much for the calm and unflappable Postal Inspector. The confinement in the small living room John Mathews later described as "a hellhole," also appeared to be becoming too much for Mrs. Mathews. In their separate ways, both of the hostages were contemplating ways to change the situation they were in. At one point during the day, John Mathews decided he would "have a go," at one of the IRA men and attempt to get a gun. The ASU had untied his hands by that point, but his feet remained bound together with pantyhose. He planned to "dive over the back of the settee," and tackle one of the men, despite the significant age and physical differences he would have experienced. The notion of "have a go" is a very British attitude to adversity, wrong doing, or criminal activity in terms of a member of the public wading into a situation to try and bring it to a successful end. The same spirit had been demonstrated by Inspector John Purnell, having a go at the lone IRA man. The message of "having a go" at one of the IRA was nodded, twitched and gestured between the couple. Mrs. Mathews, obviously alarmed at the notion, shot her husband a look that left him no doubt about her views on the endeavor. Her reaction probably saved their lives. John Mathews did not go over the back of the couch and attempt to wrestle a handgun from one of the ASU, a move that would have almost certainly proven fatal. In a likewise fashion, John Mathews dissuaded Sheila from her plan to "crash out of the balcony window," and attempt an escape. He had picked up on her intentions and signaled her to not go through with it. They resigned themselves to sitting out the siege and see what the unfolding drama would bring them.

With the level of frustration growing in the ASU, along with the nervousness of the hostages, the tension in the cramped quarters of the small room was growing palpably. The tension would increase further as the six adults turned to watch the BBC six o'clock evening news on the television. The headline feature of the news was the showing of a prerecorded interview with Mrs. Joan Royce, the sister of Sheila

Mathews. Royce was being fed questions by the interviewer and was allowed to make several direct statements to her sister. The session had been previously recorded at a Police section house. Commander Roy Habershon had agreed to the idea after members of the family had enquired if there was anything they could do to aid the police in the siege negotiations. The Met was not about to turn down a psychological Trojan horse of that nature, as the impact on the couple, and more importantly the ASU, could not be underestimated. There, on the TV screen would be another person, a loved one, telling the ASU that the two people they had hostage were human beings, that they were loved. They were parents, brothers, sisters, and had a family that yearned for them to be safe. This was a well-planned media coup by the Met.

Royce made an impassioned appeal to her sister to not lose heart. She described how John and Sheila's two daughters were holding up under the strain of the siege. She was confident that the IRA men would do her no harm as they also had parents "more or less of your age," and that their own mothers and fathers would be thinking about the situations their boys were in. Royce related that the family had a pre-Christmas reunion planned for the following Saturday, so everyone was hoping the siege would be over by then as the family was so looking forward to seeing them. She was sure that "the men will let you go," and that they would be able to attend the party. Speaking about the ASU, she said "I plead with them, please, please, please let Sheila and John go." The interviewer asked Royce what the ASU could hope to gain from keeping the hostages in the flat. Royce responded that she felt there was nothing the men could gain by continuing to hold her sister and brother-in-law hostage, "they're two innocent people," and that it was unfortunate that their flat had been picked as the place for the IRA men to hold out. Royce relayed to her sister the level of effort the police were going to in order to bring the siege to a safe conclusion, "what is going on outside, Sheila, is quite fantastic." The interviewer asked Royce to summarize her message for the hostage takers holding her loved ones inside number 22b. Royce repeated her plea for the safe release of the hostages, "I'm sure that all of them [ASU] have hearts," she said, "I can only plead with them, please let Sheila and John go." There was nothing, nothing more to be gained from continuing the siege, she added as a final comment.

There is no available record of the actual reactions of either the hostages or the hostage takers to the news broadcast. All we can state is that the broadcast was viewed by the six adults in the apartment living room, and that the emotional and psychological reactions of the Mathews and the ASU can only be speculated on as part of this unfolding drama. From a psychological perspective, the impact of seeing and hearing a close family member plead with the ASU for their release would have been immensely significant for Sheila Mathews, a person we have already noted as being emotionally sensitive. We cannot know for sure how the impact of this psychological reaction would have manifested itself on Sheila Mathews in front of her husband and the ASU. Did she become overly emotional and tearful? How would the scene played out in front of the ASU? Would her reactions to the broadcast have impacted the ASU? Would their impressions of the Mathews change because of the messages from Joan Royce, and would her comments about their own parents impact the Irishmen? Many questions remain about the effect of that broadcast, but there is no doubt that it had a significant impact on the way the remainder of the siege would be played out. It certainly added to the pressure and tension the ASU were experiencing. But, did the Met deliberately use Joan Royce to make an emotional appeal to the captives and the hostage takers in the full knowledge it would create an increased level of psychological and emotional tension in the flat? The answer to that has to be yes, as in examining the transcripts of the broadcast, it is clear that the interviewer's questions were designed to elicit a specific response from Joan Royce, with the interview appearing stage-managed from the outset. The impact on the ASU of watching the broadcast, and the reaction of the hostages as well also cannot be known, but again we can look at the psychological element. The IRA men had viewed a national broadcast, featuring a family member of their hostages, pleading for the release of a loved one. They would not have been immune to the impact of the messages, given the growing pressure from the Met and the constant refusal of their demands. This was not a case of the classic Stockholm syndrome setting in on either side, as Mrs. Mathews later stated she disliked Imbert for being "too nice" to the ASU. However, being faced with a TV broadcast with Mrs. Mathews sister pleading for their release so that they could attend a family gathering, invoking images of parents and families, it would have had an impact on their actions, even if only for a short time. The ASU still wanted food, and they were becoming increasingly frustrated with Imbert and Nevill for not meeting their demands to be fed. They had also gone without cigarettes, which would be adding to their edginess. The broadcast would be one of the proverbial straws to break the ASU's spirit, but at the same time it would make them more belligerent.

With the news broadcast over, Imbert called Tom to resume discussions. His tone was deliberately taunting to the Irishman, again visiting the history of the political situation. He invoked the memory of Wolfe Tone, questioning how the original founder of the Republican movement would view their actions. The renewed pressure on Tom, with another lecture from Imbert following close behind the Royce broadcast, was taking a toll on the IRA man. Imbert continued to press, feeling Tom was at a psychological disadvantage and wanting to force home the ego-denting tactics. He asked Tom what Daithi O'Connell, the IRA chief of staff, would think of their actions in taking a middle-aged couple hostage in their own home. It would be viewed as "kids stuff," he taunted, and what would the rest of the IRA think of them? What would they think of such a pathetic performance from this ASU, holed up in a flat, surrounded by police, and not letting the hostages out? Imbert continued to pressure Tom, deliberately belittling him, increasing the anger and sheer frustration being felt by the IRA man, feeling that Imbert was running the show and calling all the shots. The phone suddenly went dead at Imbert's end, as Tom slammed the handset back onto the base unit. That was not an unusual way for conversations with Tom to be terminated, so Imbert reasoned, and so the Detective calmly waited to start the process all over again.

Looking down on the balcony of number 22b from his third-floor flat, Imbert stared in utter disbelief as he watched the balcony door open and saw the field telephone base unit and handset sail out of the door and arc upwards, launched into the air by an enraged Tom. The field telephone glinted in the floodlights as it reached the peak of its trajectory and then fell to the street, smashing to pieces on the road fifteen feet below. Imbert later confided that as he sat there, frozen to his seat, he was dreading the sound of a gunshot as the ASU executed a hostage in the apartment. He also feared for his job, "I thought I'd be back on the beat the following day," he later told the author.

The pressure and sheer frustration at the situation had caused Tom to react explosively to Imbert's probing. The combination of all the frustrating refusals of food, the televised emotional outpourings from Mrs. Royce, the reactions of the hostages to the appeals made on their behalf, and finally being "lectured" by Peter Imbert had all proved to be too much for Tom to endure and remain calm. In one defiant act of control, he had removed the only source of confidential communications from Imbert's use. Denied the phone link, Imbert was forced back into the street below the balcony with a hand-held loudhailer, in an effort to reach the ASU and conduct some damage control. His attempt at communication was met with a barrage of verbal invective-laden abuse from Tom and his comrades, who were evidently in no mood to converse with the negotiation team. In an effort to bring events back under the control of the Met, Imbert ordered that a supply of hot vegetable soup, coffee, and cigarettes to be lowered to the balcony of 22b. In doing so, he was attempting to offer the ASU a sign that the talking between the two sides should continue. He was still very concerned that the apparent anger displayed by Tom would be transferred in some way toward the hostages. If violence did occur, it would trigger a rapid escalation of events as this would force the Met to a "tactical" resolution to the standoff. Given the political situation the British government would be faced with if the siege turned bloody, that had to be avoided at almost any price.

Officers in the apartment above lowered the supplies to the balcony window of 22b. Imbert hailed the ASU to alert them to the arrival of the long awaited and often-demanded supplies of food and cigarettes, for which he was asking nothing in return. But, to the astonishment of the police, and the very real concern of the psychological team, the ASU in a remarkable display of discipline and restraint, ignored the food container that gently knocked on the balcony window as it swayed in the light evening breeze. They were proving to the Met exactly how tough a crew they could be. They ignored the food in an effort to demonstrate to Imbert, and the negotiation team, that they were not the ones running the show. It was pure bravado, because at the end of the day the Met were in control of the situation, but it was a very effective demonstration of their resolve and a warning shot across the bow of the Met negotiators that they were to be taken seriously. They would, from this point forward, turn the police tactics back on the Met. They had been demanding food, and had been refused by the police unless they gave up a hostage. Now the police wanted to send in food and cigarettes to the ASU and hostages, so the ASU would refuse the gesture in an act of defiant control. All things considered, it had not been a great day for the Met. The field telephone link had been lost, courtesy of Tom, and they appeared to have pushed the ASU a little too far in the negotiations. How best to move forward would be the key questions for the police that evening. The people in 22b had still not received any food and this was now becoming a major concern to the psychological team. The behavior demonstrated by Tom and the ASU, angrily swearing at Imbert from the balcony, could only get worse the longer they went without nourishment. The key thing for the negotiation team for the next day would be to get the ASU to accept food; otherwise the standoff had a very real chance of coming to a tactical resolution. The SAS were very busy at their Chelsea barracks, practicing with their mock-up of the living room. The history of past tactical resolutions to hostage standoffs did not bode well for the hostages. The early 1970's had seen a rash of hostage situations around the world that had been less than successfully resolved by force. In just two examples of such situations, sieges at the Attica State Prison on September 8, 1971, and at the Munich Olympic Village on September 5, 1972, culminated in bloody police assaults having catastrophic results. These high-profile events raised serious questions concerning the failed police and military responses. These incidents were far from isolated. Over the same period, 760 of 1000 hostage deaths occurred during tactical rescue attempts. With such a disturbing record for rescuing hostages alive, the thought of the Metropolitan police responding to rescue alive anyone held captive would have seemed questionable, as the cure was often worse than the disease. Worse still was the potential political fallout for any such failed rescue that the Wilson government would have to face. In reality, the hostages had a greater chance of being killed by any armed rescuers than they did of walking out alive. The Mathews, held captive in the living room, would have been blissfully unaware of that statistic, as were the Met.

With the container of food still hanging outside the apartment window, DAC Wilford Gibson addressed the media at a press conference at 222 Marylebone Road. He summarized the exasperation felt by the negotiation team, "It may be that they don't trust us at this stage," he commented to the media. Trust would need to be rebuilt with the ASU, and quickly, but with no direct means of communication, this was to prove a significant challenge for Imbert and Nevill.

WEDNESDAY DECEMBER 10TH

The hostages and the ASU had gone without food for over four days, but the change in tactics adopted by the Irishmen meant that whereas before they were the ones demanding supplies, they were now not willing to accept the repeated offers of food from the police. The six adults in the living room of number 22b were all sleep deprived as well as hungry, due to the uncomfortable and deteriorating conditions inside the room and the noise that came in from the outside, such as the growling and barking of the police dogs. The high intensity spotlights trained on the windows of the flat made the curtains appear transparent, bathing the room at night with a bright, cold light. They were each experiencing differing degrees of stress and anxiety, with the hostages worrying about their safety and the potential future actions of their captors as the siege continued into yet another day. What would have been the ASU's main concerns and continued motivation to hold on? They may have been wondering when GHQ would intervene and carry out the widely expected retaliatory action to secure their release. The Met fully expected the IRA to carry out some action or other; the question remained when and where? The ASU knew they were not going to be allowed to walk out the front door and be given a safe passage to Heathrow, and they had known that since the first phone call O'Connell (Tom) had made to the police on the Saturday night. He would later tell Jim Nevill that they never expected to have their demands for a plane satisfied by the police, that it was "just a try." So what was driving the ASU to stick it out if not for some kind of intervention by GHQ? There was one key driving motivation for the men to hold out, without food and in increasingly uncomfortable surrounds, and that factor was evidence. The two flats shared between them at 99 Milton Grove, in Stoke Newington, and at 21 Crouch Hill both contained an arsenal of explosives, timers, detonators, bolts and ball bearings, weapons and ammunition and a slew of highly incriminating documents, such as target list and names and address of prominent people who were to be attacked. There was also a key ring taken from the McWhirter crime scene. All of this material would clearly link them to the bombing and shooting campaign they had been energetically pursuing for the past fifteen months. The police would be able to collect a considerable amount of evidence from the two locations and create a very strong case against them for all the bombings and shootings they had been unable to solve. It was in the ASU's interest to hold out as long as possible to give GHQ enough time to have other operatives go to their unoccupied flats and remove all the "tools of the trade," as they would later describe the stash. If this act alone was all that GHQ could pull off, they hoped, then holding out would be worth it. The Met would have no knowledge of this expected plan as they searched for the ASU's base of operations.

However, holding out so that the IRA could retrieve all the equipment from their flats would not be enough to prevent the police from prosecuting the men. The Met already had conclusive forensic evidence of their involvement in certain aspects of the campaign of terror on the streets of London. The M1 carbine and Sten gun had been linked to prior shootings, and Duggan had in his possession the .357 Astra magnum revolver he had used to murder Ross McWhirter. It would also not go unnoticed that they had been seen shooting at Scott's and had used armed force to resist police capture, and were holding two people against their will. These acts alone would ensure they would spend a very long time at "Her Majesty's pleasure," as prison terms were jokingly referred to in the UK, once arrested, charged and tried. The ASU could not know when, or if, GHQ would attempt to empty their respective addresses, so holding out was their only option, but the longer they did so while depriving the hostages of food, the greater the likelihood of some form of intervention by the police to free the Mathews.

The actions of the ASU in the running gun battle of Saturday night had made an impact on the general public and their elected representatives in Parliament, in terms of revisiting the whole issue of capital punishment. The last two people executed in Britain were put to death for murder in 1964. Public disquiet at a series of high profile miscarriages of justice, involving capital cases, pushed Parliament to vote to abolish the death penalty for murder as a five-year experiment in 1965. A subsequent vote in 1970 made the ban permanent, but the death penalty remained in force for treason and "piracy with violence." The events of the past few months had seen renewed calls for the reintroduction of hanging for death caused by acts of terrorism. A vote was scheduled for Thursday December 10th, 1975 in the House of Commons with a motion put forward by Mr. Ivan Lawrence, Conservative MP for Burton. The motion was signed by over fifty Conservative party backbenchers and seven United Ulster Unionists and referred to the "cold blooded and barbaric" assassination of Ross McWhirter. The upcoming debate on the reintroduction of capital punishment had triggered much public discussion both in favor and in opposition to the death penalty for crimes of terror. One argument, played out in the editorials of a prominent national newspaper, examined the role of the IRA terrorists in the "war" against the British establishment in their fight of a unified Ireland. Acting in secret and out of uniform, they were analogous to fifth columnists waging a guerrilla war behind enemy lines. In wartime, such combatants would be executed if captured. Therefore, the argument continued, the terrorists should expect to receive the death penalty after going through the due process of the law, a luxury not offered to their ilk in a real war that faced summary execution on the battlefield. Death penalties are intended to act as a deterrent, but would this be the case for all terrorist organizations? Counter arguments, viewed through the lens of post September 11th (World Trade Center) and July 7th (London underground and bus bombings) sound strangely prophetic today. What if the terrorists did not fear death, and actually viewed dying for their cause as an act of martyrdom? The IRA may not be the only future terrorist organization the British government would have to deal with, given the spate of Middle East terror episodes to that date. However, if the death penalty was introduced, could the IRA just enter into an escalation spiral of tit-for-tat killings in return for every IRA member put to death by the state? To some, the thought of bringing back the death penalty for any crime, and triggering such a cycle of killing, was abhorrent and something the government should not consider no matter how dire the IRA situation became. The Archbishop of Canterbury, The Most Reverend Donald Coggan, along with eleven other prominent church leaders, wrote an impassioned letter to the editor of The Times, published on Wednesday December 10th, the day before the parliamentary debate. The Archbishop viewed a need for the nation to avoid seeking justice through retribution, believing that the sanctity of life was indivisible and that Britain, in adhering to that principle, would contribute to a more "sane and humane world." Mrs. Thatcher, leader of the opposition Conservative party, shared no such sentiment. "Those who have committed these crimes against humanity," she stated, "have forfeited the right to life."

The right to life for the hostages was Peter Imbert's prime consideration on the fourth day of the standoff. The reversal of tactics by the ASU had presented Imbert and the negotiation team with something of a dilemma. He needed to be able to communicate with the men in the flat if he was to have any chance of getting them to take in food for themselves and the hostages. He did have the option of just lowering a container of supplies to the balcony window, as he had done on the previous day, but this would only provide the ASU with another opportunity to publicly defy the negotiator, and have the media report the event back to the ASU, thereby bolstering their resolve even further. That was not an acceptable option. Imbert and the team faced three communications-related challenges they would need to address, and quickly, if the Met were going to regain overall control of the siege strategy.

The first problem was the rather one-directional communications with the ASU. Since the very public rejection of the field telephone unit, Imbert and Nevill had been forced into using a handheld loudhailer, addressing the ASU from the street below the balcony and because everything the negotiators said to the ASU over the loudhailer could be heard by everyone in the surrounding area, there was no opportunity for quiet conversations and the subtle cajoling Imbert was so good at. The loudhailer was just a high-decibel blunt instrument, not suited for the type of work Imbert and Nevill had in front of them. Tom, on the other hand, had the luxury of either ignoring the transmissions from the bullhorn, which happened a lot, or replying in a voice that only the team in the street below could hear. This placed Imbert at a tactical and psychological disadvantage, as all of his transmissions could be heard by the press gallery, but the only thing they heard from the ASU were Tom's shouted invectives, and not his spoken replies.

The second problem facing the Met team was the degree of visibility both the ASU and the press had of the front of the Balcombe Street apartment block. Their concerns over this were many. For one, the Met were sending people in and out of the building and having to use shouted commands to the firing teams to take up position and cover the officers making a dash in or out of the building. The shouted commands presented the ASU with the chance to take a hasty potshot at the officers as they made a run for it. The Met were also concerned about giving the ASU full view of the street below the flat. Mindful of a possible break-out by the ASU, as suicidal as it may have appeared, they needed to create barriers around which the IRA men would have to maneuver to escape, giving the SO19 snipers a better chance of taking them down. Any such barriers would serve double duty by obscuring the scene from the press. After all, a tempting prize for the ASU was parked right outside the main entrance to the apartment building, and that was the car belonging to John Mathews. With the passage of time, the ASU could view a breakout as an increasingly viable option, especially if there was an accompanying action taken elsewhere on their behalf by GHQ. There was a growing concern that this was precisely what they were intending to do, based on snippets of conversations captured by the C7 surveillance team, so the screens were a high priority for the uniform branch to organize.

The third challenge was relatively simple to solve and had been considered earlier in the week. The ASU still had full access to the continued TV coverage of the siege on the two broadcast networks, and were able to follow in detail events and images portrayed on the news. This only served to bolster their resolve as they watched the news coverage of their now defiant tactics, and it also served to give the ASU situational intelligence with regards to the state of the street outside the building. The visibility issue, problem number two, could be solved by erecting large plastic sightscreens. But, in doing so, the Met didn't want the ASU seeing that activity on prime time TV news. So, from a tactical standpoint a decision was made to disconnect the electrical and gas supply to the flat. This would deprive the ASU of the television for news and the record player for entertainment. The surveillance teams and the officers outside the living room had reported that some evenings the ASU had played, over and again, Engelbert Humperdinck records. The Mathews were obviously fans of the singer and had a collection of his recordings. It is not noted if the surveillance teams were also fans, and it is quite possible that the ASU were using the music to drown out the sounds of their voices so they could have conversations that would not be overheard by the police. It may also be the case that they just plain liked Engelbert Humperdinck. A lack of mains electricity would force the ASU to ration the use of the battery powered transistor radio in the living room, focusing on hourly news bulletins rather than listening to music for entertainment. So, by cutting off the power, the Met would also be heightening the boredom and sense of isolation experienced by the men in the room. The temperature would also start to drop, once the gas supply to the four-element fire in the tiled living room fireplace was removed. The ASU had been keeping the windows of the flat open, probably to help alleviate the growing stench coming from the chemical toilet. They would be forced to balance between the smell and the dropping temperature in the room.

The Met technical team came up with a solution to the communications problem by suspending a microphone over the balcony of 22b from the flat above. They made sure that it was close enough to pick up spoken words, but far enough away to avoid being grabbed and pulled down by a member of the ASU. The microphone was connected to speakers that faced out into the street, so that any words coming from the men, as they communicated with the negotiation team, would be broadcast to the same audience hearing Imbert's words over the loud-hailer, leveling the playing field between the two sides.

To solve the signaling problem to the firing team covering movement in and out of the apartment building, the police introduced a two-color flag signal system. Green for ready and go, red for hold or stop, signaled by an officer in the doorway of the main entrance, making it virtually impossible for anyone inside 22b to see which flag was being used at any given time. With the new signal system in place, the Met began to ferry in sandbags to the flat. These were piled up against the outside of the living room door inside the flat for two reasons. Firstly, the Met were unsure if the ASU had any explosives with them inside the room. They were demonstrated explosives experts, and if they did have a device and decided to detonate it in an act of self destruction, the sandbags would afford the officers outside the room a degree of protection from the blast. Secondly, the bags would serve to make it impossible for the ASU to make a quick exit from the room. If they opened the door, they would be faced with a wall of sandbags, which would require a considerable amount of time and effort to deal with, but not before the police could take action against them, possibly going through the balcony window, although any tactical ingress to the room would have been performed by the SAS. Going into the living room was an option the police had not discounted, despite the inherent risk to the hostages. The SAS were preparing to be deployed from their barracks in Chelsea, should the negotiators feel they had to go in. Getting food into the living room had become the chief concern of the psychiatric team and the senior leadership they were working with, and Peter Imbert was being told by his superiors to get food into the hostages. Dr. Peter Scott was working directly with DAC Gibson, as explained by Peter Imbert: "Mr. Gibson had overall tactical command of the uniformed officers and the whole situation. Mr. Gibson would come and see me every morning and say something like, 'here, look Pete Scott has advised that we don't give them anything,' or, 'he has advised we give them something so that's what we are going to do, so you get on with it and arrange it!' I knew it was Peter Scott who was advising so we trusted his judgment. And of course, as a Detective Superintendent, when you've got one of the most senior officers in the force telling you what to do, you do it!"

The concerns regarding getting food into the hostages was covered by Commander Roy Habershon in an interview broadcast on the BBC radio news that evening at 6:00pm. Firstly, Habershon outlined the now almost certain belief that they were dealing with four terrorists and not three as originally thought earlier in the siege. The police were also certain that one of the men in the flat was Michael Wilson, who was wanted for murder. This, Habershon explained, was not his real name, and good detective work was helping the Met track down the identities of the other three involved in the Saturday night shootout and the IRA terror campaign over the past year and a half. Habershon went on to state that the overriding concern was still for the wellbeing of the hostages. He continued on to state that there would come a time when the medical advisors would tell the police that the lack of food was endangering the lives of the hostages. At that point, Habershon explained, the police would have to take a decision to put food in the room, "one way or another." Asked by the BBC's Denis Frost if this could mean police officers entering the living room, Habershon stated that it was a possibility as any threat to the life and safety of the hostages would be taken care of by the police.

Imbert had to get the ASU to accept food into the apartment. He had taken his prodding commentary to Tom over the phone onto the street in a far more public forum, again questioning the actions of the ASU and how these would be viewed by the IRA. No response or reaction was heard from the ASU. Imbert requested that a clipboard and pencil be lowered to the balcony of 22b, in an effort to have the ASU write out issues or requests they did not want to have broadcast out over the loudspeakers in place outside the building. Again, there was no response from the ASU. Finally, Imbert, over the loudhailer, informed the ASU that he wanted to send in Valium tablets for the increasingly distraught Mrs. Mathews. A container was to be lowered to the ASU containing the drugs. However, Imbert and the team took a gamble. They lowered a larger than expected container of sandwiches, hot coffee, and the drugs for Sheila Mathews to the balcony of 22b, with the Met hoping that once the ASU, and the hostages, took the container into the apartment they would weaken and accept the food. Supplied by the Met's fingerprint division, the container had a smooth plastic surface and was positioned over the balcony in a way that would require a significant amount of handling to get it into the flat. The Met were hoping they would obtain additional fingerprints when the container was returned. The ASU retrieved the container from the rope suspending it outside the balcony door, with Tom handling the container and transferring it inside the living room. The police team waited nervously, wondering if their gamble would work and the ASU would accept the food.

The sound of male voices shouting inside 22b could be heard from the street. After a minute or so of the shouting the food containers, with the sandwiches and soup untouched, came arcing out of the balcony door in the same fashion the field telephone handset had done the previous day. The container hit the street and spewed out the supplies inside, and a stream of invectives was directed at the negotiation team by the ASU. The Irishmen had again publicly demonstrated their resolve to play the police at their own game, while holding out for some sign from GHQ, in a rather futile attempt to exert control over the negotiation team. As a rather blunt reminder to Tom as to who actually controlled the situation, the utilities were disconnected, removing the power and heat from the flat.

The rejection of the food was a setback for the Met, although the ASU had allowed Mrs. Mathews to keep the tranquilizers, an act that was almost certainly as much in their interest as her's. Mrs. Mathews later said that, by that point in the siege, the hunger was bothering her less. "After a few days," she said, "you do not mind. I didn't feel much like eating." The ASU had also kept some of the cigarettes included in the delivery, before launching the container back at the police.

The Met had made little real progress in getting the ASU and hostages safely out of the flat, during a highly frustrating day for the negotiations team. The ASU appeared to be becoming more defiant in their dealings with Imbert and Nevill and had clearly demonstrated their resolve to hold out, even if this now meant literally throwing food back at the police. This in turn would serve to increase the Met's concerns about the ASU's state of mind and stability. The disconnection of the utilities to the flat was a calculated risk taken by the Met in an effort increase the sense of isolation experienced by the ASU. The added impact of losing the only heat source to the flat would also make it increasingly uncomfortable in the room, despite all the body heat from the six adults and the increasing cold would accentuate the impact of the hunger the IRA men and the hostages were experiencing. Cold, hungry, and with an increasing sense of isolation, the question the Met were asking was how much longer could the ASU hold out? Would GHQ be able to get a signal or message to the ASU, via the media, so they could arrange an orderly end to the stand-off? Had the Met made a mistake further isolating the ASU and increasing the level of discomfort they were experiencing? The siege was reaching a critical stage for both sides, with the ASU becoming outwardly more hard-line, but having to deal with increased deprivations, some now self-imposed, others courtesy of the Met. The next few exchanges between the Met and the ASU would be critical. Imbert and Nevill had to get through to them to avoid the increasing likelihood of a tactical resolution to the siege. If they could not get food into the flat in the next 24 hours, the resolution to the stand-off may very well be taken from their control and handed over to the military, with the inherent increased risk that the Mathews would not survive the event. The following day would call on Peter Imbert and Jim Nevill to reach deep into their collective intuitive bag of tricks to get the ASU to talk with them, and to get the men to accept the food they were being told by superior officers the hostages must receive.

THURSDAY DECEMBER 11TH

The setback of the previous evening, with the ASU throwing food out into the street, had spurred the negotiation team to start again early the morning of Thursday December 11th, day five of the siege–day five and the hostages and hostage takers had been cooped up in the close confines of the living room together for five nights. They were unwashed, smelly, cold, weary and very hungry. Conditions in the small room at this point in the stand off would have been appalling. The stench of the chemical toilet would have permeated the room with its putrid odor. Mrs. Mathews was in constant pain with her back from being forced to sit curled up in the armchair she had been confined to since the start of the siege. She was in pain and anxious. The Valium she had been given would have been less effective than the doctors would have hoped, due to her lack of nourishment. It was a very uncomfortable situation for her.

Jim Nevill, in the street with the loudhailer, attempted to rouse Tom in an effort to get the IRA man talking. Nevill needed to get the ASU to soften their adopted hard-line and allow food in for the hostages, and the ASU. To the delight of the negotiators, Tom engaged with Nevill in a dialogue, full of pauses and silences, but it was a breakthrough that Nevill was going to push. He had Tom talking, and the negotiating team needed that to continue to the point where Tom would agree to the acceptance of the urgently needed food supply. Tom refused to answer some of Nevill's questions, and also refused to make any comment, when asked, on the condition of the hostages. They discussed the conditions inside the living room, and it became apparent that things were pretty dire. Nevill offered to send Tom a new chemical pack for the toilet, and some fresh drinking water. After a short pause, the IRA man agreed to have the supplies passed down to the balcony. The negotiation team passed the message to the uniformed officers in the apartment above to send down the agreed supplies.

Using two metal buckets, the replacement chemical toilet pack and drinking water were lowered to the ASU. The buckets were taken into the flat through the balcony door, where they were unloaded and passed back outside. It is worth noting that the first chemical toilet pack was stowed under the drinks cabinet in the living room and not removed and returned to the police. The empty buckets were hauled back up by the uniformed officers in the flat above. The Met team was delighted, as this marked the first time they had managed to get the Irishmen to willingly accept anything into the flat since the previous Sunday. Hopes were raised that the hard-line Tom and his compatriots had been adopting could be softening under the pressures of the previous few days. Their first night in the flat without power and heat may have contributed to a noticeable softening of their attitude toward the negotiators. Would they accept food, now that they had taken something from the Met? The ASU had demonstrated to the police their willingness and determination to endure, to that point, the deprivations of the standoff situation. It did not appear that they had psychically harmed the hostages, although Tom's lack of communications on their condition would have been a concern to the negotiation team. Commander Roy Habershon commented on that point during a press conference that morning.

Habershon stated that he firmly believed the hostage takers had not "laid a finger in anger" on the hostages. He remained confident that the five-day stand off would still end without bloodshed. Habershon went on to add, giving the ASU something of a sideways compliment, that the IRA group in 22b were a determined band of men who were "quite capable" of withstanding the long siege. It would appear the ASU had come a long way in the senior leadership's opinion over the course of the siege, rising above the "vulgar criminal" categorization of the previous weekend.

One factor that was essential in helping the ASU withstand the pressure of the lengthening siege was the degree of cohesiveness they had as a group. Acting under the leadership of O'Connell, they had behaved as the disciplined well trained unit that they were. The psychology of group behavior was working in their favor. Psychologist Irving Janis described how group cohesion can increase in already well integrated groups under conditions of hardship or pressure from outside groups. Cohesiveness also increases when group members are frightened and face a difficult decision with serious ramifications. The other members of the ASU had demonstrated their deference to O'Connell, particularly Eddie Butler in his role as both Mick and Paddy, by seeking his approval rather than responding directly to any questions from the negotiation team when he was on the field telephone. The clear leadership, coupled with the time the men had been operating together, helped the group function as an increasingly cohesive unit. As the group stuck more and more closely together against the pressure applied to them under the siege conditions, their own self-image and identity as a disciplined urban guerrilla unit would have been enhanced. This would work in conjunction with a principle known as in-group/out-group polarization, as under siege conditions, the cohesiveness would have given the ASU an increased sense of "we-ness," the strong "us" bond they felt facing an adversary of "them"–the Metropolitan police. In their minds they were Irish Republican Army freedom fighters, and the Met were the face of the British Establishment they had been attacking in their clubs, pubs, restaurants and homes. The Met, "they," were the enemy, the other team, the opposition. In their belief set, the ASU–the "we" or "us"–were striving for a centuries-old goal of an Ireland without the heel of British oppression, a united Ireland where the Catholic population in the north would have equal housing and employment rights and the same opportunities the Protestant majority enjoyed, equal voting rights, and a right to self determination. One country, not divided into an Irish republic and the six counties in the north as it had been since the days of Michael Collins and the bitter civil war of the early 1920's. The British would call them "Fenian bastards" and they would have equally hateful terms for them in return. In a protracted terror campaign, erupting into violent peaks as the politicians argued and failed to reach terms acceptable to all parties, sometimes the protagonists on both sides lose sight of the basic root causes of the problem as they become gripped in a sectarian spiral of escalating tit-for-tat reprisals. It is all too easy for either side to demonize the other, while simultaneously draping themselves in the flag of nationalistic pride and patriotic cause. The psychology of polarized groups, where the "other" side is always less worthy than your own, has always been at the root of such conflicts whether it was the 1970's mindless tribal violence of rival football fans, Protestant or Catholic paramilitary groups, or state-sponsored war. It would have been relatively easy, from an ideological standpoint, for the ASU to summon up decades, if not more, of real or perceived "reasons" to justify what they had carried out on the British mainland, while stoking the fires of their own resistance to the police and renewing their own self-serving indignation and hatred for the British. Such justification could have included the believed collusion between the RUC and the Protestant fighters, the gunning down of Irish Catholics by the British Black and Tans, Internment and whatever other demonizing factors they could pull from their collective memories of Republican lore, taught to them by fathers, brothers, uncles from an early age. Recollections of Bloody Sunday became a strong motivator for many a young Irishman to join the IRA in order to strike back at the British. The four men in the flat with the two hostages were no exception. They were believers in the Republican cause–they had to be to carry out the deeds they had performed over the previous months in their relentless and prolific campaign of terror waged against the British public. None of the group was either sociopathic or psychotic, so it takes a believer to place a nail bomb or high explosive device in a situation where he knows, with absolute certainty, that it will kill, maim or seriously injure innocent civilians. Some may have argued it was a form of cowardice and the act of a mindless killer, but it takes a believer to give up any semblance of a normal life, living undercover among the enemy, plotting death and destruction while evading capture or death at the hands of the police. In the same manner, the police, the British public and the press regarded them as murdering, ruthless villains. One man's freedom fighter is another man's terrorist–right and wrong would depend on which side of the argument you happened to be on, but the cold hard facts were difficult to avoid. They had conducted a widespread campaign of violence, killing many and wounding hundreds, all in a cause started so long ago. However, it is not our job here to pass judgment on the IRA men and the bloody mayhem they unleashed, but to look the psychological motivations for their actions and what drove them to stay the course in a siege situation. As mentioned earlier, Mr. Mathews was shocked at the reaction to his questions put to the four IRA men on the first night of the siege, with the ASU blaming the British for all that was wrong with the world. It helps to hate your "enemy," and they evidently did so with a vengeance. The IRA men appeared indifferent toward their hostages, rarely speaking to them or addressing them directly after the outburst on the Saturday night. There was little evidence of the bonding associated with the phenomenon known as the Stockholm syndrome, where hostages from a dependent bond with their captors. It is just possible that the Met were hoping, given the length of time the six adults had been confined together, that such a bond would have developed. If so, it would have made shooting the hostages all the more difficult. It is possible the four Irishmen were impacted by the TV broadcast featuring the impassioned plea by Joan Royce, as the Met had not received any threat-related demands from the group. They could have made counter demands to Peter Imbert, when he offered food for Mrs. Mathews, to shoot one of the hostages if their own demands were not complied with. They had not done that and in fact the Mathews, as the ASU were surely aware, were the sole reason the ASU had not been overrun by either the police or the SAS. If the food situation did not change, and quickly, there was no assurance they would not be subjected to a tactical assault.

Food. It was all coming down to the nourishment of the hostages, and the potentially hunger-driven impaired judgment of the ASU. Peter Imbert took over the loudhailer duty and relayed messages to the hostages of support and hope from friends and family. The couple's plight had gripped the nation's attention, thanks to the extensive coverage of the siege in both the print and broadcast media. However, not everyone agreed, or appreciated, the intense media focus on the unfolding events in Balcombe Street, with some fearing it was bordering on the reckless. In one letter to the editor of The Times, from a retired General of the British Army, it was pointed out how "delighted" the IRA would be at having such close media attention to their cause, where the press openly discussed what alternatives were open to the IRA, what the return actions could be on both sides, and the dangers that were still to come. The writer drew a parallel with WWII, remembering a poster depicting Herman Goering, reclining in the overhead luggage rack of a British train, with the caption "the enemy is also listening." The writer was not to know the level of cooperation between the media and the police that would continue to be a vital element of the siege.

Imbert's messages of support to the hostages did not elicit any response from the ASU inside number 22b. In fact, apart from the initial early morning exchange of words between Jin Nevill and Tom, and the acceptance of supplies, very few signs of movement from inside the flat had been noted that morning. The enforced occupants were quiet and subdued. Little could be gained from the continued use of the loudhailer, other than the messages of support to the incarcerated couple. The ASU appeared to not want to talk back.

It remained an urgent priority of the Met to have food of any kind sent into the flat. The medical team was becoming insistent that the hostages receive some form of nourishment, and it was believed that giving the ASU food would help move the negotiations along as well. But, previous attempts to send food into the flat, by lowering a container of food to the balcony door without the agreement of the ASU, had resulted in the consignment being hurled back at the police in a very public display of defiance. Imbert and Nevill could not afford to have that happen again. The negotiation team had to find a tactic that would either persuade or intimidate the ASU to take in the supplies when they were offered again. The question remained, what tactic would work on the ASU?

Behind the scenes, steady police work was helping to piece together a better picture of the key terrorist suspect Michael Wilson. The Met and their counterpart in C3, the Irish Republic's counter terrorism branch, were mystified as to why they did not have any record of the IRA man on file. He was obviously an experienced IRA operative, having been involved in operations in the Irish Republic, such as the art robbery and subsequent shootout with Garda forces. He had been linked, through forensic evidence, to the bomb factory at Fairholme Road, the shooting of Ross McWhirter, and the chase and shootout on the previous Saturday. Someone had to know his real identity, and at some point something triggered a vague recollection or recognition in members of C3. It may have been the artist's impression of the wanted man, developed by the Met, and published by the national media. The artist's drawing, developed by working with eyewitnesses such as Rosemary McWhirter and the landlord of the Fairholme Road flat, did have a striking resemblance to Harry Duggan. The officers from C3 opted to search the files of known IRA operatives reported to have been killed over the course of the previous few years. Their deaths would have caused their files to be removed from the list of active subversives in the Republic and the northern six counties. Their suspicions proved to be correct. They found a match to a Harris Duggan junior of Feakle, County Clare, wanted by the Irish police for a string of offenses, all uninvestigated due to his apparent death. Officers from C3 paid a visit to his father, Harris Duggan senior who also lived in Feakle, where they collected photographs of the younger Duggan. His father related the story, as told to him, of his son's apparent death while on active service for the IRA in the North in 1974. Officers from C3 suspected that the news of the younger Duggan's death had been planted by a police informant, working on behalf of the Provisional IRA, resulting in his records being lifted from the active list.

Peter Imbert recalled the event, "There were reports that he had been killed in action in the north and had been buried. That's why when we got fingerprints and sent them over [to Ireland] they were not compared with Harry Duggan's prints. They had removed his records from the fingerprint records, because he was dead. I don't know who the poor devil it was they buried in his place!"

Duggan, a Provisional "unknown" had been identified. The discovery would force C3 to go over the records of other "dead" IRA operatives to see if any other unidentified sleepers were out and about and operating under the radar. They had good reason to be concerned. The Provisionals, in the creation of Michael Wilson, most likely did so with the full knowledge and help of the British system, of the time, for issuing passports to British citizens. Viewed from the perspective of modern times, the system was alarmingly simple to cheat. The Provisionals would have looked for someone born in Britain around the same time as the person they were looking to create a new identity for, in Duggan's case October 1952. They would find the desired identity by going through churchyards looking for a death, preferably as a child, of someone born that year. They would then have made an application for a duplicate birth certificate from St. Catherine's house, in London, the central storage repository for all such documents in the British Isles, and something that genealogy researchers would routinely carry out in the course of their investigations. Certificate in hand, a simple forged signature and stamp of the issuing parish would be added, something that could be done with a simple block letter hand printing set. The birth certificate, along with photographs, completed application form and fee would be sent to the passport office, who would issue a new passport in the name of Michael Wilson. It was that simple. With Duggan identified, police on both sides would be looking for any known associates of the IRA man, in effort to establish the identities of the rest of the ASU.

It had been a long day of little activity inside the flat. Peter Imbert had continued to make broadcasts on the loudhailer, passing on further messages of support and encouragement to the hostages. With the urgent need to get food into the hostages, he turned his attention to Tom and the ASU in an effort to get them to talk. He was not having much success. After consulting with the medical team, the negotiators decided to try a variation on the food delivery attempt of the previous day. Imbert arranged for a supply of hot soup, sandwiches, coffee and cigarettes to be brought to the apartment above number 22b. He could not afford to have Tom publicly ignore another attempt by the police to have supplies sent into the hostages. If that happened, then the public would be concerned that the Met were losing the initiative in the negotiations, with the ASU stubbornly stonewalling with Imbert and Nevill. He had to get them to accept the delivery, and mentally rehearsed the words he would use over the loudhailer to address Tom in a way that, he hoped, would force the IRA man into accepting the food. He had to try a different approach, the pressuring and cajoling he had been able to do over the field telephone was history and now he had to continue with the loudhailer as a blunt instrument in the process of communicating with the recalcitrant group in 22b.

The first container was lowered into position by an officer wearing a headset, so he could hear instructions passed to him by the negotiation team. The time was 8:00pm. The container swayed back and forth on the end of a rope, level with the balcony window. Imbert addressed the ASU leader directly, "Tom, your comrades cannot make a decision on this. This is a public announcement, the press will know the food is for the hostages and you are refusing it!" No reaction was seen or heard from the IRA men in the flat. A very tense ten minutes passed with the container of food still untouched, or acknowledged by the ASU, hanging outside the window. It appeared the situation was going to be a repeat of the day before. The Met senior leadership were being insistent that the food should go into the flat, but if the ASU were not going to cooperate, it had to be wondered how many more attempts they would allow the negotiation team before they decided to escalate the situation and use force.

Undeterred, Imbert tried again to get the ASU to talk to him, urging Tom to open the window. On the loudhailer again, Imbert made a second public appeal, "I presume you are taking responsibility, Tom, to deprive these people? The food is on doctor's orders for Mr. and Mrs. Mathews."

Finally Imbert had gained Tom's attention, with the Irishman coming to the open window. Imbert informed Tom that he was sending in food for five people as "you told me, Tom, there were five people in there." Tom responded to Imbert, asking him how he knew for sure the number of people in the flat. Imbert replied, "how many are there? These are all the sandwiches you are going to get!"

The tension was reaching a peak at the scene, as the image of the hanging food container and open window was a direct repeat of Wednesday and the ASU showed no signs of accepting a delivery this time either. Imbert waited for some reaction from Tom. Everyone on the police team was holding their breath, mentally urging the ASU to take in the container of food. When would they respond?

The silence was shattered by a shrill, piercing scream from Sheila Mathews. "Take it!" she yelled at the top of her voice, the situation finally proving too much for her to take. There was a short pause where nothing could be heard from the flat. Then Tom, speaking to Imbert, suggested that perhaps they should send in food for seven. Imbert agreed to make it food for six, knowing full well the request was a ploy from Tom to get more food, now that they had decided to accept the police supplies. Food for six was a good compromise, so Tom agreed to Imbert's counter offer. Tom manhandled the first container into the flat, and the officers above commenced lowering two further containers. By 8:15pm, the last container had been passed into the living room. Inside, Mr. and Mrs. Mathews later related how the ASU made them consume some of the food and drink first, as a precaution against the food being laced with drugs. Satisfied the food was edible, the ASU consumed their share of the food–their first in at least 108 hours. After eating, Sheila Mathews was allowed to move from the armchair to the couch and swap places with her husband, where she could stretch out and ease the pain in her back.

The Met team was understandably pleased with the result of that exchange. They had made a significant breakthrough in getting the ASU to accept the supplies after several days of belligerent resistance from the men. What would Friday bring? Was the acceptance of food an indicator that the ASU were moving back to a more reasonable position? The negotiation team had to wonder if this gesture on the part of the ASU was the preliminary step toward a possible capitulation, or would they now be more willing to release Sheila Mathews. She had become an increasing liability to the ASU, with her highly audible scream that afternoon acting as a catalyst to the ASU accepting the food. Maybe that would be an angle that Imbert and Nevill could exploit the following day, offering the men a way of handing off the female hostage in a manner that would look good for them. After all, Habershon had already told the ASU they would do themselves good by releasing Mrs. Mathews. They could but hope, as they started to formulate their strategy for the following day, that the next day would build on the success achieved on the Thursday and be even more productive.

During the food transfer, the uniformed branch brought in a truckload of scaffolding, planks and plastic sheets in order to erect the first of the two sight screens outside the apartment building to block off the view of the ASU and the Press. The first sightscreen was erected to the north of the apartment building that evening and stretched across Balcombe Street from both sides and extended thirty feet above street level. The uniformed branch intended to erect a second such screen the following day.

As events in Balcombe Street wound down for the evening, the Parliamentary debate on capital punishment for terrorist acts of murder came to a conclusion, with the members of the house on a free vote and not one dictated by party lines. The motion was defeated with 361 voting against the motion and 232 in favor, a majority of 129. During the preceding debate, both the home secretary Roy Jenkins and his shadow cabinet opposite number, Ian Gillmore, had both spoken eloquently against the motion. Mr. Gillmore talked about the concerns of entering a retaliatory cycle of IRA revenge killings, which would only produce more act of terrorism. Mr. Jenkins praised the police at Balcombe Street for their response to the siege in being, "patient, resourceful, disciplined and determined." Mr. Jenkins, in winding up the debate, said it would be wrong to view the call to reinstate the death penalty as a "sign of toughness," while resistance to the call should also not be viewed as a policy of softness toward terrorism. He promised the House there would be no amnesty for terrorists and that he recognized, in a shot at Sinn Féin, that no political excuse existed for "cold blooded murder." As expected there were many MP's also as passionate toward the passing of the motion, including the Conservative MP for Stafford and Stow, Hugh Fraser, who had narrowly escaped being killed by the ASU when the bomb they had placed under his car exploded prematurely, killing Professor Gordon Hamilton-Farley. Fraser was adamant that the British government should have available the "severest penalty" in the death sentence. It did not go unnoticed by some members of the House that the debate and vote was exactly one year to the day of the previous Parliamentary debate on the same topic. It was also noted by others in the House that during the debate one year previous, the now trapped ASU had made a bomb attack on the Navy and Military Club and had also shot at the Cavalry Club.

The ASU, having had their first food in five days were faced with working out their next move with the Met, balancing their actions against what GHQ may have in store for them. Across the street in 20 Dorset Square, Imbert and Nevill felt a measure of success in getting Tom to take in the food supplies. They too had to wonder what the next day would bring, and how the ASU would react to any of the tactics they were contemplating. The soup and sandwiches would have improved their spirits, and given them some much needed nourishment, but what would they do next?

That night, lying in bed, Imbert would go over in his mind the conversations with Tom, working out his plan for Friday, searching and reaching for the words he would use with the Irishman, looking for maximum impact while at the same time worrying over the conversations of the past few days and the impact that his words may have had on the ASU. What if he had said something that was fermenting in the imagination of Tom, something that would trigger the ASU into violence? He would be haunted by these thoughts for some time, going over the conversations, tugging at the threads of his words, unraveling them in a search for something, anything, that may push Tom past the point of no return. The SAS were ready to go in, if Sir Robert Mark gave the order, and so Imbert had to get the hostages out before a military deployment became a tactical choice the senior leadership deemed necessary, cutting the negotiators out of the process as the SAS went in shooting.

FRIDAY DECEMBER 12TH

Friday, day six of the siege, and the last day of the working week for the office workers in the Balcombe Street area who were still having to check in and out with the uniformed officers outside their workplaces. The Met were maintaining a high level of vigilance as they still believed GHQ had the capability to pull off some type of operation, to either create a diversion, or force the British government into another standoff to free the ASU. There were only nine more shopping days before Christmas. If the siege dragged on, there would be the question of IRA strikes on the Christmas shopping crowds as they bustled their way around the bitter cold London streets.

Inside number 22b, little thought was being given to the Christmas holiday. Some of the food from the day before had been saved, and Mrs.

Mathews later described eating a sandwich with a cup of coffee as breakfast that Friday morning.

Jim Nevill opened up the communications of the day at 7:30am, using the loudhailer. He asked how the hostages were doing and was told by Tom that they were "okay." That was an improvement over past enquiries as to the well-being of the couple, so Nevill pushed Tom by asking if he could speak with either of the hostages. Tom refused to allow any conversations with the Mathews and did not give Nevill a reason, just a firm "no." Not wanting to lose the flow in the communication, Nevill asked if a relative of Sheila Matthews could come and speak with her. The response from the IRA man was somewhat noteworthy. After considering Nevill's request, Tom turned him down, stating that Mrs. Mathews would find the experience too upsetting, hinting at the probable reaction she had to the TV appeal by her sister. Tom did not have to qualify his denial of Nevill's request, but the fact he did is a clear indicator of the power of Joan Royce's broadcast on the previous Tuesday, and the impact Sheila Mathews's reaction must have had on the others in the flat. So, on that Friday morning, Tom told Nevill that no, relatives could not come and speak with Sheila Mathews, as she would become too upset, and by implication the rest of the people in the flat would have to deal with the resulting emotional reaction. It was, in retrospect, both a highly compassionate action toward Mrs. Mathews, and one also intended to insulate the ASU and Mr. Mathews from the aftermath of such an event. The action showed that the group of IRA men, while not bonding with the hostages, at least connected with their emotional reactions, and how that, in turn, impacted their response. So no, there would be no conversations with relatives. Nevill continue the dialogue, urging Tom to convince the ASU to come out, to stop the siege and release the hostages. He carefully avoided using the language of surrender, as both he and Imbert had worked all week to avoid the psychologically negative term. Nevill told Tom they would be doing themselves a favor if they released Mrs. Mathews, but again this received a negative response, as did Nevill's request to send in a replacement field telephone to the ASU. Finally, Nevill asked Tom if they needed fresh drinking water to which Tom replied "yes." It had been a difficult, halting exchange between the two men that had lasted twenty two minutes.

Following the conversation with Nevill, something changed for one or all of the IRA men in the flat. Six days of being confined to the small living room of number 22b, six days of pressurizing negotiations, six days of bad sleep, little food, nervous hostages, the continued foul stench of the chemical toilet, being cold, dirty and with a limited supply of cigarettes, it was all becoming too much for the ASU. Six days of waiting and hoping for some signal from GHQ that they were going to get them out. They needed a sign, anything, to let them know that the IRA leadership had not abandoned them. Frustrated, angry, or just plain terrified, one or more of the ASU snapped, and convinced the rest of the group to go along with the plan they had talked about under the cover of the record player. They had had enough, they would not take anymore. They were an Active Service Unit, highly trained and still armed, and they had been inactive for six days while the police tried to crack their will and grind down their spirit. They decided they were going to break out, as the Met had feared, and John and Sheila Mathews, as human collateral, were going to be the means of their escape. They pooled their available cash, giving them £10 each in case they became separated once they were outside the apartment. They divided up the remaining ammunition–.38's for Butler and Dougherty, .357's for O'Connell and Duggan–and put the bullets into empty cigarette boxes, which they placed in their pockets. The hostages were untied and made to walk around the room, to get their circulations flowing and to ensure they would be able to walk unaided. Mr. Mathews was made to put on one of the ASU's jackets in an effort to confuse the police once they got outside. Their plan was simple. They would exit the flat holding tightly to Mr. and Mrs. Mathews, each with a gun barrel placed in their mouth, and they would tell the police that they would shoot the hostages if the police prevented them from reaching Mr. Mathews' car, parked out front, and driving away. Butler later told Jim Nevill, when asked, if the plan was to drive to Heathrow and hijack a plane, but Butler told Nevill that they hadn't really worked out what they were going to do at that stage. Getting out and driving away was the key first step, which would entail getting out of the living room door, blocked with sandbags, past the armed officers and the dogs inside the flat, down the stairwell to the front door of the building, out the door under the watchful marksmanship of the SO19 snipers, round the sight screen to John Mathews' Ford Cortina, bundle everyone into the car, and drive away with flat tires. Simple, if viewed through a very narrow and rationalized mindset driven by desperation. We cannot be absolutely certain for the reason the change in tactic by the ASU took place, to go from stubborn resistance to making a bid for freedom. Maybe they reasoned GHQ was not going to get them out, and so they would either get out on their own or go down fighting. In any event, they had resolved to break out in what would have been an almost certain suicidal bid for freedom. However, the decision, and the preparations they were making to execute the plan, would trigger a remarkable chain of events.

News of the ASU's plan to break out would have been conveyed to the negotiation team and the senior leadership by the surveillance team and the officers outside the living room door. Imbert and Nevill had no secure means of communicating with the ASU, and even if they did what would they say? We know you're going to break out, so pack it in and don't be so stupid? They had to find a way of getting a message to the ASU that they were in deadly peril, at risk of being killed as they attempted to make it to the street. But what could they say that would make it absolutely certain that the IRA men would realize that they meant business, and that time was running out for them? What would they fear, above all else, that would ensure their capitulation? The Met was also running out of time, as the ASU were planning on starting a chain of events that would almost certainly result in some, if not all of them, being shot by the SO19 snipers, or the other armed units, with the probable resulting death of the two innocent hostages. The second sight screen had not been erected, allowing a full view for the press, near Dorset Square, of the events as they unfolded. They would be handing the IRA a propaganda opportunity of major significance.

Peter Imbert later commented on the breakout plan of the ASU. "I think what they were thinking about doing was getting into Mr. Mathews' car, which was parked outside the main doors to the apartment block. But, we had taken precautions over that and had put a big plastic screen right across the street, so they'd have needed a lot of courage to come out, make a go for the car and get away. They would have been captured or shot before they got to the car."

The Met team needed to present the ASU with an option to give up, while still inside the flat, by making the odds of their survival appear so dire that there was no way they would go on with their plan to break out of the flat. They would not know about the barricaded living room door. They would not know the car had been tampered with, and could possibly only guess at the number of rifles and hand guns that would be pointed in their direction as they attempted to get out. The Met needed to get a scenario in the minds of the ASU that would ensure their capitulation in the face of overwhelming odds, and get it to them fast. The question was, how?

The message delivery solution was the government controlled BBC. At a hastily convened press briefing, broadcast at 1:00pm that Friday, DAC Peter Walton, talked with the BBC's David Lay. The BBC news man described how the police had not discounted the possibility of a shootout with the IRA men, and that the police had announced that a detachment of soldiers from the Special Air Service was on standby and ready to go into the apartment. DAC Walton confirmed the situation with the SAS, "yes, they are on standby," he confirmed, emphasizing that "all possibilities are being considered." The SAS were ready to go in, if ordered to by the police who were in tactical command of the situation. Mr. Mathews later said that they had all heard the broadcast on the transistor radio, "there was a mention that the SAS were on hand."

The SAS are the elite of the elite in the world of the Special Forces. They had been practicing storming the flat in the mockup they had built at their Chelsea barracks. The IRA men would have been very aware of the ruthless efficiency of the Army's band of elite trained killers, well practiced in close quarter armed combat. Any assault by the SAS would be rapid, hard, and probably over before they could react. Stun grenades would temporarily blind and confuse the ASU, followed by armed troopers who would target each man and shoot to kill. They would not get out alive. Sir Robert Mark was prepared to sacrifice the hostages as noted earlier, but to actually send in the SAS and kill the IRA men would have been a political nightmare for the Wilson government. But, we are left to speculate if the deaths of the IRA men would have been a propaganda tool the IRA would use against the British. Would their "execution" at the hands of the SAS turn them into martyrs, to be immortalized forever in Republican lore? Would that serve the cause better than having the ASU languish in a high-security prison for the rest of their lives? The harsh reality facing the ASU was plain and simple. While GHQ trusted them to not reveal operational details if captured by the British, they were, as a unit, expendable. No matter how valuable they may have been to the IRA, others would come along to take their place in the ongoing struggle. Maybe this realization that they were indeed expendable, and probably already written off by their leadership, caused a rapid change of heart in the ASU. The possible realization that they had been abandoned to the mercies of the Met, plus the BBC insight to their potential fate, gave the ASU three options to choose from. They could carry out their plan and breakout, with a high probability of being shot by the police in the process. They could continue to hold the Mathews as hostages and wait for the SAS to come crashing, unannounced, through the balcony window with their flash bang grenades and automatic weapons. Neither of these options gave them much chance of survival. The only option that would get them out alive was to give in. Surrender. Give up. Give Imbert and Nevill what they wanted, give up the hostages, sit in a cell in Paddington Green police station and face a lengthy interrogation on their past misdeeds. A brief trial, then they would spend life in Parkhurst prison, or some other high-security jail in the British Isles. It was over.

There is no paper trail or even a direct willingness on the part of the police officers involved at the time to attribute the 1:00pm BBC news broadcast as anything but a coincidence. None of officers involved at the time and interviewed by the author acknowledged the BBC as being primed by the Met. However, Sir Robert Mark did refer to the practice working with the media so that specific questions would be asked of the police during press conferences, so that the police could get across a point or comment and make it sound as though it was not a pre-scripted response. Nevertheless, the subsequent impact that the 1:00pm broadcast had on the ASU is undeniable in terms of the reaction they had to the content. Having weighed up all the options, Butler would later tell Nevill and Imbert that the ASU felt the odds were against them, and so giving in was the only real option left open.

The ASU must have debated these options for about thirty minutes after the end of the BBC broadcast. Shouting out of the balcony window at 1:45pm, Tom asked Imbert to send in another land line, a key breakthrough for the Metropolitan police. Imbert and Nevill were thrilled; Tom wanted to talk in private. This was the key psychological moment the negotiation team had been striving for all week. The police scrambled to bring in the extra field telephone kept in reserve, and the replacement field telephone was lowered to the balcony of 22b. Peter Imbert called to Tom on the loudhailer, as he later recalled. "They requested a new field telephone, so I said over the megaphone, 'it's outside the window now Tom, so reach out and get it. The most important thing about this one is don't muck about with it or throw this one out the window because we haven't got any more left!' That was true, we'd have had to ask the Army for one, and that would have been embarrassing."

With the new field telephone in place, Tom wasted no time in making an opening gambit with Peter Imbert, taking the experienced police officer a little by surprise. "After the second field phone had been passed to them," related Imbert, "Tom said to me, 'what are the terms for our surrender?' That was the first time during the week that either of us had used that word. I had avoided using the term surrender because it sounds like one is crowing over a victory. Myself and Jim [Nevill] had consistently avoided using it but he [Tom] used it that morning. I replied, 'you're not mucking me about are you?' But, that's when we started negotiating about how that [surrender] was going to happen. That was most definitely a key psychological moment–we knew they were going to come out and that was the end of it."

Tom had opened the door for Imbert to now control the orderly collapse of the siege. He negotiated with Tom in sorting out the details of the hostage handover and exit of the four Irishmen from the flat. Imbert and Tom reached an agreement on how they would move forward. First, Sheila Mathews was to be released. Once she was safely in police hands, Imbert would have a hot meal sent into the flat for the four IRA men and their remaining hostage. He would allow them time to enjoy their first hot meal in days, and then they would release Mr. Mathews and come out one at a time, after showing that they were unarmed. They would walk out onto the balcony and climb across the dividing railing that separated the balcony of 22b from that of the flat next door.

Tension and anxiety was building on both sides. Getting everyone out without incident was to prove a very nerve-racking experience for the negotiating team. Imbert was deeply concerned that someone would misread an action or gesture and start shooting. People had been wound up for a considerable amount of time, so things would have to move at a controlled, measured pace, with only one person, namely Imbert, calling the shots. Peter Imbert later recalled the concerns he had. "Then of course we had the most difficult and sensitive part of the operation–getting them all out one-by-one and getting them out safely, so that nobody did anything silly, either the terrorists or our chaps. You can imagine Mr. Mathews coming out onto the balcony and waving to the public, and somebody thinking he's going for a gun, not knowing he was the hostage rather than a terrorist."

It was time for the ASU to release Sheila Mathews. Tom, in another positive gesture towards the hostages, asked Imbert if it would be okay for somebody to help Mrs. Mathews walk out onto the balcony and to the dividing railing, and she was feeling weak and needed support. Imbert agreed, providing the ASU man helping her demonstrated he was unarmed. Tom agreed, and Eddie Butler emerged from the balcony door, hands raised. Satisfied, Imbert told Tom to have the ASU man bring out Sheila Mathews, who was dressed in a green floral housecoat and red stockings. Butler, supporting her right arm, helped her toward the dividing railing. Imbert became concerned as he could not see Butler's left arm, obscured from his view. Imbert told Tom to have the ASU man raise his left arm. Tom called to Butler through the door, "Eddie, raise your left arm," and Butler complied. Mrs. Mathews was left at the balcony dividing railing by Butler, who backed away and then turned around with his hands raised. He moved back into the flat. The time was 2:15pm.

Mrs. Mathews was left alone outside, in a gentle drizzling rain, for about a minute. Two officers from the flat next door stepped out onto the balcony. One covered the balcony of 22b with a handgun, while the other helped Mrs. Mathews across the railing. Minutes later, escorted by a female police officer, she was seen scurrying across Balcombe Street to a waiting ambulance, from where she was rushed to University College Hospital for a checkup. Detective Inspector Ron Chapman was asked to ride in the ambulance with Mrs. Mathews in order to conduct a tactical debriefing. He was to record this on a small Dictaphone machine, to gain situational intelligence regarding the insides of the flat in case the police still had to resort to an assault on the building. As Ron Chapman recalled, "I didn't get to talk to her much, because it was a very short run to the hospital. Once we got in there she was whisked off by a large number of doctors and nurses who told me that I would have to wait in order to talk with her!"

At the request of the police team, news of the ASU agreement to release Mrs. Mathews was held back by the BBC. They agreed to hold off announcing the negotiated release of Sheila Mathews until the 3:00pm news broadcast. The BBC were fully aware that the ASU were following events on the radio, and so agreed to the police request to delay the report, as they were concerned that broadcasting of the news real-time could impact the work Imbert still had to do to get the ASU and Mr. Mathews out of the apartment safely.

Good to his word, Imbert had a large metal container of food lowered to the five remaining men in the flat. The first hot meal they had eaten all week consisted of sausages, Brussels sprouts and potatoes. Imbert, as he said he would, allowed the men time to enjoy their last meal outside of a British prison environment. Their future meals would be courtesy of Her Majesty's Prison Service.

At 3:50pm, Peter Imbert called Tom on the field telephone and asked the Irishman, "Who is going to come out first?" Imbert wanted to secure the release of Mr. Mathews, but Tom was reluctant to release his only remaining hostage, fearing it would leave the ASU exposed to an attack once the civilian was out of the room. Imbert and Tom discussed the order of release and agreed that Mr. Mathews would come out in the middle of the group, leaving only two of the ASU in the flat without a hostage, a workable compromise for both sides.

The ASU made themselves makeshift hoods to obscure their identity. They disarmed and placed all their loaded handguns and ammunition on the floor by the television set. As part of their preparations to end the siege and surrender to the police, Mr. Mathews later stated that the four IRA men used whiskey from the drinks cabinet as a means of cleaning their teeth. The four men had not touched any of the alcohol in the flat since the beginning of the siege, demonstrating considerable discipline and restraint in doing so, given the conditions they were facing. We are, however, left with the question as to why they used whiskey to clean their teeth, before being taken into custody, as this would have left a considerable odor of alcohol on their breath as they gave themselves up to the police.

Eddie Butler was the first to emerge onto the balcony at 4:15pm with hands raised. He was covered by marksmen in the adjoining building, and by officers on the adjacent balcony. Butler was transferred to the flat next door and into a police van in Balcombe Street, where he would wait for the rest of the ASU to join him.

Tension was rising in the Met teams as the end of the six day stand-off was in sight. Imbert had to keep the situation calm, as there were a lot of fingers on triggers, and all the guns were trained on the balcony of 22b. The armed officers, conducting the transfers, were evidently in a rush to get them all out quickly and were becoming increasingly nervous, as Peter Imbert later described. "When they were finally coming out of the flat, there was a lot of noise in the background. The Assistant Commissioner was near me at the time and said, 'who's doing all the bloody shouting?' In fact it was the firearms team in the next flat yelling, 'come on, come on! Next one, next one, next one!" I had to say to O'Connell, 'don't take any notice of anyone but me.' What I didn't want to have happen was to have people who'd been trained to kill [the Met Firearms team] and had been waiting a week getting a bit jumpy."

Officer A and his partner from the SPG were called around to the front of the building to cover the exit of the ASU, along with the firearms teams, as he later recalled, "so, we actually saw them come out, which was nice for us. It was only the second time we had seen them, only this time they were unarmed and with their hands above their heads, which was also nice!"

At 4:16pm Hugh Dougherty transferred from number 22b in the same manner as Butler. John Mathews followed Dougherty, and cautiously made the walk across the balcony to the waiting officers ready to receive him. Peter Imbert was very concerned at the level of tension in the police teams. "When Mr. Mathews came out," he said, "I insisted he kept his hands over his head, as I didn't want him waving to the public and the lads down below thinking he'd got a gun or was doing something. I didn't want that to happen. So, it wasn't only the terrorists one was keeping calm but your own colleagues as well."

Like his wife, John Mathews was rushed to University College Hospital for medical examinations. Detective Inspector Ron Chapman was still waiting at the hospital in order to speak further with Mrs. Mathews regarding conditions inside the flat. He made a phone call to the incident room to pass on the limited amount of detail he had obtained, as he recalled, "I then learned it was all over. Mr. Mathews had just been released and the hostage takers were in the act of being talked out of the flat."

Peter Imbert, on the phone with Tom during the transfers, asked the Irishman about the location and condition of their weapons, so that they could be located by the police once the ASU had transferred out of the building. Peter Imbert later related the exchange: "They had a number of different weapons in there with them and they were loaded. I said yet another silly thing when I said to O'Connell, 'where are the weapons?' He told me where they were, as though I knew the inside of the flat intimately, saying they were by the TV. I asked him if they were loaded and he replied that yes, they were. I said to him, 'don't touch them, don't touch them!' They'd had them for over 12 months or more themselves, and had been using them, and there I was warning him not to touch them!"

Duggan was the next to leave the flat at 4:20pm. Imbert, in his final words with Tom on the field telephone told the Irishman he would see him down at Paddington Green police station in a while. Tom replied, "yeah, see you down the nick." With that last exchange, Imbert and Tom hung up the phone. Walking away from the phone, O'Connell emerged from the flat at 4:24pm and along with his four comrades was later transferred to Paddington Green for initial processing.

The Balcombe Street siege was over without a single shot being fired. Imbert and Nevill could congratulate themselves on a very good result. So many things could have gone wrong, right down to the last-minute, but they had achieved the objective they had set out to complete on the previous Sunday–the safe extraction of everyone in the flat. The Met were jubilant, as they had finally captured the IRA gang that had been so elusive, and destructive, for so long. The current wave of the IRA attacks in London had been brought to an end, but the IRA would not take this defeat lightly. Other units would replace the four men for sure, the question was when?

With the ASU in police hands, the sandbags were removed from the front of the living room door. Several officers shoulder charged the door to break it down, as it had been propped shut from the inside. The scene that greeted them was one of squalor and mess, made all the worse by the stench of the two chemical toilet packs still in the room. Food containers, thermos flasks and food wrappers were strewn around the floor. It would take a considerable effort to clean up the place and make it fit for Mr. and Mrs. Mathews on their release from hospital, if they could face coming back to the scene of their six-day ordeal.

At 5:00pm that afternoon, the Home Secretary Roy Jenkins was shown the inside of the living room at number 22b and the conditions the hostages had faced and endured for the siege duration. He praised the police for their success in avoiding a shootout and getting the IRA men and hostages out alive. He praised the end of the Balcombe Street siege as a "giant tribute" to the work of the Metropolitan police. Their strategy of wait-and-see had been vindicated. "We were generous with our patience," he told the press, "but generous with nothing else." Jenkins, and the Wilson government, could breathe a collective sigh of relief. The strategy of the Met, as executed by Imbert and Nevill, had avoided a politically damaging incident by sidestepping the tactical option and ending the siege in a peaceful manner. The hostages were alive, and the police had the IRA's most valuable and prolific ASU on their way to cells in Paddington Green for interrogation by the two officers who had been seeking them since late 1974. It was an excellent result for the Met, and the Wilson government, and Jenkins had every right to be happy about the outcome. It avoided a potentially embarrassing political situation and robbed the Provisionals of a propaganda coup in the possible killing of four young IRA men on the streets of London. The SAS were not required to make a tactical resolution to the siege but, according to Peter Imbert, had something to say on the negotiated settlement. "One or two of my friends in the SAS said to me, 'you jammy bastard[4]–we wanted to go in and get them out!' That may have resulted in a very different outcome."

At University College Hospital, Dr. Howard Baderman informed the press that Mrs. Mathews' condition was satisfactory, but that she was "weak, shaky and very weary." She had requested some tea, toast and cigarettes. John Mathews arrived at the hospital two-and-a-half hours after his wife, and was said to be in good spirits, drinking cup after cup of tea. In a gesture to the couple's bravery and stoicism over the past six days, they received flowers and a personal note from Sir William Ryland, chairman of the Post Office. The Queen also sent a personal message of congratulations to the couple who, after being reunited, were placed under armed police guard in adjoining hospital rooms for the evening. Before they settled down for the night, their first bed rest in a week, they were reunited with their two daughters, Jill and Pat, and Sheila's sister Joan Royce. The family party, planned for Saturday, had been postponed as the family was unsure the couple would be released by then. Besides, it would not have been much of a celebration with two loved ones being held at gunpoint.

DAC Gibson later told the press that "we had no idea they were going to surrender." The request for a field telephone was a key breakthrough, but O'Connell's opening question about terms of surrender had taken the police completely by surprise, he added. After approximately 140 hours, from start to finish, the outcome of the standoff was an outstanding success for the Met. They had taken the ebb and flow of the negotiations, dealt with the anger and stubbornness of the ASU, and prevailed in a tense standoff. As Peter Imbert would later say, "everyone was delighted, because that really marked the end of that terrorist campaign! There were others that came back later, but that was the end of this ASU."

The ASU members had been escorted to Paddington Green where they waited for the interrogations with Nevill and Imbert to begin. The siege was over, but the job was not yet finished. The police needed answers to a string of questions regarding the ASU's bombing and shooting spree over the past year and a half or so. One of the pressing and immediate demands was locating their base or bases of operation, as the police expected to find weapons and bomb making equipment which could be a danger to members of the public if not located quickly.

Imbert and Nevill arrived at Paddington Green station to begin the process of questioning the four suspects. The initial conversations were short, lasting about five minutes each. During the questioning of Butler at around 6:30pm, the IRA man was pressed to reveal the location of his address. Imbert was worried that a child may find explosives or weapons. Butler assured him that no child would find anything, but still Imbert pushed home the question, where was it? Butler relented and told him the address, 61 Crouch Hill.

Later, when asked about the interrogations of the four men and who was the most difficult to talk to, Imbert would reveal a grudging admiration for Eddie Butler. "I think possibly Duggan was the worst," related Imbert, "he was very surly throughout all the interrogations. O'Connell was the boss man, but Butler was the toughest. He's the sort of man, if one had to be doing some sort of commando raid during the war, he's the sort of man you'd prefer out of the lot [ASU] to have with you. He was the man who was going to carry it out; he would carry out the orders regardless."

Finally that evening Imbert and O'Connell met face to face for the first time in O'Connell's cell at Paddington Green. Imbert asked the IRA man, "are you the one who was doing the talking on the phone, are you Tom?" O'Connell said yes, he was Tom. Imbert continued, "I'm the one you know as Peter and have been talking to you during the week." O'Connell's reply was a terse "so?" Imbert responded, "just before you left the flat, you said you'd see me down the nick, so here I am and I think we've got a lot to talk about."

With the initial interviews conducted, the day was winding down for all involved. John and Sheila Mathews were resting in hospital. The ASU were in their cells in Paddington Green, and Imbert and Nevill would go home to their families safe in the knowledge they had done an outstanding job. Everyone was safe, and the wait-and-see strategy had paid off.

Butler had given the police his address, but Imbert and Nevill had yet to extract more details from him regarding who he was living with at 61 Crouch Hill, Islington. The Bomb Squad would need to move fast to secure the location and extract as much forensic and other evidence from the building before the site became contaminated by members of the public, such as an unsuspecting landlord. The question on Butler's mind, having given up his address, would be related to one of the reasons he and the other ASU members held out so long in number 22b. What would the police find when they arrived? Had GHQ, as hoped by the four IRA men, arranged for other operatives to clear out all the explosives and weapons from the flat, leaving the police with little evidence? Butler, like the other IRA men now in custody, would be left to wonder. There had been no reported efforts to secure their release from the siege location, so would the IRA have gone to the trouble to clear out the two flats? Had they really been abandoned by GHQ? The result of the police search would reveal the answers to that question and they would find out very soon. The police were also somewhat surprised that the IRA had not attempted to make some form of effort to spring their top team. The potential for a counterstrike by the IRA had been in the forefront of the Met's thinking during the siege, but nothing had taken place. When asked about the lack of intervention by GHQ during the siege Peter Imbert answered, "I think the reason it did not happen was the IRA philosophy toward the ASU's in the field. They were a team, and I think the IRA could trust them not to give away secrets, but they were expendable. That would be one team gone, but there would be other teams that would take their place. They were ruthless at the command level as well."

The Home Secretary Roy Jenkins summed up the result to the press that evening. "It shows the policy we have been pursuing in this situation and that is our general sweet patience."

NOTES

1. For obvious security reasons, Nevill did not refer to any of the officers involved in the chase by name. It would be several weeks before the British public would learn of the heroism of John Purnell and Phil McVeigh.

2. From this point in the siege narrative, O'Connell will be referred to as "Tom."

3. The author is grateful to Mr. John Purnell for sharing this anecdote regarding his former boss, George Howlett. Mr. Howlett retired from the Metropolitan Police with the rank of Commander in 1992.

4. "Jammy bastard" is a well used British slang term for someone who is considered lucky.

doi:10.1300/J173v08n02_01

FIGURE 15. December 12, 1975. At 2:15pm, Sheila Mathews, aided by Eddie Butler, transfers out of 22b.

Source: History by The Yard / Metropolitan Police. Used with permission.

FIGURE 16. At 4:15pm, Eddie Butler is the first of the ASU to come out of 22b and transfer into police custody.

Source: History by The Yard / Metropolitan Police. Used with permission.

FIGURE 17. Inside 22b at the end of the siege. Note the chemical toilet on the left, behind the makeshift privacy screen

Source: Empics–Press Association. Used with permission.

FIGURE 18. From the left, Hugh Dougherty, Joe O'Connell, Eddie Butler and Harry Duggan after their arrest on December 12, 1975.

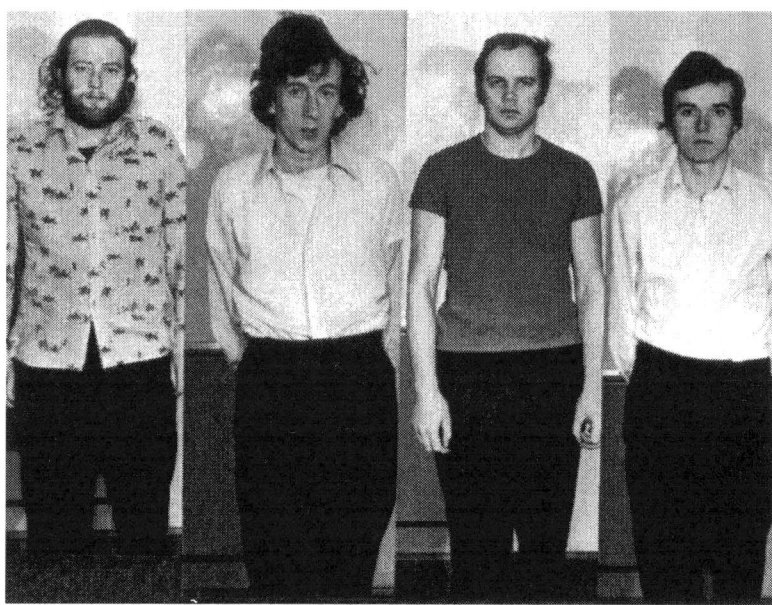

Source: Empics–Press Association. Used with permission.

FIGURE 19. A cheerful Sir Robert Mark (left) and Detective Chief Superintendent Jim Nevill as they display to the media the haul of weapons taken from the ASU at Balcombe St. and found in their safe houses.

Source: History by The Yard/Metropolitan Police. Used with permission..

FIGURE 20. 1: 5.56mm caliber Armalite rifle. 2: M1 carbine. 3: Mark II Sten sub-machine gun. 4: .45 Star semiautomatic pistol. 5 and 6: .357 Astra magnum .7 and 8: .38 Smith and Wesson. 9: M1 carbine–note the modification to the wood-work to allow the stock to fold up.

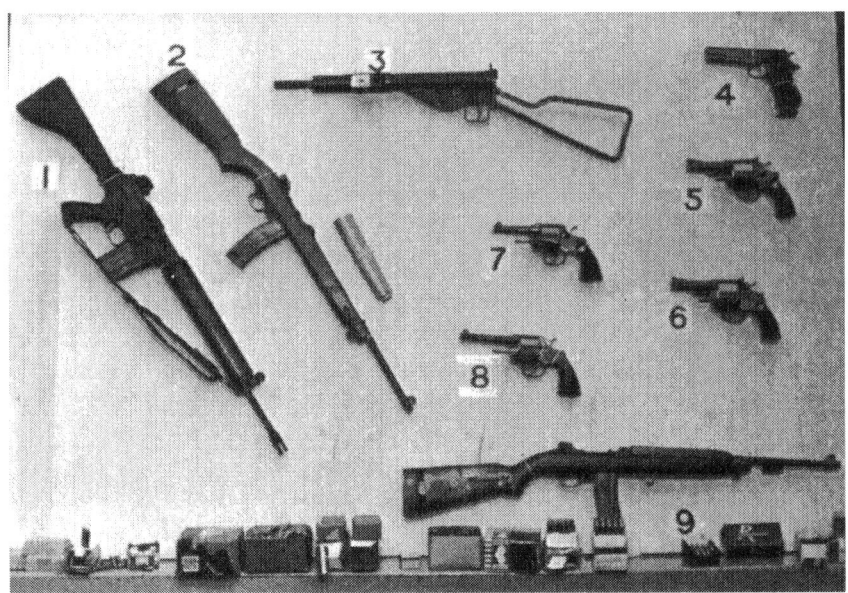

Source: History by the Yard / Metropolitan Police. Used with permission.

FIGURE 21. From the left, Inspector John Purnell, Detective Inspector Henry Dowswell and Sergeant Phil McVeigh after receiving the George Medal from the Queen at Buckingham Palace.

Source: John Purnell. Used with permission.

FIGURE 22. The author with John Purnell, GM QPM, in February of 2007 after retracing the route taken by Purnell and McVeigh as they gave chase to the ASU on December 6th, 1975.

Source: Monica Hatch. Used with permission.

FIGURE 23. Lord Peter Imbert, QPM, in uniform as Her Majesty's Lord-Lieutenant of Greater London.

Source: Peter Imbert. Used with permission.

Chapter 6

Post Siege Events

Following their capitulation at 22b Balcombe Street, the four members of the ASU were held in cells at Paddington Green police station and under the powers granted to the police under The Prevention of Terrorism Act, Imbert and Nevill could hold the four until December 19th without charging the men. Each of the ASU were questioned by Imbert and Nevill on a number of occasions between the 12th and the 31st of December. The key pieces of intelligence the Bomb Squad officers needed from the men related to the location or locations of their living accommodations, so that any terrorist related materials could be recovered by the Police and examined by the forensic teams to determine any link between the material and past terrorist attacks.

It had taken Peter Imbert and Jim Nevill approximately one minute to persuade Eddie Butler to reveal his address at 61 Crouch Hill, with Butler obviously mindful of Jim Nevill's comment about innocent people possibly being harmed by the ASU store of munitions. However, Butler had no idea as to the state of the apartment he had revealed to the Bomb Squad. The primary motivation for the ASU holding out for six days in number 22b was the faint hope that other IRA operatives would have been sent to the two addresses and cleared out all the ASU's weapons and equipment. In revealing the address so quickly, Butler was taking a gamble, as he was unsure what the police would find when they arrived at his flat. Butler had given the address to Imbert and Nevill at around

[Haworth co-indexing entry note]: "Post Siege Events." Moysey, Steven P. Co-published simultaneously in *Journal of Police Crisis Negotiations* (The Haworth Press, Inc.) Vol. 8, No. 2, 2008, pp. 235-244; and: *The Road to Balcombe Street: The IRA Reign of Terror in London* (Steven P. Moysey) The Haworth Press, Inc., 2008, pp. 235-244. Single or multiple copies of this article are available for a fee from The Haworth Document Delivery Service [1-800-HAWORTH, 9:00 a.m. - 5:00 p.m. (EST). E-mail address: docdelivery@haworthpress.com].

doi:10.1300/J173v08n02_02

6:20pm, and by 7:30pm Detective Inspector Ron Chapman was standing outside the door of the flat shared by Butler and Dougherty. Ron Chapman recalled the event, "Ken Howorth, an explosives expert with the Bomb Squad, went with the team to Crouch Hill. The ASU had the upstairs flat and there were a number of tenants in the large three-story house. We were relying on Ken to examine the door to the flat and check that it wasn't booby-trapped. It wasn't, so we entered the flat."

It was evident to the Bomb Squad officers that the IRA had not cleared out the flat, and so Chapman and his team found a plethora of terrorist paraphernalia, including an Armalite automatic rifle and several hundred rounds of assorted ammunition, wires, fuses and detonators, documents, press clippings and a list of potential targets, books and a quantity of explosives. The police team also found bags of sawdust, and Butler would later tell Imbert and Nevill it had been used to mix with the gelignite in order to stabilize the explosive. While searching through the top floor flat, Detective Inspector Chapman made a discovery that was both chilling and gave him a sense of relief. Chapman had found a box of ball bearings and, looking at the contents, it was apparent to Chapman that there were quite a few missing, used as shrapnel in the ASU's bombs and he had seen first hand the deadly effect they had on the victims, as Ron Chapman would later recall, "It gave me a great sense of satisfaction to find that box, as having seen identical ball bearings being removed from the bodies of the two victims of the Walton's restaurant bomb, it was good to know the quantity left in the box would not be used against future targets."

Chapman also made a discovery linking the ASU to the McWhirter murder, "one of the other things we found in the flat was a key fob with a picture of the Bisto kids on it," explained Chapman, "it was a promotional advertising item. When we got back to Paddington Green police station I remember Pat O'Connor, the exhibits officer who had dealt with the McWhirter shooting, showing me a photo of Mrs. McWhirter's keys and asking me if we had found anything like them in the ASU's flat. Her keys had borne an identical key fob when stolen after the shooting."

In examining the documents and papers found inside 61 Crouch Hill, Ron Chapman found an interesting glimpse into the sense of humor of Butler and Dougherty, in the shape of a Time Out magazine computer dating form where, as Dougherty would later tell Jim Nevill, Butler had filled out the form with a deliberately wrong date of birth for Dougherty, making him out to be an old man looking for a date. It was one sign of the two men's human existence among the inhuman trappings of their terror campaign.

With the first of the ASU's flats under the control of the Met, Imbert and Nevill's most pressing need became the location of the flat used by O'Connell and Duggan, but the two IRA men were not particularly talkative to the investigating officers. Duggan's typical response to questioning would be a terse "I have nothing to say" or just stony silence as the IRA man adhered to the principles of resisting interrogation, outlined in the IRA's Green Book training manual. Imbert and Nevill would continue to question the four detainees while the forensic teams did their job on the interior of 61 Crouch Hill and on the bomb making equipment and weapons removed from the flat as evidence.

John and Sheila Mathews returned to their flat on Monday December 15th after spending the weekend at University College Hospital for tests and examinations. The couple had not suffered any physical injuries, although the psychological burden of dealing with the trauma of being held captive in their own home would weigh heavily on Sheila Mathews in particular. The Met had hired a contract cleaning company to give the flat at 22b a thorough going over before being handed back to the couple, who had struggled with the decision to return to the property. Sheila Mathews appeared on the verge of physical collapse when the couple arrived back at 22b Balcombe Street, and she needed assistance to get to the first floor flat. She had determinedly announced, while at University College Hospital, "I have got to go into the flat." Mr. Mathews apparently did not harbor any ill-will toward his captors and in fact stated that he felt "sorry for them" as they were just young men following instructions. His anger was directed at "the brutes" that had sent the four young men over to England to carry out a campaign of terror against London, that eventually resulted in the six-day standoff at their home.

During the questioning of Eddie Butler, the first of a string of issues would surface that would cause the two primary investigators, Imbert and Nevill, considerable soul-searching. Nevill had asked Butler, on the day after his arrest, to describe the first job he had carried out as a member of the ASU, to which Butler replied that the police had already put people away his first job. Surprised, Nevill asked him which job did he mean and Butler responded with one word: Woolwich. Nevill initially thought that Butler was indicating he was involved with Paul Hill, Patrick Armstrong and the other two people convicted of both the Guilford and Woolwich pub bomb's, but Butler told the surprised police officers that he had never heard of any of the "Guilford four" until they went to trial. Butler also told Nevill and Imbert that he was the cover man on the

Woolwich attack and none of the Guilford four were involved in the throwing of the bomb at the Kings arms. The report generated by the scientists at RADRA had indicated a forensic link between the Woolwich bombing and some of the subsequent blasts and defused bombs recovered across London. With confessions of guilt from all four defendants in the case, Surrey police and the Crown Prosecution Service had not surfaced the forensic link as it did not help their case against the four people who, as the Surrey police claimed, had willingly confessed to the crimes. The Met were being presented with a different view of the Woolwich attack, from someone who claimed to have been present when the bomb was thrown, and who also claimed to have no knowledge of the four people convicted of the crime. Members of the Bomb Squad had interviewed Conlon, Armstrong, Hill and Richardson and were convinced they were, in fact, guilty as charged. Butler's unexpected prison cell confession to the Woolwich bomb would be the first indicator to the Met that maybe all was not right with the Guilford four case, and that maybe Surrey police had made a mistake. There would be more surprises to follow.

The Met eventually tracked down the second address at 99 Milton Grove, Stoke Newington, on December 17th through a tip-off by a member of the public responding to Sir Robert Mark's appeal for help in locating the digs of the ASU. Despite finding nothing in the way of explosives in the flat, the bomb squad team found a large amount of incriminating material which was taken away by the exhibit officers for cataloging as evidence against the four IRA men. Among the materials collected from Milton Grove, they found copies of books that had also been recovered from 39 Fairholme Road the previous February, such as the Army List and civil-service yearbook. A comprehensive list of potential future targets was also recovered, including the names of Roy Jenkins, Ted Heath and photos and names of senior police officers including Sir Robert Mark and Commander Roy Habershon. Hidden behind a panel in the bathroom, the police found a quantity of ammunition and bomb making materials concealed under the bathtub. They found the two spent .357 cartridge cases fired during the murder of Ross McWhirter, and the hand-drawn map O'Connell had made of the site near Scotland Yard, complete with the route several Bomb Squad officers would take on their way for a drink after work. They recovered a number of press clippings and references to some of the restaurants the ASU had attacked, such as a page torn out of the Egon Ronay guide that contained a review of Walton's restaurant, bombed by the ASU in November. In all, the Met had recovered sufficient evidence from the Milton Grove and Crouch Hill addresses, coupled with the admissions of some of the ASU, to build a watertight case against the four men for the acts of terror conducted across the capital since October 1974. The forensic teams would require time to analyze and catalog the exhibits recovered from both addresses and the Met would need to charge the four men to keep them in custody, and so a series of identity parades were arranged for the 17th to further link the ASU men with events of the December 6th chase and start of the siege.

Following the identity parades, Ron Chapman had an opportunity to sit and talk with Joe O'Connell in his cell, sitting on the floor and engaging the IRA man in conversation regarding his criminal activities. Ron Chapman recalled that O'Connell seemed only too willing to discuss the activities of his particular ASU, providing they stuck strictly to that topic–O'Connell would not discuss other people or other events outside of the activities of his team. Chapman had the opportunity to form an opinion of O'Connell during this extensive conversation, which lasted through the night and into the next morning. "I'd been used to dealing with hardened criminals," said Chapman, "but he was just so completely different. He was very cool, calm, matter-of-fact and clearly an intelligent person. He was a political idealist in a way, and was in no way a regular criminal. A lot of the people in the IRA were criminal types, but he was more of an intellectual, he was more of a student type."

At 9:25am on the 18th of December, 1975, the four men were formally charged with six offenses relating to the night of December 6th and the six days of the siege, including possession of firearms with intent to endanger life, using firearms to resist arrest and the unlawful imprisonment of Mr. and Mrs. Mathews. They were to be taken before a magistrate, charged and then remanded in custody at Brixton prison where they would await trial. After the charges against them had been read by Inspector Pollard, Commander Roy Habershon pointed out to the four that their troubles had only just started. "I'd like you to fully understand the charges you have just heard are only specimen charges relating to the Balcombe Street affair," Habershon stated, "a report will be submitted to the Director of Public Prosecutions and it is very likely that other very serious charges will be proffered and I want you to fully understand that," concluded Habershon.

After the men had been charged and remanded in custody at Brixton prison, they were subject to further questioning by Nevill and Imbert regarding the catalog of crimes committed during their reign of terror on the British capital. After being charged, Butler and O'Connell became a little more talkative but Duggan and Dougherty remained men of few words. The ASU had presented the Met with a thorny dilemma regarding the Woolwich bombing, as Butler had indicated he had acted as cover man on the job and the four people convicted of both the Guilford Woolwich pub bombings had nothing to do with the attack. That assertion would cast doubts regarding the Guilford bombs, as there appeared to be an apparent forensic link with some of the later bombs constructed by the ASU. Did this mean there was a common link in the manufacture and supply of the bombs by another group of terrorists, or did it simply indicate that the wrong people had been convicted in the first place? As the Met compiled their report for the Director of Public Prosecutions and the Crown prosecution service, they received clear direction from the Crown solicitors to not link the ASU with the Guilford and Woolwich events. There had been a due process of law and four people were serving long sentences and confessed parts in the deadly attacks. It would serve no useful purpose for the Crown to also link the ASU with the crimes, so when the final set of charges was compiled and ready to be put in place, Guilford and Woolwich were conspicuous by their absence from the list of 25 charges against O'Connell, Butler, Duggan and Dougherty.

"Yankee Joe" William Quinn had been dragged before a court in Dublin charged with assaulting a police officer and with being a member of the IRA. After a tip-off that Quinn could be a wanted terrorist suspect, Adrian Blackledge, who was one of the three officers that give chase after Quinn, was sent to the Irish Republic to identify the man as a suspect in the murder of PC Stephen Tibble. Blackledge made a positive identification, but the court granted Quinn bail and so the American promptly vanished from the Republic before extradition proceedings could be put in place. The Met would not let a killer of one of their own get away for long. Detective Inspector Alec Edwards, of the Bomb Squad, contacted a counterpart in the San Francisco police. They knew Quinn hailed from that part of California and had strong links the Irish Republican community in the bay area and so Edwards requested that the SFPD keep an eye out for William Quinn and to contact him if he did, in fact, pop up in San Francisco. Detective Inspector Edwards was in no hurry, figuring that Quinn would eventually get careless, lazy or just plain home sick and feel it was safe, at some point, to return to his roots. When and if he did, Edwards would be on a plane from London to arrest the suspected killer of Stephen Tibble, the Met's young fallen officer, whose selfless act of heroism would be marked by a simple stone memorial at the junction where he was shot that fateful day in February 1975.

Several British lawyers, concerned at a possible miscarriage of justice in the Guilford four trial, started to question the case. The ASU were also making known their concerns over the possible wrongful convictions and viewed the situation, leading up to their trial, as an opportunity to take issue with the entire notion of British justice. Under normal circumstances, any captured IRA group would have refused to acknowledge the authority of a British court and its ability to try members of the IRA and, as such, would have withdrawn from any participation in the proceedings. Transferred from Brixton to Wandsworth prison, the ASU requested a meeting with Frank McGuire, Member of Parliament for Fermanagh and South Tyrone in Northern Ireland, ostensibly to highlight the conditions under which they were being held. At a meeting with McGuire on May 27th 1976, Butler, O'Connell and Duggan agreed to make a statement about Guilford and Woolwich, providing Brendan Dowd, convicted on three counts of attempted murder after his July 10th 1975 shootout with police as he tried to resist arrest, would also be permitted to make a statement. McGuire subsequently met with Dowd who agreed to make a statement on the Guilford and Woolwich events, as along with O'Connell, he had claimed he had participated in both attacks. The four IRA men met with Guilford lawyer Alistair Logan and retired police Inspector James Still and gave a detailed statement regarding their participation in the two bombing events.

The ASU came to trial at the Old Bailey on January 24th, 1977, facing a total of 100 indictments, with each defendant charged with 25 counts of murder and bombing from December 1974 to December 1975. Each of the four men refused to answer a guilty or not guilty plea, with O'Connell stating, "I refuse to plead as the indictment does not include the two charges concerning the Guilford and Woolwich pub bombings–I took part in both–for which innocent people have been convicted." Similar statements were made by both Duggan and Butler.

The judge for the trial of the ASU was Mr. Justice Cantley, who had presided over the trial of Brendan Dowd in 1976. This action had gained him the dubious honor of being added to the ASU's hit list and surprisingly, in view of this, Justice Cantley did not step down and excusing himself from trying the four defendants despite learning he was listed as a future victim, an action that raised many eyebrows in legal circles at the time. The trial continued until February 7th, when the prosecution closed and rested their case. The court was informed by the Defense Council, Richard Harvey, that no witnesses will be called by the defense but that instead Mr. O'Connell would read a statement made on the behalf of the four defendants. It is worth quoting a section of O'Connell's address to the court: "we say that no representative of British imperialism is fit to pass judgment on us, for this government has been guilty of the very things for which we now stand accused. This government carried out acts of terrorism in order to defend British imperialism and continues to do so in Ireland. We have struggled to free our country from British rule. We are patriots. British soldiers in Northern Ireland are mercenaries of British imperialism. Yet none of them has ever been convicted of the murders of unarmed civilians which they have committed in Ireland. We ask the members of the jury to consider this paradox. We are all four Irish Republicans. We have recognized this court to the extent that we have instructed our lawyers to draw the attention of the court to the fact that four totally innocent people are serving massive sentences for three bombings, two in Guilford and one in Woolwich, which three of us and another man now imprisoned have admitted that we did. The director of public prosecutions was made aware of these admissions in December 1975 and has chosen to do nothing . . . We do not wish to insult members of the jury when we say that they are not our peers. An English jury can never be the peers of Irish men and women. We will be judged only by our countrymen. Any verdict or sentence from this court is nothing more than the continuation of the hypocrisy of British rule in Ireland and the injustice it has inflicted on our country and its people. We admit to no 'crime' and to no 'guilt', for the real crime and guilt are those of British imperialism committed against our people. The war against imperialism is a just war and it will go on, for true peace can only come about when a nation is free from oppression and injustice. Whether we are imprisoned or not is irrelevant, for our whole nation is the prisoner of British imperialism. The British people who choose to ignore or swallow the lies of the British gutter press are responsible for the actions of their government unless they stand out against them. As volunteers in the Irish Republican Army we have fought to free our nation from its bondage to British imperialism, of which this court is an integral part."

The result of the ASU's trial was not the resounding success the Met had hoped for at the outset. As they had intended to do from long before the trial started, the ASU and their defense team had raised doubts about the integrity and legality of the Surrey police prosecution of the Guilford four, and the five women and six men of the jury did not find the four IRA men guilty on all counts as the police as hoped. The jury found the four men not guilty of the bombs at Putney High Street, the Charco Grill and the Caterham Arms. They were also found not guilty of the bomb at the Trattoria Fiore and the September 1975 explosion at the Portman Hotel.

The not guilty verdicts were a stunning blow to the police, given the forensic evidence they had collected, together with the statements from the four men regarding their involvement in the events. The four were also found not guilty of murder at the Hilton Hotel explosion, with the jury reducing the charge to manslaughter because of perceived delays in the police passing on the warning to the Hilton. But it was the Caterham Arms pub bombing, the almost exact replication of the Guilford pub bombs, that surprised the police the most. O'Connell's address to the courts had obviously made an impact on the jury, as during their deliberations they had asked for a transcript of the speech, but this request was denied by the judge as O'Connell's address to the court was not regarded as evidence. After the trial, one of the jurors spoke out about the proceedings, ". . . we were, in a way, rebelling against being railroaded by the court into unanimous verdicts of guilty: as if we were just there to rubberstamp what the court, the prosecution and the police wanted: as if it were all a foregone conclusion. Some of us got very upset. We thought that it was immoral . . . we definitely felt that at least some [of the defendants] were connected with Guilford and Woolwich."

The Guilford and Woolwich issue would continue to echo for several years before coming to a head again in the courts but, despite their impassioned admissions of guilt, the four members of the ASU would not be charged with any offense relating to the two controversial episodes, with the Crown prosecution service and the Director of Public Prosecutions preferring to keep any reference of the events away from their charge sheets. With the trial over, it remained for Justice Cantley to past sentence on the four men. Butler, O'Connell, and Duggan each convicted on 20 counts, were given 12 life sentences, 21 years for manslaughter, six 20-year sentences and one sentence of 18 years. Dougherty was convicted on 18 counts and received 11 life sentences, 21 years for manslaughter, five sentences of 20 years and one of 18 years. Each of the four men came individually into court to be sentenced. Duggan, gripping the dock rail, faced Justice Cantley and said, "I'm not listening to any of this English rubbish!" O'Connell just listened expressionlessly until Justice Cantley had finished passing sentence, then turned and shouted, "up the Provo's" before being taken back to his cell. Dougherty just called out to his sister in the public gallery, "good luck Mary."

It was finally over. The cat-and-mouse game between the Bomb Squad and the IRA had, for a time, come to an end. The bombings, shootings, all the fruitless searches, the murders and the chases, all finished. The ASU were going to spend the rest of their lives behind bars, with Justice Cantley's recommendation that they serve at least 30 years incarcerated in British top security jails. With the ASU behind bars, many people could move on and pick up the pieces of their shattered lives, impacted by the events of 1974 and 1975. The young soldiers who had been crippled for life in the pub bombings, the widow of PC Tibble, Captain Goad and Ross McWhirter, the emergency service personnel who had the grisly task of recovering bodies and body parts from the bomb scenes, and all the families of victims who had lost loved ones impacted by the terror campaign could move on, knowing the perpetrators would be behind bars for the rest of their lives. The IRA campaign in London had been brought to a halt by combination of luck, timing, ingenuity and bravery on the part of the officers of the Metropolitan Police. Mr. Justice Cantley, in his summing up, had praise for the bravery of Inspector Purnell and Sergeant McVeigh, Inspector Dowswell, Major Biddle and many others. "I want to now commend men of true worth, unarmed policemen who faced and chased these criminals, and the bomb disposal officers . . . who staked their lives against the chance to make a bomb safe for others," he stated.

Justice Cantley concluded with the statement, "I realize that there were other policemen who showed great courage and devotion to duty who were not identified in the trial. I hope they received the recognition they undoubtedly deserve. The public is very fortunate to have the protection of men such as these."

doi:10.1300/J173v08n02_02

Chapter 7

Observations
on the Balcombe Street Siege

Joe O'Connell and his three companions did not set out on the night of December 6th with the express purpose of taking a middle-aged couple hostage in their own home. Their target was a shooting attack on Scott's seafood restaurant and possibly other unknown targets in the West End. It is interesting that the four men chose to attack the restaurant with gunfire rather than with a thrown or placed bomb. This is probably best explained by the leak of the police dragnet operation in the London *Evening Standard* newspaper that outlined how the Met intended to flood the streets of London with unarmed plainclothes police officers, on the prowl for the IRA men. Pausing outside a restaurant to fire from automatic and semiautomatic weapons would take less time and expose the ASU to less risk of being apprehended than if they stopped and got out of their vehicle to mount a bomb attack. They also chose to use the folding stock M1 carbine and the WWII era Sten gun as the primary weapons during the attack and had the Sten fail on Butler again without firing a shot. Although the failure of the submachine gun probably save the lives of several police officers later that evening, we are forced to question the wisdom of the ASU's strategy in depending on a notoriously unreliable weapon, just because it was easily concealed in Butler's canvas bag. Nevertheless, the ASU did rely on the Sten; it

[Haworth co-indexing entry note]: "Observations on the Balcombe Street Siege." Moysey, Steven P. Co-published simultaneously in *Journal of Police Crisis Negotiations* (The Haworth Press, Inc.) Vol. 8, No. 2, 2008, pp. 245-261; and: *The Road to Balcombe Street: The IRA Reign of Terror in London* (Steven P. Moysey) The Haworth Press, Inc., 2008, pp. 245-261. Single or multiple copies of this article are available for a fee from The Haworth Document Delivery Service [1-800-HAWORTH, 9:00 a.m. - 5:00 p.m. (EST). E-mail address: docdelivery@haworthpress.com].

Available online at http://jpcn.haworthpress.com
doi:10.1300/J173v08n02_03

jammed and was stowed away, along with the functioning M1 carbine, in Butler's canvas bag, and the four men drove away from Scott's. We do not know if they had other targets for that night or if they had been responsible for an incendiary device that went off in a shop doorway in Oxford Street. We do know that the car was spotted during the attack by two officers involved in Operation Combo and that their subsequent radio transmission triggered a chain of events that eventually had the four IRA men fleeing on foot, down the steps from Rossmore Road, after a brief firefight with armed police. Initially splitting into two groups, the four men joined up again at the junction Ivor Place and Balcombe Street and continued their flight from the law. Watched by several bystanders, the four men ran up the stairs to number 22 where they attempted to exit the rear of the building but failed to find a way out. They wasted precious seconds looking for an escape route and would have been greeted by least two armed police officers if they had attempted to exit the building by the front door, as Officer A and his partner from the SPG had taken up covering positions outside the building with the shootout in Rossmore Road only too fresh in their minds. The ASU had trapped themselves in the building and any attempt to escape by the front door would have put them at a tactical disadvantage and they would have been shot, arrested or both if they had tried to escape to the building with the rapidly escalating police presence in the street outside. Their only option was to head for the flat with lights on, as that would afford them human collateral in the form of hostages. Breaking into an apartment that did not appear to have anyone at home, and barricading themselves inside, would have made them an easy target for an armed response from the police, but as we have discussed this would have then presented the Wilson government with a severe political headache.

The initial call to the police, by O'Connell, and subsequent rejection by the police of any demands made by the IRA, fell into the expected script of a hostage standoff situation of opening gambit followed by outright rejection, i.e., I have A and will give it to you if you, in return, give me B. No, I will not give you B, but you will give up A immediately.

O'Connell knew his opening gambit would be rejected, and in doing so Ernest Bond would also have realized that the police would be in no position to give or receive anything until the situation regarding hostages had been evaluated. It should be noted that O'Connell did not give police a deadline by which they had to come up with his demands. Deadlines can work against both sides in a hostage situation. If a hostage taker issues a deadline to the negotiation team, then a number of events can occur. Firstly, the negotiators may tell the hostage takers that their demands cannot be satisfied in the time allowed, forcing the hostage takers into either extending the deadline or taking punitive actions against the hostages, or threaten to do so if the negotiators fail to meet the conditions of the new deadline, thereby forcing both sides into an escalating spiral of missed deadlines and reprisal threats. Secondly, the hostage takers deadline could be satisfied by the negotiators, but that would put the law enforcement team into a position of conceding to the hostage takers demands and timeline, rather than having the hostage takers accept a compromise position from the police. We must not forget that hostage negotiations are never about a win-win solution, they cannot be as a mutually beneficial resolution to a hostage standoff is neither possible nor desirable. In most cases, it would be highly undesirable to allow hostage takers to achieve an unchallenged escape and full immunity for their crimes in exchange for the safe release of the hostages. Although such a resolution would totally satisfy the demands of the hostage takers, it would result in a scenario unacceptable to the police and the public they serve. So, in many hostage situations, deadlines are either not given or allowed to expire without acknowledgment by the police to avoid painting the hostage takers and negotiators into a psychological and tactical corner.

From the negotiators standpoint, the Balcombe Street siege could not have got off to a worse start from a psychological perspective. Four highly trained and skilled urban guerrillas had been referred to as "vulgar common criminals" by Sir Robert Mark, who had also bluntly broadcast that the only destination the men could look forward to would be a cell in Brixton prison. It was not publicly mentioned, but judging by Sir Robert's private views on the expendability of the hostages, a mortuary slab was also a perfectly acceptable alternative destination for the ASU. Imbert and Nevill, coming into the role of negotiators, would have to work with the psychological team and the Met senior leadership to develop a unified strategy to deal with the IRA men. The Spaghetti House "dry run" had given the Met a chance to practice their elected strategy of isolating the hostage takers, but the Balcombe Street siege was different in that it was a highly charged political opportunity for both the Wilson government and the IRA leadership, all closely watched by the Unionist movement in Northern Ireland. The Wilson government desperately needed a bloodless resolution to the siege in order to avoid worsening the political situation, in the light of increasing international scrutiny and possible future censure if things went badly wrong. By virtue of the political chain of command, this desired outcome would pass down from the Prime Minister and the Cabinet to the leadership of the Met through the office of the Home Secretary. The desire for a nonviolent end to the standoff would drive the tactics and strategy available to the Met, which in turn would translate into a broad outline script for the negotiating team.

There was a spectrum of options the Met could use against the ASU as they attempted to talk the men out of the confines of number 22b. They could launch an all out tactical assault, without warning, with no attempt to negotiate with the IRA men, which would probably have cost the hostages their lives and created a nightmare for the government. They could have opted to do nothing, no negotiations, and no offers of compromises and just waited to see what the ASU would do. That again would have presented a serious risk, as the police would not have been proactively trying to control the hostage takers and influencing their moves regarding the hostages, leaving everything up to chance. They could opt to negotiate with the ASU without making or offering any concessions to their demands, or they could move toward a position where the negotiations were accompanied by some small concessions toward the IRA men. Their final option would be to negotiate with the men and lie about concessions they had no intention of making real, in order to manipulate the hostage takers. In general, negotiators dislike lying to hostage takers unless they absolutely have to in order to save a life in imminent danger. The prevailing view is that lies will, at some point, be discovered and future negotiation situations compromised if the hostage takers know the police team has a track record of lying to get what they want.

The besieged IRA men also had a spectrum of options of their own, but theirs was a little starker in nature. They could naïvely hope for a negotiated settlement with the police, achieving their tongue-in-cheek objectives of safe exit and passage to Ireland in exchange for the hostages. This was highly improbable as an option, as the IRA men rightly recognized from the outset. At the other end of their spectrum they had option to make a break for it, and shoot their way to freedom, resulting in the almost certain death of the ASU members and their hostages. As they wanted to prolong the siege long enough to allow for some assistance from the IRA, it would be in their best interest to keep calm, keep the hostages alive and listen to what the police negotiation team had to say. Looking at the events of the siege, we can see that the police position started out as one of negotiate but refusal to allow concessions, that eventually moved to a position of allowing the ASU to achieve small concessions in response to their larger demands. The ASU started out with a large demand, somewhat tongue-in-cheek, and then moved to a reluctant set of talks with the police, to a position of defiance that eventually led to the final phase of the siege, where they sought out from the police the terms of their surrender. Hostage negotiation events typically follow four distinct phases of Contact, Bargaining, Agreement and Conclusion. Examining the siege at Balcombe Street, and comparing the event with other similar situations, we can construct a more detailed model of how the police and the negotiation team handled the situation to bring about a bloodless resolution to the armed standoff. The model breaks down into the six elements of contain, control, collect, communicate, concessions and conclusion and we will examine each of these in turn.

(1) CONTAIN

The first steps carried out by the police at Balcombe Street included the closing off access both into and out of the siege area. This involved two stages, creating an inner and outer containment zone. The outer containment zone, in this case, included the area just south of Dorset Square to Taunton Place at the north end of Balcombe Street and extended west to include Boston Place which runs parallel to Balcombe Street at the rear of the building. Drivers were required to leave their cars and exit the zone with the police maintaining cordons at each of the zone's perimeters to regulate entry and exit into the area. The outer containment zone played an important role in keeping the press and TV crews at a telephoto lens distance away from the siege location. Having learned this valuable lesson at the Spaghetti House siege, this prevented a media feeding frenzy to occupy buildings that would provide prime coverage locations: these locations would be used by the police to set up sniper cover, observations posts and negotiator's flat for Nevill and Imbert. Control of the outer containment zone would also require the evacuation of all residents from their homes, inside the zone, to temporary accommodations for the duration of the siege, both as a safeguard for the general public and as a means of providing tactical accommodation for the police.

The inner containment zone incorporated the apartment building, the flat at number 22b, down to the living room the ASU had chosen as the place to hold out against the police. The police would occupy the flats surrounding number 22b, giving the officers from the C7 Technical Support team the opportunity to gather intelligence via their electronic surveillance tools. The inner zone would eventually be secured by the external barricading of the living room door with sandbags, preventing the ASU from making a rapid exit with their hostages and providing the officers in the flat with some degree of protection from any explosion that may have been set off inside the room.

(2) CONTROL

With the inner and outer zones established and maintained, the next step for the Met would be the control of everything that either entered or exited from the inner containment zone, including information, food, water, heat, power and people. This level of control would be used to create and maintain a sense of dependency in the hostage takers.

Control may be a strong term when it comes to discussing the relationship between the police, the broadcast media and the press, but this is precisely what the Met did at Balcombe Street. In order to have the broadcast media act as an asset rather than a liability, the Met primed reporters with questions to ask of senior officers at press conferences, held during the siege, so that carefully measured responses could be given to ensure the right message would be sent to the intended audience inside number 22b. The same is true of the carefully staged TV appearance of Joan Royce, as she publicly pleaded with the hostage takers to release her sister Sheila, a deliberate move designed to psychologically influence the ASU to be more humane toward the hostages if things had deteriorated between the ASU and the Met.

The police also ensured the media messaging was carefully controlled, in order to avoid passing any tactical information to the ASU the police did not want them to have, and used the same principle to convey the message to the group that they were under the imminent threat of a tactical assault by the SAS, thereby creating the psychological tension that resulted in the rapid collapse of the siege.

Imbert and Nevill used the inner containment zone to pass the ASU water and chemical toilets, not at the request of the IRA men but on a planned basis to further reinforce the sense of dependence they had created through the isolation of the hostage takers, further emphasized by the eventual disconnection of the services to the apartment. The police team had complete control of the environment the ASU experienced, but as we have seen they had little control over the behavior of the men, which increased the need for the police to gather intelligence from the flat as the siege continued.

(3) COLLECT

Information is the prime currency of the hostage negotiator. Without information regarding the situation unfolding in a crisis event, such as an armed hostage standoff, the negotiators are working in the dark. It is, therefore, imperative that the negotiation team and the police backup units use all means available to them to gather as much intelligence as they can on the hostage takers, and the hostages, and as fast as possible. They need to understand the number of hostage takers in the event the situation requires a technical resolution. They need to collect intelligence on the hostages, such as names, ages and family connections in order to be able to build a picture of the people being held captive, and to use this picture when, if appropriate, discussing the hostages with the hostage takers. In the Balcombe Street siege, the police used a reverse flow of intelligence through the TV appearance of Joan Royce to paint a picture of Sheila Mathews as a sister, a mother, wife and beloved family member, all of which served to humanize the hostages to ASU who also had mothers, sisters, and loved ones.

The negotiation team at a hostage situation also needs to collect intelligence on the availability of media reporting to the hostage takers inside the inner containment zone. A golden rule adopted by many hostage negotiation teams is to make the initial assumption, until proven otherwise, that the hostage takers have access to *all* the reporting on the siege, which will impact the downstream communication strategy as it is determined precisely what level of communications are available to the hostage takers. Information also needs to be collected on any armaments the hostage takers may have in their possession. Do they have automatic weapons or handguns? Do they have explosives or hand grenades? This level of detail is critical in order to prepare any SWAT or military teams going into the inner containment zone in the event of a tactical deployment. If they are armed, what about the psychological state of mind of the hostage takers? Are they suicidal and looking for a murder/suicide event with the hostages, or looking to become victims of the increasing phenomenon of death-by-police-officers, by provoking the officers on the scene to shoot-to-kill in order to protect the hostages? Each scenario requires a careful, measured and very different response from the negotiation team, who also needs to know if the hostage takers are politically motivated or criminals in a bungled robbery, whether the standoff was deliberately planned, such as the 1980 Iranian embassy siege, or a siege of opportunity such as the events of Balcombe Street. The two scenarios are very different, particularly if the deliberate hostage takers are foreign nationals with differing societal values to those of the negotiation team. For example, in negotiating with "Tom" Peter Imbert was dealing with a man with a similar societal experience–i.e., white northern European male whose first language was English. The concept of martyrdom was not part of the central doctrine of the IRA man, and so personal survival would have been a strong psychological driver in his conversations with Imbert. It is all well and good to die for your cause, but the Western mindset, regarding self-destruction or sacrifice, hinges on what the author would refer to as the George Patton principle. The crusty US General once told his troops, "no bastard never won a war by dying for his country. He won it by making the other poor dumb bastard die for his." Unlike some Middle East Islamic sects, martyrdom is not gloriously rewarded in heaven in the doctrines of Catholic or Protestant religions. O'Connell and Imbert would both be operating under the same set of societal and psychological "rules" regarding this point. The desperate plan to break out of the flat on the last day of the siege may have contradicted this philosophy, but this was most probably driven by increased frustration, food deprivation and a pervasive sense of inaction and helplessness in a unit trained to take action. If Imbert and Nevill had been dealing with foreign nationals, with the inherent communication and language issues that invariably accompanies such situations, the outcome of the Balcombe Street siege could have been very different.

(4) COMMUNICATIONS

As with the collection of situational intelligence, communication is the key tool the hostage negotiator has in dealing with any hostage takers. At the core of every hostage standoff, the basic requirement of the situation is to pair a negotiator with the person or persons in crisis so they can return to a state of psychological and emotional stability through communication. A practiced negotiator, using active listening, skillful communications and allowing the passage of sufficient time, will allow the stability to return to the hostage takers and reduce the initial tension in a standoff. Part of this process is for the negotiators to understand the perceived grievances, and subsequent demands, of the hostage takers. It is particularly important to establish if the negotiation teams require language specialists to speak with any non-English-speaking hostage takers. If this is the case, it is important that the "interpreter" is a native speaker of the required language or possesses a high degree of fluency, in order to understand colloquialisms, slang and inflection nuances that could otherwise be missed. This is critical, as negotiators rely on conversation to build rapport with hostage takers and as the primary tools of conversation, words, represent the key ingredient, but not the only component of conversation. Voice inflection, tone, and speed of delivery all play an important part in the communication and negotiation process, in which the negotiator it is trying to establish a "hook": a topic of emotional and psychological meaning to the subject. In effect, lives may depend on the ability of the negotiator to converse with and listen to the hostage takers, hence the critical importance, if dealing with non-English speaking hostage takers, of have very proficient interpreters on hand to work directly with the negotiation team. This factor is still important even when dealing with foreign nationals who have a basic command of the English language, as they will tend to reason in their native language and translate back into English. This cognitive process can create critical misunderstandings that can cause a siege situation to spiral rapidly out of control. By way of example, the diplomatic mission of the then Secretary General of the UN, Kurt Waldheim, to Iran during the 1980 student occupation of the US embassy in Tehran is a good case in point. Waldheim flew to Tehran in an effort to bring the protracted occupation of the US embassy to an end and free the US personnel that had been held hostage. The Iranian TV and radio networks greeted Waldheim at the airport on his arrival and broadcast his message of intent to the Iranian people, "I have come as a mediator to work out a compromise," stated Waldheim. His words were translated into the Persian language Farsi and beamed around the country to a nation curious about the UN Secretary-General's visit. Kurt Waldheim had nothing but good intentions for his visit to Iran, but his choice of words backfired on him. Waldheim and in the rest of the English-speaking world knew only too well what it meant to be a mediator working to reach a compromise, but in the Persian language the message did not travel well. In Persian, a mediator is a meddler, someone who barges in uninvited to interfere in someone else's business, and the word compromise has no positive connotation. So, what the Iranians heard was, "I have come to meddle, uninvited, in this matter and compromise your integrity." One hour after his arrival the UN Secretary-General's motorcade was stoned by angry Iranian citizens. This may be an extreme example and the Iranian news agencies may have been conveniently amnesiac in their possibly politically motivated translation, but the point remains that there is always the chance that some nuance of meaning can be lost in a translation, with potentially deadly results in a hostage standoff situation.

One aspect of the communicate factor comes back to the management of the news media at the siege location. The needs of the modern media, with 24-hour news coverage on cable TV and Internet feeds means there is always an appetite to cover breaking news as it happens, live from the scene. Police psychologist Dr. James Greenstone, of the Fort Worth Police Department in Texas, is one of the world's foremost experts in the handling hostage crisis situations. Dr. Greenstone commented to the author that his phone rings constantly with calls from the TV news networks whenever a hostage or barricade situation occurs as "what bleeds, leads," he said. The needs of the media to fill their time slots cannot be allowed to compromise the work of the hostage negotiation teams on the scene and this is a recognized principle among some of the media. The Poynter Institute of Journalism advised media reports to adhere to a number of key guidelines when reporting from hostage situations. These include avoiding the description, with either words or images, of any information that could divulge the tactics of positions of SWAT team members, outside the siege location, to the hostage takers inside. It also advises the media to challenge any intuitive reaction to "go live" from the scene, unless there are strong journalistic reasons for a live, on-the-scene report. This is something the police and negotiation teams need to coordinate with the media on-site, as a strong journalistic reason may not be compatible with the strategy and tactics being employed, hence the need to keep the media beyond the outer containment zone unless the police *want* to show a particular scene to hostage takers for tactical or psychological reasons. All this boils down to limiting what the media reports, to avoid tipping off the hostage takers, via TV, radio or Internet links, to any developments the police or negotiators fear would compromise their efforts. There also has to be an eye on future hostage events. The rise of the Internet and video sharing websites makes the task of developing a terrorist network communication strategy far easier than in previous generations. Substantial strategic and tactical information can be gleaned from watching and studying video of past tactical interventions and such video can easily be posted on the Web and passed around between activist cells. The modern media, inadvertently, may just be helping future terror groups to nullify established hostage scene tactics employed by law enforcement groups, so it is in the public interest to have the media resist showing a "scoop" on a hostage scene, as future lives may be compromised by such actions.

There have been several notorious live TV coverage episodes of hostage standoff interventions. Several TV networks broadcast coverage of the disastrous FBI and ATF raid on the Waco compound of the Branch

Davidians in April 1993, showing scenes of agents being fired upon, and being hit, by cult members shooting through the roof of the building as a law-enforcement teams attempted to gain access. TV coverage of the FBI and ATF agent's movements would have been available to the cult members holed up inside the compound, allowing them to react and respond to the real-time images.

The final moments of the May 1980 Iranian Embassy siege in London, where the SAS stormed the building at Princes Gate, was famously broadcast live by the BBC, interrupting the prime-time bank holiday Monday live coverage of the world snooker championship in the process. The coverage of the raid was a huge tactical liability, but the Thatcher government wanted the world to see the black-clad SAS troopers charging into the embassy with their unwritten orders to use deadly force against the hostage takers, killing five of the six in the process. It was a political use of the media that was outside the control of the police at the scene. The TV coverage was timed such that the detonation by the SAS of the shaped charges, designed to blow in the armored glass windows, and the troopers descending on ropes from the roof to rapidly enter the building, could all be seen not only by the British TV viewers but by the entire world. In order to emphasize the political nature of the live coverage, the then Home Secretary William Whitelaw, a staunch political ally of Margaret Thatcher, stated at a press conference the day after the raid, "the operation, and I think the people of this country and many in the world will think so too, was an outstanding success, and it shows that we in Britain are not prepared to tolerate terrorism in our capital city. The world must learn this."

The communicate element does contain a caveat for the negotiation teams involved in any hostage standoff situation. If the surveillance teams, such as C7 at the Balcombe Street siege, are successful in bugging the inner containment zone, a rich source of intelligence may be gleaned through the surveillance of conversations between the hostage takers, and also possibly between the hostage takers and their captives. This presents the psychological teams with the opportunity to assess the state of mind of the hostage takers and feed back to the negotiators ideas to further push the talking along towards a solution. However, the negotiators have to self-censor to ensure that no intelligence gathered through the use of surveillance techniques leaks over to their conversations with the hostage takers, as they will quickly work out that they are being watched or listened to. However, any intelligence gathered from the inner containment zone, together with any other intelligence on the hostage takers, should be used by the negotiation team to look for, and exploit, any common ground that may exist or that can be fabricated. This is not the same as lying to the subjects and is a legitimate influence tactic that can be employed to generate some small degree of personal contact between the negotiators and the subjects. By finding something that the hostage taker values and aligning their views accordingly, providing the issue is not of a subversive nature or supporting the hostage taker's perceived grievance, the negotiators can draw out the hostage takers on the subject in careful, measured steps creating a small link between the two sides. Psychologically, we tend to warm more towards people with similar perceived interests to our own, and are therefore more likely to make concessions to these people when asked to do so.

(5) CONCESSIONS

Crisis or hostage negotiation has the primary purpose of leading the hostage takers to be satisfied with a continuum of relatively small concessions from the negotiation team. Initial demands are declined and smaller alternatives are proffered to the hostage takers in return. This tactic is amply illustrated by incidents where the hostage takers make outlandish demands for large sums of cash and a jet aircraft for an international escape, but settle for a statement of their position to the media and judicial considerations in return for the safe release of the innocent parties. The negotiator's role is to get the hostage takers to accept small concessions and build on these to get larger ones. Each concession, considered on its own merits, would not appear very large but they act in an additive fashion, rather like the individual steps on a staircase. Each step is not that big or difficult to take, and the increase in height is relatively small, until we look back and see just how far down the floor is from where the staircase started. In such a fashion, the negotiators can move the hostage takers from a major demand to being satisfied with a set of relatively small concessions.

Examining the six days of the Balcombe Street siege, we can see how Imbert employed of the concession tactic with O'Connell. The ASU demanded free passage to Ireland, and Imbert countered with the offer of a hot meal in exchange for the release of Mrs. Mathews. In turn, the ASU demanded a hot meal, and Imbert offered the men soup instead. Eventually the ASU played Imbert at his own game by refusing to accept deliveries of sandwiches from the police. This was that ASU's attempt to counter the efforts made by Imbert and Nevill to have the men feel increasingly powerless and diminish their perceived ability to influence the outcome of the siege. One key factor to the concession strategy Imbert and Nevill employed with the ASU featured the avoidance of certain words and phrases with O'Connell while negotiating with the Irishman. As with all good negotiators, they avoid using the word "no" when faced with a specific demands from O'Connell, as this would have shut down the conversation, increased O'Connell's frustration and, potentially, impacted the safety of the hostages. Rather than using "no" or other negative words, the negotiating team would respond with a lesser offer that may have been a subset of the initial request, and in doing so, the words used to the ASU would not dismiss or invalidate the initial request, but would present O'Connell with another set of options. Imbert and Nevill also worked diligently to avoid using terms such as "give in" or "surrender" as these would sound like the negotiators were gloating over the captivity of the ASU. Imbert used phrases such as "when you come out," as this would give the ASU some semblance of dignity, given the fact that there was no way out of 22b for the men other than through a controlled exit under the cover of police marksman or a suicidal break-out attempt.

The passage of time also helped to erode the salience of the ASU's initially high demands. After several days without food or cigarettes, obtaining these desired commodities became more real, more immediate than any thoughts of transportation to Ireland. Although the IRA men inside 22b knew they were not going to obtain a safe passage to the Republic, it is worth remembering the temporal dimension if dealing with hostage standoff situations. Time plays a critical role in the developments inside a hostage situation with regard to the unfolding relationship between captors and hostages. Although the hostage/captor bonding phenomenon known as the Stockholm syndrome did not appear to be a factor in the Balcombe Street siege–it is hard to bond with people who are trying to ignore you–time does play an important factor in the hostage's ability to survive a siege event. It has been noted that in groups of hostages who survived the first three days of a siege, 86% would be released unharmed at the end of the siege. Of the remaining 14% of cases, only 3% would be killed by their captors while 11% would die as a result of armed interventions by SWAT teams or Army Special Forces.

The steps of control, contact, communicate and concessions form an iterative process that both the negotiation team and the hostage takers enter into that form the basis of the negotiation process employed to bring the siege to a hoped-for bloodless conclusion. Some of the stages may be skipped during any given cycle, but the iterations end when the negotiations team feel they can move to the final stage of conclusion.

(6) CONCLUSION STAGE

In the Balcombe Street siege the conclusion came after the four-man ASU had made a decision to use the hostages as human shields and exit the flat at gunpoint, making for the Ford Cortina, owned by John Mathews, parked outside the apartment building. Their escape plan had not been developed much beyond getting out of the flat and out to the car, indicating a degree of desperation on the part of the IRA men. The police had deflated the Cortina's tires and so it would not have been capable of sustaining any speed. It is also likely the police had taken other steps to further disable the vehicle, such as removing the rotor arm from the distributor rendering the car incapable of starting. The C7 surveillance teams would have passed on the details of the proposed break-out to the negotiators and the Met senior leadership team in tactical control of the outer containment zone. The senior leadership hurriedly convened a news conference broadcast on the BBC radio network, and made it known the SAS were ready to go in and rescue the hostages, should the Met team deem it necessary. The conclusion of the siege came about after the ASU had heard the news broadcast, which added to the wearing down of the ASU team both physically through lack of food and psychologically through ego-deflating tactics employed by the negotiation team. The final straw was the prospect of certain death at the hands of the elite troops of the SAS. The ASU's plan to break out contained a degree of uncertainty as to the outcome of their actions and, as such, would give them the opportunity to rationalize their prospects of surviving such a bold move, given the overwhelming police presence outside the apartment building, bolstered by the cohesive nature of their relationship as a tight knit team. In facing a raid by the SAS, there would have been no opportunity for the four men to have any chance of survival, and so they folded the hand they had been playing with Imbert and Nevill for six days and capitulated. At no point during the siege had the two negotiators lied to the ASU about their prospects, and it was the IRA men who initiated the conclusion of the siege by asking for the terms of their surrender.

Not all armed standoffs end in such a control conclusion. At the Iranian Embassy siege in London, tactical command of the standoff transferred from the Met and the negotiation team led by Superintendent

Fred Luff to Colonel Michael Rose, of the SAS, after the execution of a hostage, the Iranian press attaché Abras Lavasani. At that point, Superintendent Luff's role became one of supplying the leader of the six armed terrorists with disinformation about efforts to provide the group with safe passage, via bus, to Heathrow Airport. Luff had been put in the position of negotiating while-lying-about-concessions in order to distract the terrorists as the SAS made ready to storm the building.

The six stage model, as described in this chapter, has been constructed from an analysis of the Balcombe Street siege and of other hostage standoff situations and is intended an illustration of the types of tactics that can be employed during such an event. There are many "how-to" books on the subject that can be reviewed for more tactical information.

The Met and the Wilson government would hail the eventual result of the Balcombe Street siege as a victory for the patient approach the police had employed against the IRA men. The negotiators had avoided resorting to force, as that would have almost certainly resulted in a bloodbath, and all the associated adverse publicity another massacre would bring to the doors of the Government. The capture of the four IRA men would mean that the Met would get them before a court, just as Imbert had hoped at the outset of the siege, and conduct a detailed post siege analysis of their own performance. The siege had been a new experience for the Met, who at times found themselves improvising tactics and strategy as events unfolded at the siege location. They had learned valuable lessons in hostage situation containment, and negotiation, and would begin to formally integrate these nuggets of information into a training program for negotiators and first responders, which is now held annually at the police college in Hendon, the establishment that supplied the six pairs of gym shoes to officers of C7 so they could creep around the hallways of the Balcombe Street apartment building in relative silence. Having to borrow gym shoes for the team is in itself an indicator as to how new this type of operation was to the Met.

While recognizing the result as a great success for the Met, the Balcombe Street siege is in some respects somewhat unique as a hostage negotiation episode. Firstly, the group concerned had been the target of an intense police investigation for almost a year and a half, with very little to show for the effort expended on the part of the police. The IRA team had created a reign of terror in the heart of the capital unprecedented since WWII, in their attacks on the British establishment, and the Bomb Squad had been almost powerless to stop them. Secondly, the ASU *wanted* to stay in the flat, after becoming trapped in 22b, in order to give the IRA time to carry out some form of action on their behalf. This objective played into the emerging wait-and-see strategy of the Met, but the police were totally unaware of the ASU's desire to stretch out the siege for as long as they could endure the conditions. The police tactic of sitting it out would have its endpoint, particularly in view of their strategy of depriving the ASU food, which became compounded by the subsequent refusal by the ASU to accept any food offered to them. The medical team would have eventually called a halt to the of-fer/refusal cycle, had Mrs. Mathews not broken the cycle by demanding that the ASU accept the food offered to them on the Thursday. Finally, the siege set the future standard of keeping the mental health specialists, such as Dr. Scott, in the background and allowing the seasoned law en-forcement officers such as Nevill and Imbert to be the direct interface with the hostage takers. There had been a trend to have the police asso-ciated psychologist or psychiatrists push themselves into the forefront of the negotiations, but it was realized this practice was not the most ef-ficient use of trained mental health practitioners. As Dr. James Greenstone stated, "often, those most skilled in crisis intervention have not been trained in any of the behavioral science disciplines. Profes-sional training may make us skilled professionals in our field, but it might not qualify us to apply what we know in ways special to crisis in-tervention." The street-smarts and coolness of Peter Imbert and Jim Nevill allowed the Balcombe Street siege to reach a highly desired peaceful conclusion. Mrs. Mathews may have later stated she was somewhat angry at Peter Imbert for being "too nice" to the IRA men, but that was all part of Imbert's approach to getting the situation under control and he probably saved her life in the process.

One lesson from the Balcombe Street siege is very clear, in terms of applying strategy and tactics to hostage situation, and it is this: because a hostage negotiation strategy is developed and applied successfully in one situation, there are no guarantees that the same tactics and strategy, applied analogously to an apparently similar but essentially different scenario, will be a successful. External forces, sometimes outside the control of the negotiation team and, at times, the hostage takers, will drive the negotiation process in a different direction to the one the origi-nal prototypical "model" was constructed around. In the Balcombe Street event, the Wilson government was attempting to resuscitate the failed power-sharing talks between the warring political factions in Northern Ireland, and could not afford to have a bloody shooting on the streets of the capital. Such an outcome would probably have resulted in an escalation in the politically-driven terrorism both in Northern Ireland

and on the British mainland. Providing the Provisional IRA with four martyrs to their cause would have been directly detrimental to future power-sharing discussions. Extraction of the ASU from the apartment, alive, was a very real political objective arguably placed, covertly, ahead of the lives of Mr. and Mrs. Mathews.

In examining any hostage situation involving political or terror-based groups, the national and international political risks and ramifications must be factored into the overall tactical and psychological strategies applied to the situation. While many police forces have extensive experience of siege tactics, at a local level, it is always a wise course of action to examine the peripheral geopolitical and psychological issues before carrying out any rehearsed or field-tested tactics. Not doing so may drive a degree of uncertainty to the eventual outcome and work to the detriment of the negotiation team, and the national and or international interests, of the home country government, with the potential for Domino-like repercussions in the future.

doi:10.1300/J173v08n02_03

Chapter 8

Postscript

With the arrest and conviction of the four members of the London the ASU and the conviction of Brendan Dowd the previous year, all but one member of the team was behind bars. William Quinn, wanted for the murder of PC Stephen Tibble, had fled Ireland and was thought to be somewhere in the United States, his home country. The San Francisco Police Department had their radar up for any sign of the wanted man, who also had a string of other alleged terrorist crimes in the UK linked to his name. If he surfaced, Detective Inspector Alec Edwards would be waiting.

One fallout of the ASU trial and conviction centered around the lack of charges made against the men for the Guilford and Woolwich bombings that O'Connell, Butler and Duggan, along with Dowd, admitted that they had carried out with no involvement of the convicted Guilford Four. This admission of guilt gave Conlon, Armstrong, Hill and Richardson reason to hope for an appeal or retrial, but only Richardson made an application for appeal within the time frame allowed after her conviction, but eventually all four were permitted to file for an appeal on the basis that new evidence had emerged in their case.

We have to look at the motivations behind the ASU's claim that the Guilford four were innocent. In this book, the Guilford and Woolwich bombings are as described by the ASU to the investigating officers after their arrests at Balcombe Street and also based on their testimony at the

[Haworth co-indexing entry note]: "Postscript." Moysey, Steven P. Co-published simultaneously in *Journal of Police Crisis Negotiations* (The Haworth Press, Inc.) Vol. 8, No. 2, 2008, pp. 263-285 and: *The Road to Balcombe Street: The IRA Reign of Terror in London* (Steven P. Moysey) The Haworth Press, Inc., 2008, pp. 263-285. Single or multiple copies of this article are available for a fee from The Haworth Document Delivery Service [1-800-HAWORTH, 9:00 a.m. - 5:00 p.m. (EST). E-mail address: docdelivery@haworthpress.com].

Available online at http://jpcn.haworthpress.com
doi:10.1300/J173v08n02_04

October 1977 appeal hearing for the Guilford four. We are therefore left asked a few fundamental questions regarding the possible political motivations behind the IRAs actions. O'Connell had told Imbert and Nevill that the IRA had been "after" Hill and Conlon for some time on suspicion of passing information to the Army. If that was the case, why would they care if possible informants, guilty or not, rotted in a British prison? We are also left to wonder what the IRA would have done with the men if they had indeed caught up with them. If, for a moment, we take the ASU's confessions on Guilford and Woolwich at face value and agree they did carry out the raids, could it be that O'Connell and his team were motivated to spare three fellow Irishmen a life in prison by publicly supporting their innocence, while at the same time ensuring the ASU received full "credit" for the mainland terror campaign? However, there is another possible motivation for the ASU to make the claim that the Guilford team did not exist anywhere except in the imaginations of the investigating officers from Surrey police. By claiming responsibility for the attacks, the ASU were implying that the Surrey police had created or coerced statements from the Guilford four in order to bring the supposed villains to justice and calm the public concerns at perceived police inefficiency. O'Connell and his team were, in their doctrine, political prisoners of war convicted by a court system they did not recognize under a system of justice they did not believe could ever be fair to Irish men and women. They had waged war against the British establishment in order to bring pressure to bear on the government to pull out of Northern Ireland and let the Irish people determine the future of the divided nation. What better way to continue to attack the establishment than by having it turn itself inside out, with claims of serious misconduct on the part of the police that allowed a massive miscarriage of justice, and subsequent incarceration of four innocent people, along with seven of their family and associates for a crime they did not commit. An appeal by the four, and their subsequent acquittal, would serve to cast serious doubts on the integrity of the British judicial system and the honesty of sectors of the British police, bringing international scrutiny on the government and allowing the Republicans to crow, on a very public stage, about the inhumanity and cruelty of so-called British justice. If a successful appeal secured the release of the four people convicted in the Guilford and Woolwich cases, it would also trigger an investigation of the Surrey police detectives involved and their relationships with members of the Met and what would have to have been the biggest police cover-up in British history. If statements had been falsified, doctored or tampered with, then a watertight conspiracy from the lowest levels of the Surrey police and the upper ranks of both Surrey and the Metropolitan police would have to have taken place. Such a cover-up would also have to have been maintained and an investigation into a possible scandal could ruin the careers of any officers found to have been involved in perverting the course of justice. It would have been an audacious ploy to pull off, but one not outside the realms of possibility for the increasingly politically savvy IRA.

Theorizing aside, the Guilford four appeal did in fact open on October 10th, 1977 before Lord Justice Roskill, Lord Justice Lawton and Mr. Justice Bernham. O'Connell, Dowd, Butler and Duggan appeared in person to give very detailed accounts of the execution of the Guilford and Woolwich attacks, although Dowd appeared confused at times and contradicted the testimony of the other three, leading the judges to believe that the three men from the Balcombe Street siege had taken time to get their story straight, but did not coordinate with Dowd, who was held in a separate prison. Despite the detail given by the four IRA men, the judges clung to the confessions and the statements made by the Guilford four while in custody, with Justice Roskill stating, "if the confessions were both voluntary and true, then the evidence against the applicants was overwhelming." This was despite the lack of forensic evidence linking Conlon, Hill, Armstrong and Richardson to the crimes. Judge Roskill, in a reference to a possible IRA conspiracy stated that O'Connell, having been found guilty and convicted of six murders, "had nothing to lose by accepting responsibility for a further seven." The judges were not able to dismiss out of hand the details of the accounts rendered by the ASU and Dowd, and so reached the conclusion that the two groups had colluded in the attacks, with Justice Roskill summing up their findings on October 28th, "we are all of the clear opinion that on no possible grounds for doubting the justice of any of the four convictions or for ordering a new trial." The Guilford four would stay in prison, despite the evidence presented to the court of appeal by the ASU members. The miscarriage of justice rumblings, however, would continue on for several years while those outside the walls of her Majesty's prisons got on with their lives.

John Purnell and Phil McVeigh, while filling out their paperwork at Paddington Green police station on the night of December 6th, had speculated about the possibility of receiving some form of Commissioner's commendation for their selfless bravery under fire. They were to be surprised by precisely what they were to receive in way of public recognition for their deeds. The British system of medals for gallantry, for non-military personnel, is topped by the prestigious George Cross

(GC) created in 1940 by the then King George in order to recognize acts of conspicuous bravery by civilians during the blitz on London during World War II. It is considered the civilian equivalent of the Victoria Cross, the military's highest award for bravery. Because of the rarity of awards of the GC, a slightly junior metal was introduced, known as the George Medal, which is only given for "acts of great bravery." In 1977 John Purnell, Phil McVeigh and Henry Dowswell were awarded the George Medal for their conspicuous bravery in chasing down the four armed members of the ASU, resulting in the six-day siege at Balcombe Street. A year earlier, Major Geoff Biddle had been awarded the George Medal for his bravery in defusing the bombs of the ASU, and PC Stephen Tibble had been posthumously awarded the Queens Police Medal for gallantry. Along with the 1977 recipients of the George Medal, Bob Fenton, Phil Mansfield, Officer A and two of his SPG colleagues were awarded the prestigious Queens Gallantry Medal for their bravery in the Rossmore Road shootout. Detective Sergeant David Waghorn received a Commissioner's commendation for his ingenuity in conceiving Operation Combo that netted the IRA terror team. The storekeeper at the police college in Hendon never received back his six pairs of plimsolls and refused to allow George Howlett to forget about them.

While interviewing Peter Imbert during the research for the book, he told the author that he has teased John Purnell down the years about his gallantry award. "I've always told him he was lucky to have got the George Medal," said Peter Imbert, "I've also told him he should have gotten himself shot, that way he would have got the George Cross!"

One prize still eluded the Met, and that was the arrest and conviction of PC Stephen Tibble's alleged killer William Quinn. In a nation where the regular police officers remain unarmed, the killing of an officer is regarded as a crime for which punishment of life-in-prison should be precisely what it says, life with no expectation of early release. He had killed one of their own and the Met would leave no stone unturned in their efforts to bring Quinn to justice once he showed his head to the police in the United States, if that was where he had fled.

In 1981, Detective Inspector Alec Edwards received a call from the FBI: William Joseph Quinn had indeed surfaced in San Francisco as Edwards had half expected. After matching Quinn's fingerprints with those taken after his brief altercation with the authorities in Dublin, and with the visual identification made by PC Adrian Blackledge, Detective Inspector Alec Edwards, accompanied by fellow Anti Terror squad officer Alan Lewis, traveled to San Francisco in 1981 to work with FBI officers on the arrest of Quinn for the murder of PC Stephen Tibble.

Quinn also had a long list of alleged offences carried out in the UK that Edwards and Lewis were all too aware of as they worked through the US court system to have Quinn extradited to face charges in the UK. This presented the officers with a dilemma, as the court system in the US viewed the alleged offenses that linked Quinn to several terrorist bombings in the UK differently to the murder charge, which went straight to the Supreme Court, with the alleged bombing offences being handled by the lower courts. Edwards and Lewis, working with the Crown prosecution service and the Director of Public Prosecutions, had a decision to make, as Alec Edwards later described, "it was a matter of deciding whether to go with just the murder charge or waiting to get the other charges referred back to the lower courts. The decision was made to just pursue the murder of PC Tibble, so the other alleged offenses just remained on file. So, because Quinn was not extradited for the other alleged terrorist offenses, we could not charge him with any of them once we had him back in the UK. All the other alleged offenses remained on file, so his trial at the Old Bailey was purely for the murder of Stephen Tibble and not for any of the other alleged offenses we would like to have put before the court."

It would take Edwards and Lewis five years of work to get Quinn back to the UK, in 1986, and ready to face trial one year later, where he made a not guilty plea to the court for the murder charge. As Alec Edwards described, "he was just an all American boy who got sucked up into the politics and joined the cause, so he said, with the terrorist charges all denied by Quinn of course."

The police had considerable forensic evidence that linked Quinn to the other alleged offences, but this could not be used in the case against him. However, with the eyewitness accounts given by officers such as Derek Wilson, who had pursued Quinn on the fallen officer's motorbike and had waited 12 years to tell his story to a court, Quinn was found guilty and received a life sentence for the murder of 21-year-old Stephen Tibble.

By the time Quinn's conviction, Peter Imbert had reached the pinnacle of his career with the Metropolitan police. The 1975 Balcombe Street siege had given the Met leadership team the opportunity to watch Peter Imbert as he went about the difficult job of talking the ASU out of number 22b. He had shown how well he acted under pressure and demonstrated considerable skills of communication and diplomacy. The success of Balcombe Street, and all the efforts that had preceded the event, would help fast track the remainder of Peter Imbert's career. In 1976, both Peter Imbert and Jim Nevill received promotions, with

Nevill promoted to Commander and placed in charge of the Bomb Squad, with the unit subsequently being renamed the Anti-Terrorist Squad, a far more fitting title for a group that would face other forms of terror in the future. Peter Imbert was appointed to the post of Assistant Chief Constable of the Surrey police force, putting him in the position prior to the 1977 appeal by the Guilford four. Imbert became the Deputy Chief Constable of Surrey before moving to the Thames Valley police, headquartered at Aylesbury in Buckinghamshire, as Chief Constable in 1979, making Imbert the youngest Chief Constable in the country at the time. Imbert would eventually return to his policing roots in London on his appointment as Deputy Commissioner of the Metropolitan police, "I recall the day in 1985 when I arrived at New Scotland Yard for my first day as the newly appointed Deputy Commissioner," said Imbert. "My ex-Royal Marine driver, wearing a smart police uniform, jumped out of the car, saluted the patrolling police officer outside Scotland Yard, and announced: 'The new Deputy Commissioner reporting for duty.' To which the Yard man saluted back and said: 'I am very pleased to meet you, Sir, but who is the little man in the back?'"

And so at the time of William Quinn's conviction, Peter Imbert had risen to the top police job in Britain with his appointment as Commissioner of the Metropolitan police and became Sir Peter Imbert after receiving a knighthood from Her Majesty Queen Elizabeth II. At around the same time, there were increased rumblings, yet again, regarding a serious miscarriage of justice in the case of the Guilford four and the Birmingham six, convicted of the Tavern in the Town and Mulberry Bush pub bombings. The Guilford four were actively lobbying for a second appeal court hearing, with their cause being helped by TV investigative reporting and MP's such as Labour's Chris Mullin, a former investigative journalist before turning to politics. The campaign to free the Guilford four centered on reported serious regularities in the manner of their confessions to the crimes, with some of the convicted claiming that the police coerced confessions from them under physical and psychological duress. The second appeal, which commenced in October 1989, focused on the confession of Paul Hill, which appeared to have been adjusted by the investigating officers who apparently did not immediately write up notes taken after questioning Hill and appeared to have colluded in the later wording of his statement. This came to light after officers from the Avon and Somerset forces, conduct an investigation into the methods used by the Surrey police detectives involved in the arrest in questioning of Hill, and later Conlon, Armstrong and Richardson. During the appeal hearing, Roy Amlott QC, on behalf of the

Guilford four, commented on the results of the Avon and Somerset police investigation, "it has thrown some doubt on the honesty and integrity of a number of Surrey police officers investigating the case . . . the Crown is now unable to say that the convictions of any of the four were safe or satisfactory." The Court of Appeal agreed with the claim and on October 19th 1989, quashed the convictions of the Guilford four and set them free after having served 15 years in prison. However, the mood in the police and in some of the national newspapers did not reflect the jubilant celebration of some on the release of the four, with one editorial commenting that the only miscarriage of justice occurred when the four were set free. Senior police officers close to the case echoed that sentiment, feeling that at some point the truth about the innocence or guilt of the Guilford four would come out.

As a result of the convention is being set aside, the Home Secretary Douglas Hurd orderly a judicial inquiry into the case as well as a criminal investigation into the actions of the Surrey detectives involved. Two of the officers left the force and three were suspended pending an investigation. The three suspended detectives were later charged with perverting the course of justice and went to trial but the charges were later dismissed and the officers went free. However, the image of the police had been tarnished by the Guilford four episode and further action in the courts, on the grounds of a miscarriage of justice, secured the subsequent release of the Birmingham six, in March of 1991.

Sir Peter Imbert retired from his role as commissioner in 1993 and became the first nonmilitary person to be appointed as the Lord Lieutenant of London, the Queens representative for the capital city, becoming Lord Peter Imbert in the process. This new chapter in Lord Imbert's life, with a seat in the House of Lords and an office in City Hall Westminster, has not changed the man who, at his core, is still a down-to-earth copper, with a heart of gold and a sense of humor to match.

John Purnell retired from the Metropolitan police in 1995, having reached the rank of Deputy Assistant Commissioner and spent the next 10 years of his career as group security director for Tesco, one of the UK's largest retail chains. John retired from Tesco in 2005 and is now enjoying retirement to the full with his wife Margaret. John Purnell was appointed Deputy Lord Lieutenant of London in March 2007, once again partnering him with his old boss Peter Imbert. Other officers involved in the ASU's reign of terror also retired, such as Detective Superintendent Ron Chapman who left the police, like many of his colleagues, after 30 years of service. After retirement, Ron discovered a dormant artistic talent and is now an accomplished painter of watercolor landscapes and village scenes in and around the county town where he lives in the South of England. Officer A, of the Special Patrol Group also left the police after 30 years and lives in quiet anonymity, with none of his current friends and colleagues knowing about his acts of bravery in the Rossmore Road shootout and Balcombe Street episode. David Waghorn, the architect of operation combo, spent the rest of his career with the Anti-Terrorist Squad, and now lives in retirement in his beloved Dorset in the South of England. Sadly, Henry Dowswell passed away one year after receiving the George Medal for his brave actions and Alec Edwards, who would have been with Henry in the Yellow Peril the night of December 6th if he had not agreed to swap duty with another officer, is currently director of an international security company based in London.

John and Sheila Mathews moved away from Balcombe Street after Mr. Mathews retired from the Post Office, buying a house in the town of Abingdon in the Buckinghamshire countryside. Ironically, six months earlier, Peter Imbert had moved to the same town after becoming Chief Constable of the Thames Valley police. The siege couple had moved just half a mile from the house owned by Peter Imbert and his wife, so naturally the police officer would visit the couple from time to time. He recalled how Mrs. Mathews didn't really like him, and she felt he had been too kind to the IRA men.

But what about the other central characters in this story, namely the Province and people of Northern Ireland? How would the story unfold for the bloodstained Province and how would the political situation play out? The ASU's campaign had been designed to pressure the British government to pull out of Northern Ireland and, in effect, trying to smash, once and for all, the single party stranglehold the Unionists had historically enjoyed in the Province. Other Active Service Units would make attacks on the mainland Britain and the Anti Terrorist Squad would continue to wage a cat and mouse battle of wits with the bombers as they continue to strike military and establishment targets and politicians. The IRA would strike against the government of Margaret Thatcher, who eventually became the IRA's most hated British Prime Minister. They assassinated Thatcher's shadow Northern Ireland Secretary, Airey Neave, with a car bomb in 1979, and narrowly missed killing Thatcher with a bomb in a Brighton hotel during the 1984 Tory Party conference. The 100-pound bomb killed five people and wounded 34. In a statement released to the press, claiming responsibility for the attack, an IRA spokesman stated, "Today we were unlucky, but remember, we only have to be lucky once; you will have to be lucky always. Give Ireland peace and there will be no war."

The political climate would change again after the 1997 elections ousted the Conservatives and put 43-year-old Tony Blair, the Oxford educated barrister and leader of the opposition Labour Party, as the new hope Prime Minister in number 10 Downing Street. Blair brought an air of determination and commitment to see a genuine and sustainable power-sharing arrangement in place, one that would include formal co-operation with the Irish Republic. Blair also had the active support in getting a peace process moving from the US President Bill Clinton, who arranged to have former US Senator George Mitchell act as the chair-man of a proposed series of multiparty talks on moving to a true power-sharing arrangement in Northern Ireland. The Reverend Ian Paisley dismissed Mitchell, saying he was "from the Kennedy stable of the Boston lobby of Republicans," which was not a very promising start to the process.

The multiparty talks started at Stormont and by January 1998 the par-ticipants were presented with a joint British and Irish document titled "Propositions of heads of agreement," that resurrected certain elements of the Sunningdale agreement which, predictably, raised the ire of the Unionists. The proposal outlined that constitutional changes could only occur on the bases of cross party agreement, the formation of an elec-toral assembly and the creation of a Bill of Rights for the Province of Northern Ireland. The document also touched on the politically thorny topic of how to handle the paramilitary prisoners, held in British jails, and then even touchier subject of disarming the IRA and the loyalist paramilitary groups, with the eventual goal of decommissioning their weapons, a proposal that would be viewed with distrust by all sides.

Tony Blair wanted the talk to move at a faster pace and so moved the discussions from Stormont, in Belfast, to Lancaster House in London, but the positioning of the Unionists, wanting to look close to the govern-ment, which was an understandable maneuver given their fervent desire to stay part of the United Kingdom, made Sinn Fein and the SDPL edgy and prevented progress from being made at the pace Blair expected. Ac-cordingly, the location moved to Dublin Castle in the Irish Republic to continue discussions under the watchful eyes of the British and Irish governments. The representatives from Sinn Fein, the Alliance Party of Northern Ireland (APNI), Progressive Unionist Party (PUP), the UUP, and the Northern Ireland women's coalition, under the guidance of Chairman George Mitchell, continued to hammer out the terms of an agreement but, as usual, things did not go smoothly. The British and

Irish governments expelled Sinn Fein from the talks, to the outrage of Sinn Fein President Gerry Adams, because of the supposed IRA involvement in the killing of two people earlier in the month of February, removing Adams and his people from the talks for 17 days.

Mitchell set a deadline for the talks to reach an agreement, urging the delegates to push for April 9th, 1998 as the day they would announce success. President Bill Clinton made calls to the Northern Ireland party leaders to encourage the politicians to come together and reach a lasting settlement. One day past the deadline, and 25 years after the proud Edward Heath had announced the success of the fated Sunningdale agreement, an equally proud George Mitchell told the world, at 5:36pm, "I'm pleased to announce the two governments and the political parties of Northern Ireland have reached an agreement." It was the Friday before Easter, Good Friday, and that would be the name the historical agreement would be anointed. After 30 years of violence, mistrust, failed talks and collapse assemblies, it had taken a young Prime Minister with behind-the-scenes politicking and public support from Bill Clinton, together with a genuine desire from Gerry Adams and Sinn Féin for a settlement, to come up with a plan that could work. Historically, the parties agreed to an all Ireland referendum to go forward to allow the entire people of Ireland to make a yes or no vote on the terms of the new power-sharing agreement that included a 105 member assembly at 12 member executive. The Good Friday agreement also allowed for the establishment of a joint North-South ministerial Council, and the formation of a Council of The Isles with members drawn from the assemblies of England, Scotland, Wales, Belfast and Dublin.

Sinn Féin, understandably cautious about the Good Friday agreement, but Adams agreed to bring the proposal before the party delegates for a vote of approval. Predictably, the UUP and Paisley's Democratic Unionist Party opposed the agreement and went on a no-vote campaign to prevent the deal from going forward but were handed a blow to their position by the UUC, the policymaking body of the UUP, who backed the agreement with 72% of delegates in favor of a yes vote. Paisley famously gained the nickname of Dr. No in his opposition to the Good Friday agreement.

In a move that was totally political, O'Connell, Butler, Duggan and Dougherty were moved by the British government from their high security prisons in Britain and repatriated to Portlaoise Prison in the Irish Republic, having served 22 years and five months in prison. The move was somewhat inspired, as the British government needed Sinn Fein to adopt the Good Friday agreement, but to do so the party would need to make a constitutional amendment to allow Sinn Fein candidates to actually take their seats in the new assembly as proposed by the agreement. A meeting of Sinn Fein delegates was called for May 10th to vote on such an amendment, and to rapturous applause from the 350 delegates Gerry Adams presented Joe O'Connell, Eddie Butler, Harry Duggan and Hugh Dougherty, hailing the four men as "our Nelson Mandela's." On hearing of the response the ASU had received from the delegates, one retired senior officer from the Met said he wished he could have shown the meeting the photographs of the dead and mutilated from the bomb scenes they created, to see if they would still cheer. The four men, in a political move to back Sinn Fein, had been released from prison for one day in order to attend the meeting and the move, again predictably, infuriated the Unionist parties. The subsequent vote on the amendment to the Sinn Fein constitution was carried by 95% of the delegates eligible to vote, ending 77 years of Sinn Fein refusal to participate in the running of any Northern Ireland government, a hugely significant milestone in the ongoing peace process.

Pockets of Unionists continue to oppose the Good Friday agreement, with divisions emerging in some of the political parties. Ian Paisley, leader of the DUP, and opposed to the agreement, accused pro-agreement UUP leader David Trimble of being prepared to "break the union," and continue to call for a Protestant no vote. However, after personal appeals by President Bill Clinton and Prime Minister Tony Blair, the first all-Ireland vote on the future of the nation since the 1916 general election took place on May 22nd, 1998, with a high turnout north of the border, as on this occasion the Catholics had not called a boycott on the process, as they had with the border poll under the government of Edward Heath. In Northern Ireland 81% of the electorate turned out to vote, 71% voting yes in favor of the agreement. In the Irish Republic, the turnout was lower, at 56%, with 85% voting in favor of the agreement. The Good Friday agreement was a resounding success with the people of Ireland and the Unionist parties having to find a way to come to terms with the new reality.

As part of the Good Friday agreement, the British government had committed to release paramilitary prisoners from the groups that had maintained a cease-fire as required by the terms of the agreement and so, on the morning of April 13th, 1999, 131 Republican and 118 Loyalist prisoners were set free. Among those walking out of the confines of Portlaoise Prison on that spring morning were the four members of the ASU, who had each served just less than 23-years behind bars for their crimes. They were free, and opinions in the general public were mixed, with many feeling that convicted murderers should not have been released as part of a political process. However, this point of view missed the fact that it was, in effect, a political process, or failure thereof, that drove men like the ASU to carry out acts of violence against the British government, and the British people, in a desperate attempt to overcome the inequalities in the political system in Northern Ireland that denied the Catholic minority a voice. Some members of the public adopted a more philosophical view, including the daughter of Professor Hamilton-Farley, killed by one of the ASU's booby trapped bombs. "I believe you must do things for the greater good," said Diana Hamilton-Farley, "yes, it was very difficult, but times move on. To continue to hold any feelings towards what these people do doesn't help me and it doesn't help anybody else."

The bitterest pill for many in the Met to swallow, as part of the Good Friday agreement, was watching the killer of young PC Stephen Tibble walk free. After serving seventeen years behind bars, both in the United States and the UK, William Joseph Quinn went free. As one officer involved in the Tibble murder case later put it, "He had done quite a bit of porridge, but it wasn't justice in the full sense of the term."

The government of Tony Blair, helped by the Irish government, continued to push both Loyalist and Republican paramilitary groups to decommission their weapons, or put them in safe storage out of reach. The dream of power-sharing and genuine collaboration with the Irish Republic would depend on drastically reducing the potential for the paramilitary of both sides to wage war on each other. Prospects for power-sharing became more promising after elections in the Province made Paisley's Democratic Unionist Party, and Sinn Fein, under the leadership of Gerry Adams, the two dominant political parties in Northern Ireland. Tony Blair, supported by the Irish government, devoted a considerable amount of effort to coax the bitter historical enemies into talking in what appeared to be a never-ending series of summit meetings. However, what eventually convinced the hard-line Unionist Ian Paisley to even contemplate the notion of compromise, a word that was barely in his vocabulary, turned out to be the remarkable effort of Gerry Adams in convincing the different factions of the IRA to reject the rule of the bomb and the bullet and, instead, strive for their objectives through the ballot box. In a triumph for Adams, the IRA finally announced on September 26th, 2005, that it was renouncing violence, had disarmed and it was this act that allowed the IRA and Sinn Féin to give Paisley and the hard-line Unionists an assurance there would be no future attempts to push the Province out of the United Kingdom through acts of force. Sinn Fein, with a nonviolent help of the IRA, had cut the political legs out from under Paisley. He could no longer fall back on demonizing of the group he habitually referred to as "Sinn Féin IRA" to publicly link the two groups together, and could no longer refuse to co-operate with a group, so he would claim, totally dedicated to the creation of a unified Ireland. The old argument, applied for decades against the Republicans, would no longer hold water as Sinn Féin had fully endorsed the peace process, backed the Good Friday agreement, convinced the IRA to give up its long history of armed violence, and demonstrated that, politically, the party of Sinn Féin was a force to be reckoned with in the Province. Like it or not, Paisley would have to swallow his pride, and to some extent elements of his political ideology, in order to catch up with the shifting politics and changing face of Northern Ireland.

Blair and Irish Prime Minister, Bertie Ahern, could see the dilemma the IRA's declaration would cause the DUP, with regard to forming a power-sharing government with Sinn Fein. Paisley had a long and very public record of denouncing Sinn Fein in almost biblical terms of evil, and had stated he would never talk to Sinn Féin, in general, and Gerry Adams in particular, having once described Adams as having consorted with the devil himself! Paisley had, in some respects, painted himself into an ideological corner and the British government and Sinn Fein both recognized the situation he was in. To make a power-sharing alliance work, there would need to be a means for both Paisley, and to some extent Sinn Fein, to save face and actually work together. Wanting to capitalize on the momentum the IRA disarmament had given the peace process, the British and Irish governments set a deadline of May 8th, 2007 for all the parties involved to put in place the Good Friday plans for power-sharing.

Subsequently on March 26, 2007, the almost unimaginable occurred in a room at Stormont Council, the once symbol of a Protestant Unionist dominated government the IRA had vowed to bring to an end 37 years before. For the first time sworn bitter enemies, the hard-line unionist and leader of the DUP, Ian Paisley, and Gerry Adams, President of Sinn Fein, sat in the same room for a face-to-face meeting to work out the details of establishing a power-sharing government. The two men did not shake hands, but the media reporters present stated that their body language was "respectful." The two men sat side-by-side to issue a joint statement on the date for the formation of the new government. Sinn Féin had wanted May 1st, but Paisley wanted May 15th. In an act that would have been deemed impossible at one point in their joint histories, the two men made a compromise and agreed on May 8th as the date.

Both Tony Blair and Bertie Ahern were delighted, "this has the potential to transform the future of this land," said Ahern. Tony Blair was equally effusive, "everything we have done over the past 10 years has been a preparation for this moment," stated Blair, mindful of his own political legacy as he prepared to step down from the Prime Minister's position at the end of June, 2007, to be replaced by his financial minister Gordon Brown. Blair's declining popularity with the British public, over the government's continued support of the war in Iraq, and his alignment with US President George W. Bush, had forced his hand and pushed his party to have him step down after 10 years as Prime Minister. Blair wanted the peace process in Northern Ireland to be his legacy and not a failed strategy in Iraq, but only time will tell how Blair will be judged through the eyes of history.

During the joint press conference, Gerry Adams punctuated events with comments in the Irish language, an action that would have previously elicited very derisory comments from Paisley, who on this occasion smiled and sat quietly as Adams spoke. Adams translated his closing comments to the press, "now there is a new start, with the help of God."

With four days to go before the official start of the new Northern Ireland government, the Protestant paramilitary group the Ulster Volunteer Force, UVF, proclaimed they would be renouncing violence and were committed to evolving into a "force for good." Many observers raised skeptical eyebrows at the announcement, given the UVF stated that while it had placed its arsenal out of the reach of the rank-and-file members, its leadership was not ready to turn over their weapons to the disarmament program, as the IRA had done in 2005. Tone of the founding fathers of the UVF, Gusty Spence, stated that this was "a real end to the UVF . . . will bring us closer to the peaceful, democratic, prosperous future that all our people deserve." But, even as it announced the end of its paramilitary status, the UVF could not resist a jab at its longtime adversary. The group stated they were renouncing violence after recognizing that Northern Ireland's position was secure in the United Kingdom after "the failure of the IRA campaign" to end British control, totally missing the point that the IRA had become more of a political force as many of its top leaders had migrated to key positions in Sinn Féin. Old enmities, it would appear, die hard with some groups.

The first meeting of the power-sharing government on May 8th 2007, also provided a photo opportunity many had thought could never have happened. Gathered in the assembly chamber of Stormont Castle, the new First Minister of Northern Ireland, the 81-year-old Dr. Ian Paisley, sat shoulder to shoulder with his new Deputy First Minister 56-year-old Martin McGuinness, once Paisley's sworn enemy in a past role as Chief of Staff of the IRA. The two men laughed and joked in front of the press cameras alongside a smiling Tony Blair and Irish Prime Minister Bertie Ahearn. We can only hope that the healing of the Province of Northern Ireland, through genuine power-sharing, partnership and cross-border cooperation, continues while we remember the 3,500 or so lives lost in the bloody sectarian violence, attacks on and by the British security forces, and the activities of the IRA on the British mainland. A new chapter has started in Northern Ireland's history. We can only hope that the memories of the Troubles remain vivid enough for all concerned to prevent history from repeating itself, as the fledgling power-sharing government stretches its wings and learns to fly.

The political situation has come a long way from the bloody days of 1974 and 1975, days that drove the IRA to send team of volunteers to bomb and shoot their way across London with impunity. The six days of the Balcombe Street siege remain as a measure of controlled hostage containment and negotiation and has become one of the gold standard for this type of police operation, made all the more remarkable by the actions of intuitive, rather than trained, negotiators. While it is true the negotiators were not aware of the hostage takers motivation to stick it out as long as they could, in the vain hope of either direct intervention by the IRA or the removal of evidence from their residences, Jim Nevill, Peter Imbert and the support team backing them did a remarkable job given the circumstances. The opportunity for the siege to go sour presented itself at all times while the four armed men continued to hold their two hostages in the flat. However, as we have noted, the negotiation team had a lot of factors going for them, some they were aware of and some they could only speculate about. At the start of the siege, they could not have realized that the hostage takers wanted to stay in the flat for several days to allow for some action to be taken by the IRA leadership. The ASU knew they had no chance of getting a car to the airport and a plane to the Irish Republic, using their initial demands as almost an expected exchange in their role as somewhat unintentional hostage takers, as after all they had gone into the apartment building looking for a way out the back, with the intent of giving the pursuing officers the slip, as had worked for William Quinn as he evaded the determined pursuit of Derek Wilson.

The negotiation team also did not initially know how many of the ASU had gone into number 22b. The failure of the video surveillance had left C7 blind but not deaf as their audio feeds continued to function.

The IRA men expected the police to be listening in on the flat, hence the Engelbert Humperdinck records used to cover their conversations and the Tom, Mick and Paddy routine they adopted, with O'Connell as Tom and Butler as the other two, keeping Duggan and Dougherty off the phone to avoid possible voice identification.

But, what Imbert and Nevill may not have known, and could only have speculated on, was the degree of sophistication and maturity they were dealing with in the members of the ASU. Despite the initial comments, at the outset of the siege, by Sir Robert Mark, the Bomb Squad had developed a healthy respect for the ASU, given the fact they had eluded capture for fourteen months despite house searches and the lucky, but tragic, discovery the bomb factory at 39 Fairholme Road, where they had escaped detection. The ASU were sophisticated bomb makers, an undisputed fact that would lead the Met to speculate on the type of urban guerrillas they had trapped inside 22b. Detective Inspector Ron Chapman's later assessment of Joe O'Connell somewhat validated the Met's earlier impression of the men, realizing that whatever Robert Mark may have said about the group, these were far from common criminals. Ruthless, calculating killers yes, but not your average IRA thugs. They had been meticulous planners, taking the time, trouble and risk in carrying out detailed reconnaissance of future targets. They had been a well trained and disciplined adversary.

The negotiation team also had the benefit of the Spaghetti House siege and the lessons the Met had learned regarding the media, helping them to eventually treat the media as an asset rather than a nuisance to be contained. While it is clear it was not partnership of equals, as such a relationship never can be in a hostage standoff situation, the Met treated the media with respect and in return the media became an essential element in the eventual capitulation of the four men of the ASU. In truth, the Met were, at times, somewhat manipulative of the media but given the circumstances, and the stakes, the overall benefit to the Met outweighed the potential impact on their future relationship should similar circumstances occur again. However, this has to be balanced against the political will and climate, as we have noted, that exists at the time of any hostage situation that places a nation under the spotlight of international attention. The governments of Heath and Wilson had come under increasing scrutiny from the international community over the handling of the Northern Ireland question, particularly from the USA. There had been a less than positive reaction in the Province to the investigation into the bloody Sunday massacre conducted by the British Chief Justice Lord Widgery, lingering sectarian resentment over the general strike and boiling outrage at the Dublin bombings. In short, Wilson and his government could not afford to have a bloody shootout with the hostage takers in number 22b, unless of course the ASU had first shot a hostage. As such, the negotiation team was having to deal with only one stand off, with the armed men in the flat, and despite the tough and some what contradictory public statements made by the Met senior leadership team, there was no direct or indirect pressure from Wilson or his Home Secretary Roy Jenkins to storm the flat, free the hostages and kill the hostage takers in the process. Despite the readiness, and apparent willingness, of the SAS to go into the flat to bring the stand off to an end, a bloody tactical conclusion to the Balcombe Street siege would have done lasting damage to the Wilson government and an unknown, and unimaginable, outcome in Northern Ireland.

One other advantage the Met negotiation team enjoyed was the in-depth knowledge of the Republican movement and history of the IRA possessed by Peter Imbert. This knowledge, although applied a little bluntly against Joe O'Connell at times, helped Imbert get under the skin of his adversary. He used the knowledge in his ego-denting tactics with O'Connell to great effect, creating tension and frustration in the Irishman, which played into the hands of the negotiation team.

The Met would take the experiences they had gained from both the ASU bombing campaign and the resulting siege and further develop their strategies for dealing with such events in the future. The Bomb Squad would be transformed into the Anti Terrorist Branch, which would later morph into the modern-day SO 15 Counterterrorism Command. Hostage negotiations would become a matter for trained officers to handle, rather than being assigned to one or two of the investigating officers on the case. As it turned out, Sir Robert handed the negotiator roles at Balcombe Street to Nevill and Imbert who, fortunately, proved more than equal to the task by virtue of their years of experience on the streets of London dealing with volatile policing situations.

In many respects the actual siege, and the resolution of the stand off at Balcombe Street, can be regarded as an almost prototypical model of how to handle armed, politically motivated, accidental hostage situation, should an event like that ever happen again! But there are hidden dangers in making such assumptions. We must remember that the hostage takers had a motivation to extend the siege, which the Met officers could not have known. They were also native English language speakers and, therefore, would follow the spoken and unspoken elements in their dialogue with the negotiation team with no difficulty. Apart from dialect and slang terms, there would have been little room for misunderstanding, within Imbert and Nevill not requiring a translator and all the risks that would entail. There are also risks in a belief in our own infallibility, believing that the tactics resulting in a success in one situation can be applied successfully to a different, but analogous set of circumstances. Having built a model of the Balcombe Street siege, in order to be successfully applied to other such situations, the conditions present in the new event must be factored into the thinking of the response team. Not doing so is a recipe for disaster. The social psychologist Dr. Dietrich Dörner styled this type of failure as the Rumpelstiltskin principal. A new situation, such as those found by the Met at Balcombe Street will normally result in the decision-making groups going through a basic three-step analysis, i.e., given the prevailing conditions, if I take the following actions, I should achieve the following expected result. If this chain of logic works the first time it is used, it will naturally be applied to subsequent analogous events. But, because "it" worked before gives the user an increased risk in the belief that "it" will work again and so the first step, evaluation of the conditions for the new event, may be omitted with deadly consequences for the hostages, hostage takers or the police response teams involved.

In many respects the siege of Iranian embassy in London, during six days in May 1980, can be regarded as a failure in both logic and of the initial tactics employed by the Met in an effort to replicate the success of the Balcombe Street siege and apply the model developed in 1975 to a new and different set of circumstances. The hostage takers were not native English speakers, with only one having a rudimentary grasp of the language. The political climate, with the rather right-wing government of Margaret Thatcher in control, was very different to the conditions existing during the government of Harold Wilson, and Thatcher wanted to send a message to the world that London was not a soft target for terrorists. The Met subsequently found themselves facing not one but two standoffs, as while they desperately try to talk hostage takers out of the building, the SAS was preparing to storm the embassy with their unwritten instructions from the government to prevent the incident from spreading beyond the building.

We have, at times, dwelt on the nature of the hostage takers involved in the Balcombe Street episode, acknowledging the grudging admiration demonstrate towards the men by some of the officers involved in the siege and the campaign of terror leading up to December 6th, 1975. The IRA men were not common criminals, some have said. So we must also state that many of those who sought to capture the ASU, and take them into custody, were not common or average police officers as many exhibited great courage in the face of danger. We have noted the bravery of the officers involved in the Rossmore Road shooting, such as Bob Fenton, Phil Mansfield, Henry Dowswell and flying squad driver PC Peter Wilson. The unrelenting courage of John Purnell and Phil McVeigh, as they gave chase to the armed IRA men, cornering the men in 22b Balcombe Street. The cool courage under fire demonstrated by Officer A and his SPG team of colleagues as they exchanged fire with the IRA men, and the calm and collected professionalism of the bomb disposal officers such as Captain Roger Goad and Major Geoff Biddle, to mention but a few. However, it is not just courage in the face of bullets or unexploded bombs that distinguishes the hundreds of officers from the Metropolitan police and the other police forces across Britain, or any other country. It is a determination and dedication to duty, day in and day out, to protect the public that they serve, to keep the streets of our cities safe from the terrorist's guns and bombs. But it also takes a special kind of courage to do your job, knowing you are on a terrorist hit list. Peter Imbert, as part of the Bomb Squad team responsible for the capture and incarceration of the IRA's most prolific team of urban guerrillas, would have been a natural revenge-inspired target for the terrorists as the Commissioner of the Metropolitan police. While researching material for this book, the author was fortunate enough to meet with Lord Peter Imbert, at his invitation, in his office in Westminster. The meeting was the first of several long in-depth conversations on the IRA terror campaign and the subsequent Balcombe Street siege, which included a guided tour of the streets of London where Lord Imbert pointed out all the pertinent locations impacted by the IRA's ASU. As we drove past Scotland Yard, Peter Imbert recalled the discovery of the map made by Joe O'Connell that showed at the route taken by Bomb Squad officers to their local pub. I commented that it must have been a sobering moment to discover he was a potential target of the ASU. Yes, said Lord Imbert, it was sobering but that was not the closest call he had with the IRA during his career as a Metropolitan Police officer. I asked Lord Imbert which episode came to mind. After pausing for thought he replied, "the most sobering thing I had with the IRA was when I was going to the Royal Overseas League in St. James to give a talk on terrorism. I was then Commissioner of the Met at the time. About a quarter of an hour before I was due to speak, I was still scribbling out my notes. My driver came in and told me there was plenty of time, as there had been a bomb hoax in the hall. I said fine, that gives me a while longer. I asked him to tell me when were ready. He came back about half an hour later to tell me it was actually a real bomb! What had happened was that the manager of the hall we were going to speak in had gone around the room to check it. He'd straitened up the curtains, straitened up the chairs and then noticed that the top of the podium was somewhat proud of its base. He tried to push it down, but it wouldn't move. He opened it up and inside was a plastic box with black tape round it. So, holding it up, he asked the BBC and ITV camera crews if it was their's. He asked the BBC crew, and they said no, it wasn't their's. The ITV crew announced it was not their's either and that they were getting out! The bomb squad was called and found it was a viable bomb. I was interviewed later that day–and you know how in life you say some foolish things? The interviewer asked me, 'what were your thoughts when you found out that it was a bomb and could have killed you and all of the others in the front row waiting to speak?' I replied, 'I should have worn an old suit!' "

The closing remarks on this chapter in Metropolitan police history will go back to the words of Justice Cantley who concluded the trial of the ASU with the statement, "I realize that there were other policemen who showed great courage and devotion to duty who were not identified in the trial. I hope they received the recognition they undoubtedly deserve. The public is very fortunate to have the protection of men (and women) such as these."

The formation of the new power-sharing government in Northern Ireland, it is hoped, has closed the book on a very bloody and violent chapter in both British and Irish history. The operations of the IRA during 1974 and 1975 may very well represent the peak of the "traditional" type of terrorism of the era, with dedicated terror operatives evading capture at the hands of equally dedicated and ingenious members of a city police force. Modern-day 21st-century terrorism has seen a dramatic shift in the way subversive organizations ply their deadly trade, with the suicide bomber replacing the time bomb and the thrown bombs of the latter part of the 20th century. The days where unarmed police officers give chase to armed terror suspects are, probably, long gone, and the notion of an armed terrorist standoff, involving hostages, quaintly old fashioned. However, we cannot forget that terrorism, and hostage taking, will always be with us in some shape or form, but the two may have moved to a mutually exclusive position. The post-September 11th world has seen a radial shift in the nature of international terrorism, with many of the perpetrators willing, or expecting, to die along with the innocent people they take "captive." I use the term deliberately to distinguish the temporary holding of civilians, such as during the attacks on the World Trade Center in New York, as opposed to the measured, deliberate practice of holding others hostage. In the first case, the terrorist has no intention of either freeing the captives or sparing their lives, as they are a temporary means to achieving their ultimate, bloody goal. In a hostage situation, the perpetrators are holding the innocent parties as a temporary collateral bargaining chip, with the accepted script of some form of exchange underscoring the tempo of the event. It may be, from a police crisis negotiation aspect, that hostage situations of the type carried out by the IRA in Balcombe Street, on a high profile international stage, are a thing of the past, relegated to a bygone age by "hostage takers" who are all too willing to cut the throats of their victims, on video, for later viewing on the Internet and satellite news organizations. We may well have move to a place where the skills of the police and counter terrorism squads focus on the detection and apprehension of terror suspects before they commit their acts of violence, as after the fact leaves little for them to either investigate or prosecute. This new place may also feature the skills of the hostage negotiator working at the municipal, county or state level as they deal with the local and domestic hostage standoff situations, with terrorist-driven events, such as Balcombe Street, a faint memory from a time of relative innocence.

BIBLIOGRAPHY

Adams, G. (2001). Before the Dawn. Mount Eagle Publications Ltd.

Betz, J. (1982). Moral Considerations Concerning the Police Response to Hostage-takers. Ethics, Public Policy, and Criminal Justice.

Bew, P. and Gillespie, G. (1999) *Northern Ireland A chronology of the Troubles 1968-1999*. Dublin: Gill and Macmillan Ltd.

Burke, F. V. Jr. (1995). Lying during crisis negotiations: A costly means to expedient resolution. Criminal Justice Ethics, Vol. 14.

Cialdini, R. (1993). Influence the Psychology of Persuasion. New York: William Morrow.

Coogan, T. (2002). The IRA. Palgrave Macmillan.

Coogan, T. (1995). The Troubles: Ireland's ordeal 1966-1996 and the search for peace. London: Hutchinson.

Davidson, T. (2002). To Preserve Life: Hostage-Crisis Management. Cimacom.

DiVasto, P. V. (1996). Negotiating With Foreign Language-Speaking Subjects, The FBI Law Enforcement Bulletin, June 1996.

Dörner, D. (1997). The Logic of Failure–Recognizing and Avoiding Error in Complex Situations. Perseus Books Group.

Fiske S. & Taylor S. (1991). Social Cognition, New York: McGraw-Hill.

Greenstone, J. (2005). The Elements of Police Hostage and Crisis Negotiations: Critical Incidents and How to Respond to Them. New York: The Haworth Press.

Greenstone, J. & Leviton, S. (2001). Elements of Crisis Intervention: Crises and How to Respond to Them. Wadsworth Publishing.

Griffin, J. (2003). Hostage. Andre Deutsch Ltd.

Hart, M. (2004). The Irish Game. Walker Publishing Inc.

Hatcher. C., Mohandie, K. & Turner J. (1998). The Role of Psychologists in Crisis Negotiations. Behavioral Sciences and the Law, Fall.

Heath, E. (1999). The Course of My Life. Coronet Books

Hill, A. (2005). The Birmingham Pub Bombings. Firepower, West Midlands Fire Service. Autumn (issue 86).

Hogg, I. (1978). The Complete Illustrated Encyclopedia of the World's Firearms. A & W Publishers Inc.

Kee, R. (1989) Trial and Error. Penguin Books Ltd.

Maloney, E. (2003). A Secret History of the IRA. W. W. Norton & Company.

Mark, R. (1978). In The Office of Constable. Harper Collins Ltd.

Morgan, K. (2000). The Oxford Illustrated History of Britain. Oxford University Press.

Moysey, S. (2004) The Balcombe Street and Iranian Embassy Sieges–A Comparative Examination of Two Hostage Negotiation Events. Journal of Police Crisis Negotiations. Vol. 4(1). The Haworth Press.

Pemlot, B. (1993). Harold Wilson. HarperCollins Publishers Ltd.

Ruben, J., Pruit, D., & Kim, S (1994). Social Conflict. New York: McGraw-Hill.

Slatkin, Arthur (2005) Communication In Crisis And Hostage Negotiations: Practical Communication Techniques, Stratagems, And Strategies For Law Enforcement, Corrections, And Emergency Service Personnel. Charles C. Thomas.

Steele, B. (1995). Guidelines for Covering Hostage-Taking Crises, Prison Uprisings, Terrorist Actions. A Poynter Institute Handout. Florida: The Poynter Institute.

Thompson, L. (2006). Hostage Rescue Manual: Tactics of the Counter-Terrorist Professionals. Greenhill Books

LIST OF GOVERNMENT DOCUMENTS

Cabinet Minutes Confidential Annex (Top Secret). CM(72). Thursday 3 February 1972. Cabinet meeting notes relating to the Lord Widgery enquiry into the Bloody Sunday shootings. UK Public Records Reference PREM 15/1001.

Memo from Sir Alec Douglas-Home, Foreign Secretary, to Edward Heath, Prime Minister. (Secret and Personal). PM/72/10. Monday 13 March 1972. Document outline Home's opposition to Direct Rule. UK Public Records Reference PREM 15/1004.

Transcript of telephone conversation between Mr. Faulkner and the Prime Minister.T103/7215. Wednesday March 1972. Heath invites Faulkner to Downing Street in order to inform him of Direct Rule decision. UK Public Records Reference PREM 15/1004.

Notes of a Meeting with Representatives of the Provisional IRA (Top Secret). Wednesday 21 June 1972. UK Public Records Reference PREM 15/1009.

Telegram from Edward Heath to Liam Cosgrave (Secret). DUB/FO 005/02. Monday 2 April 1973. Edward Heath looking for additional cooperation between security forces in Northern Ireland and those in the Republic of Ireland. UK Public Records Reference FC0 87/247.

Notes of a meeting at Chequers between William Whitelaw and Edward Heath (Confidential). Monday 2 July 1973. Meeting to discuss the Northern Ireland Assembly election held on Thursday 28 June 1973. UK Public Records Reference PREM 15/1693.

Notes of meeting held at Chequers (Secret). Friday 24 May 1974. Meeting between Harold Wilson, Brian Faulkner, Merlyn Rees and Gerry Fitt to go over the worsening situation in Northern Ireland caused by the UWC general strike. UK Public Records Reference PREM 16/147.

Memo from Merlyn Rees to Harold Wilson (Top Secret). Monday 27 May 1974. Reese outlines to Wilson the desirability of having the Executive of the Northern Ireland Assembly resign. UK Public Records Reference PREM 16/148.

Memo from Harold Wilson (Top Secret). Thursday 30 May 1974. Wilson lays out his concerns for dealing with the aftermath of the UWC strike. UK Public Records Reference PREM 16/148.

Memo from Home Secretary Roy Jenkins to the Cabinet. IRA terrorism in Great Britain (Secret). C(74)139. Sunday November 24 1974. Reese outlines his proposal for the prevention of Terrorism Act. UK Public Records Reference CAB 129/180.

Notes of Margaret Thatcher's meeting with the Prime Minister Harold Wilson–briefing on Northern Ireland situation. (Confidential). Wednesday 11 September 1975. UK Public Records Reference PREM 16/520.

WEB SITES AND ELECTRONIC RESOURCES

BBC News Archives
www.news.bbc.co.uk
Birmingham pub bombings:
http://birmingham999.co.uk
Communist Party of Great Britain
http://www.cpgb.org.uk
Conflict and Politics in Northern Ireland (1968 to the Present)–The Cain Project:
http://cain.ulst.ac.uk
The Dublin and Monaghan bombings:
http://www.dublinmonaghanbombings.org
FBI and ATF raid on the Branch Davidians at Waco, Texas:
http://www.firearmsandliberty.com/waco.massacre.html
The helicopter Song:
http://celtic-lyrics.com
The History of Scotland Yard:
http://www.historybytheyard.co.uk/
Metropolitan Police
http://www.met.police.uk.
The Margaret Thatcher Foundation
http://www.margaretthatcher.org/
The Royal Engineers Museum and Library
http://www.remuseum.org.uk

doi:10.1300/J173v08n02_04

Index

Page numbers followed by an *n*, *f*, or *p* indicated notes, figures, or photographs.

24834043R00173

Printed in Great Britain
by Amazon